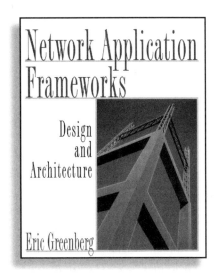

Praise for Network Application Frameworks

This book is destined to change the way networks and their applications are developed. It is required reading for my staff. For carriers wishing to understand how their networks impact customer applications and how their networks can be enhanced to improve the customer experience, this book provides the answer.

> **VAB GOEL**
> DIRECTOR OF IP NETWORK ENGINEERING
> & ADVANCED TECHNOLOGY
> QWEST COMMUNICATIONS

This is required reading for IS staff, network designers, and application development managers. Greenberg's book is not only an expansive reference on new and legacy technologies, but it clearly shows how to successfully design networks and their applications together—making this the network-centric computing book everyone's been looking for.

> **ERIC VAUGHN**
> DIRECTOR OF ELECTRONIC COMMERCE
> FANNIE MAE

It's rare to find one book that covers this much ground so effectively. Greenberg addresses topics of great importance to the enterprise. And in the final analysis, he successfully articulates the basic truth—that the network and its applications are indeed one.

> **JEFF TREUHAFT**
> DIRECTOR OF PRODUCT MARKETING
> NETSCAPE

No other book covers so many areas in network security with so much depth and breadth. This is a must-have book for IS professionals, network designers, and development managers who must be proficient in all of the technologies covered in Greenberg's book. This book is a classic.

> **DR. PRAKASH AMBEGAONKAR**
> PRESIDENT AND CEO
> E-LOCK TECHNOLOGIES INC.

Praise for
Network Application Frameworks

Network
Application
Frameworks

Network
Application
Frameworks

Design and
Architecture

Eric Greenberg

ADDISON–WESLEY

An Imprint of Addison Wesley Longman, Inc.

Reading, Massachusetts • Harlow, England • Menlo Park, California
Berkeley, California • Don Mills, Ontario • Sydney
Bonn • Amsterdam • Tokyo • Mexico City

Many of the designations used by manufacturers and sellers to distinguish their products are claimed as trademarks. Where those designations appear in this book, and Addison Wesley Longman, Inc. was aware of a trademark claim, the designations have been printed in initial caps or all caps.

The author and publisher have taken care in the preparation of this book, but make no expressed or implied warranty of any kind and assume no responsibility for errors or omissions. No liability is assumed for incidental or consequential damages in connection with or arising out of the use of the information or programs contained herein.

The publisher offers discounts on this book when ordered in quantity for special sales. For more information, please contact:

AWL Direct Sales
Addison Wesley Longman, Inc.
One Jacob Way
Reading, Massachusetts 01867
(781) 944-3700

Visit AW on the Web: www.awl.com/cseng/

Library of Congress Cataloging-in-Publication Data

Greenberg, Eric, 1963–
    Network application frameworks : design and architecture / Eric
Greenberg.
        p.   cm.
    Includes bibliographical references and index.
    ISBN 0-201-30950-5
    1. Computer networks.   I. Title.
TK5105.5.G73   1998
004.6—dc21   98–30709
                                                      CIP

ISBN 0-201-30950-5
Text printed on recycled paper.
1 2 3 4 5 6 7 8 9 10—MA—0201009998
First printing, November 1998.

Contents

Writing a book is an adventure. To begin with, it is a toy and an amusement; then it becomes a mistress, and then it becomes a master, and then a tyrant. The last phase is that, just as you are about to be reconciled with your servitude, you kill the monster, and fling him out to the public.

Winston Churchill

Preface

This book provides a comprehensive road map for understanding the design, architecture, and inherent integrated nature of modern and legacy networking and application technologies. The audience for this book includes IS managers, systems engineers, software designers, network engineers, system administrators, network managers, systems architects, senior technologists, and senior management.

By reading this book, you will be introduced to a wide range of highly relevant enterprise networking and application technologies. Armed with this knowledge, you will be able to design new systems that better meet functional, performance, and operational objectives. For existing deployments, your ability to isolate poor performance to either the network, the application, or both will be improved. In addition, you will be able to design networks and applications that more seamlessly and efficiently integrate legacy technologies with modern ones.

To understand the purpose of this book, let's consider the following scenario:

> The company's sales staff has called a meeting with the Information Systems (IS) department to discuss the increasingly poor performance of their worldwide sales processing application. The IS group has brought the folks responsible for the network to the meeting as well. The networking people blame the application developer, arguing the application must be at fault, and, vice versa, the developer claims the network is slow. Furthermore, there is a desire to integrate the sales processing application with other corporate systems, and there is confusion and disagreement on exactly how to achieve that. The networking people claim the systems cannot be integrated due to differing incompatible protocols, and the application folks want to rewrite everything but do not have the time or resources for that approach.

Problems like these have existed for years, but we are now entering a new era in which less and less tolerance exists for this isolated approach to network and application design.

Distributed object technology, directory services information embedded within the network, vast connectivity, a huge base of older legacy technology that must be further integrated, and a host of other technologies we will discuss in this book are producing a tighter coupling between the network and its applications. This means that our old habits of separating network and application design, which never worked well anyway, will no longer work at all. The functionality, efficiency, performance, reliability, and security of the network and its applications are so intertwined that designing them in isolation will repeatedly result in networks and applications that miss the mark in too many ways—over budget, underperforming, poorly integrated, and too expensive to maintain.

As a result, there is a growing need for technical professionals to understand how both networks and applications behave together, as one. Like those systems-level hardware designers who are more concerned with how chips and boards work together than they are transistors and capacitors, there is a need to look at the design problem from a higher level of abstraction.

In this new tightly coupled era, one of the greatest challenges is the integration of existing (legacy) technologies with open multiplatform standards-based ones. To ignore what is installed across the enterprise today and just speak of what is new is to be unrealistic. This book places heavy emphasis on the understanding of legacy technologies and their role as part of an integrated heterogeneous open standards-based networking and application environment.

Can We Really Cover All That?

It is fair to ask ourselves this question. With all the information explored in this book, plus its associated sea of endless details, is it practical to address all the subject matter here, or is it necessary to decompose it analytically, step by step, detail by detail, topic by topic, and span thousands of pages? Covering this many topics is a formidable challenge for both the author and the reader.

I have discussed this problem with many people over the years and have found that there are three general classes of responses:

1. The *Naysayers* are people who argue that it cannot be done. They look at me, from within their safe insulated and, in my opinion, overly simplistic world, and state that it is not practical to expect one person to understand enough about both applications and networking technologies. They argue human beings are not mentally capable of such things. These are separate areas of study and require individuals who solely focus on one or the other. That is the way it has been, and that

is the way it will always be. And, they add, there are "detailed people" and "architectural people" and the two do not mix.

2. The *Curious* are those who usually are very receptive. They start off the discussion by giving me the benefit of the doubt. Their questions generally take the following form: What is the perspective, viewpoint, mental discipline—the magic if you will—involved in cultivating a deeper understanding of both?

3. The *Burned* are people who have experienced firsthand the scenarios I described earlier. They have been in the meetings where the network engineers and the application developers clashed and the system did not work. These people demand a copy of the book and usually our discussions last three to four times longer than we anticipated. They also ask me about viewpoint and discipline: How do you get to the bottom of problems in such complex systems, given that we agree it must be done?

Relative to the Naysayers, I perhaps have more confidence than they do in the capabilities of technical professionals and management. I think they can indeed grasp this. I also believe that detailed and architectural people do mix. I rebel against the belief that systems and architectural folks do not need to be bothered with details, despite the fact that I have had titles in my career such as Systems Architect. I believe in having such people and positions, but the moment they think that they are the only ones who worry about architecture and that they do not need to worry about details, then the project is guaranteed to be in for some serious trouble. People responsible for the system must have a good understanding of concepts, architectures, and, yes, indeed, details. Details keep them honest. If you can't worry yourself with details such as the bytes of overhead for a packet or configured maximum packet and retransmission values for your applications and protocols, then you cannot architect well, in my opinion.

For those who ask about the magic, the secrets of a mental discipline that will help one cut across such a wide range of topics, in search of the key details, but not all the details, I offer more of a psychological argument. I often refer them to such abstract perspectives as those from a famous Chinese philosopher, Lao Tzu, an acquaintance of Confucius and historically accepted by many as the author of an approximately 2,500-year-old famous text entitled the *Tao Te Ching*. Lao Tzu wrote with great eloquence about *Tao*, or the *Way*. In his book, he infers that the nature of everything in our universe escapes extreme rationalization and overly analytic definition. All that exists reflects a certain flexibility, or softness, and, free from a desire to know each and every detail in our world, but instead to know its concepts (its flow) as well as the select details that guide it, we are then free to realize its mystery. The Tao is hidden but always present and is filled with infinite possibilities.

Keeping Lao Tzu's perspective in mind, let's consider again the aspirations of this book. Given that any single topic explored here can alone justify hundreds and occasionally even thousands of pages of explanation, how can its goals be met?

I believe the answer is rooted in perspective. For everyone I have come to know who takes true ownership for the quality of a given network and its applications together, I have observed that their problem-solving approach and psychology consistently include a virtually indescribable freeness while brainstorming, coupled with a willingness to dive deeply, looking for that one detail that, when brought to the surface, reveals the fundamental insight they are after. They seem instinctively to know which details to pursue and which to leave alone. Their instincts tell them where to dive.

Their thought process is not purely top-down, nor is it entirely bottom-up. Both techniques are applied at different times. The best problem solvers I have met do not fashion themselves purely as architects or simply as programmers or network engineers. Instead, they see themselves as thinkers. They are willing to own the entire problem, not just a piece of it, and, at the same time, they have the sense and fluidity about them to know when and where to focus. They know how to maintain their buoyancy, regardless of the infinite number of details involved, because they focus only on those details that matter.

I believe, consciously or not, these people have a sense of what Lao Tzu was writing about—they have found a Way. And, while I may not grasp or proclaim with great certainty that this book successfully shows this Way, I will admit to you that, in writing it, I envisioned harmonizing with it, and I envisioned sharing it with you. We will dive together, and select which details are relevant for our design and architecture study and which we will choose to leave alone. And, in doing so, we will explore a great expanse of networking and applications technologies and prepare ourselves for the new connectivity paradigm of our era—the design and architecture of *network application frameworks*.

Book Organization

Our study of network application frameworks will be organized by technology provider and open standards, with emphasis on solutions offered by Netscape, Microsoft, Novell, and IBM as well as important open standards from organizations including the IETF, OMG, IEEE, ISO, and others. Table 1 summarizes each chapter in the book.

Table 1 Summary of Book's Chapters

Chapter	Title	What's covered?	Why should I read this chapter?
1	What Is a Network Application Framework?	We'll define the term *network application framework* and introduce important concepts, including objects, directory services, transaction processing, security, and other topics.	A firm grounding in the basic components of network application frameworks is essential. It seems everything is going the way of object orientation, distributed computing interactions of value are quite often performed as transactions, directory services provide fundamental information required for the network and its applications to work together, and the need for security is self-evident.
2	Core Network Application Framework Technologies	We'll study the fundamentals of modern security protocols and techniques including SSL/TLS, IPSEC, X.509 certificates, public key cryptography, and Kerberos, which Microsoft is incorporating into the Windows environment; we'll explore distributed computing and the object Web by looking at CORBA and IIOP as well as RPC; we'll learn about directory services, the "glue" between the network and its applications, including X.500, LDAP, and their relationship to one another.	Obtaining a systems-level view of technologies including CORBA/IIOP, SSL/TLS, public key cryptography, and Kerberos allows you to better design applications that leverage them and networks that support them. For example, knowing the sequence of information exchanges for a Kerberos login and subsequent credentials presentation helps you understand better where to place Kerberos servers in the network. Likewise, understanding how objects might discover each other over the network helps you guide your distributed object architecture and network support.

Table 1 (continued)

Chapter	Title	What's covered?	Why should I read this chapter?
3	The TCP/IP Protocol Suite	We'll look at the TCP/IP protocol suite from the perspective of performance, efficiency, and security, combining these elements to understand design impact on applications and networks.	It is one thing to know of the TCP/IP protocol suite, and entirely another to have a view onto its performance, efficiency, and security. There are many TCP/IP-based applications deployed today that are running very inefficiently and insecurely and that are burdening their underlying networks unnecessarily. More than just a tutorial on this protocol suite, this chapter provides an analysis of the protocol suite, intended to guide you in your design and architecture efforts so that your implementations may reflect efficiency and security.
4	IP Routing	This chapter summarizes advanced IP routing topics, offering both a tutorial and design and architecture analysis. Advanced topics include OSPF and the routing protocol used in the backbone of the Internet, BGP-4.	The traditional view of "knowing a routing protocol" is to memorize how the routers are configured and how the routing protocols basically operate. For true design and architecture, though, one might need to answer deeper questions. For example, which routers carry a heavier processing (CPU) and memory utilization burden than others? What do example network topologies look like when using these routing protocols, and what are their pros and cons from a performance and efficiency perspective? And how about topics such as CIDR and VLSM? In this chapter, we'll explore these topics and others.

Table 1 (continued)

Chapter	Title	What's covered?	Why should I read this chapter?
5	Internet Protocol Version 6 (IPv6)	The IPv6 protocol is presented, including new addressing formats, autoconfiguration capabilities, and its relationship to IPv4.	Despite its challenges, a surprising number of IPv6 implementations are becoming available. The protocol offers a number of benefits in the areas of address management and autoconfiguration.
6	The Open Group Distributed Computing Environment (DCE)	We'll study DCE in order to get an idea of what a well-rounded distributed computing environment looks like.	While DCE itself has not received significant deployment, its impact has been widespread. For example, the upcoming Microsoft NT 5 server product offers an important feature also supported in DCE—Kerberos. By understanding DCE, you know a good model against which you can measure other frameworks and approaches.
7	Microsoft and WOSA	Microsoft's network and applications technologies and the Windows Open System Architecture (WOSA) are presented.	Microsoft dominates the desktop landscape today and is working to do the same with its server products. In this chapter, we'll learn how Microsoft's technologies work with each other and also look at the way they compare and interoperate with those from other vendors and from open standards bodies.

Table 1 (continued)

Chapter	Title	What's covered?	Why should I read this chapter?
8	The NT 4 Directory Service	The NT 4 directory service defines the way access control and security are configured for users, groups of users, and resources within the Windows environment. In this chapter, we'll study design techniques using the NT 4 directory service and also consider its pros and cons.	A recurring theme throughout this book is one of the importance of directory services. They are fundamental to managing users and resources within the enterprise, and their importance is increasing rapidly. We'll learn in this chapter the strengths and weaknesses of the NT 4 directory service, laying the groundwork for the reader to compare this service offering to the next one from Microsoft, called *Active Directory*, as well as to other offerings, including Novell NDS, LDAP, and X.500.
9	NT 5 Active Directory Services	Microsoft completely redesigned its directory services with the release of NT 5. In this chapter, we'll look at this redesign and compare it to its predecessor, the NT 4 directory service.	NT 5 presents some serious questions to the network and applications professional. With the availability of very competitive alternative products and associated open standards including LDAP, there is now a sense of choice about where to go next with your enterprise infrastructure. Further commit to Microsoft, ride the line of open standards, or go fully with some other vendor—what is the next best step? This chapter, coupled with others in the book, help provide you with the information you need to make your own decision.

Table 1 (continued)

Chapter	Title	What's covered?	Why should I read this chapter?
10	Novell NetWare	We'll study the networking and applications development technologies offered by Novell NetWare, covering versions from 3.x through 5.	Contrary to the belief of some, Novell is not off the map, by any means. Its NDS directory services product offering is stellar in many respects, and few can compete with it. Novell's massive installed base as well as its substantial network server-side market share make it an important part of most network and application designs.
11	IBM	IBM computer products and architectures including mainframes and mini-computers will be covered, as well as SNA. Issues associated with legacy mainframe integration into a TCP/IP environment and the Web will be addressed. Important techniques for networking legacy IBM mainframe systems are studied, including spoofing and SDLC/token ring conversion.	IBM remains a leader in high-end transaction processing. In order for electronic commerce to meet its potential, IBM solutions must be integrated onto the Web and enterprise applications and networks. Traditionally, knowledge of IBM mainframe technology and networking capabilities has been limited to the select few experienced IS professionals who have been in the industry long enough to have experience with it. This chapter endeavors to make this knowledge available to a wider audience.

Table 1 (continued)

Chapter	Title	What's covered?	Why should I read this chapter?
12	Design Rule Summary	A structured summary of the design and architecture rules and observations presented in the book is provided.	This chapter serves as a quick reference guide for key information presented in the book. It provides readers with one place where they can go to get their memory quickly refreshed on a particular topic or to identify one or more key details that are more easily visualized in this summary format.

Notice that every chapter in this book begins with a *mind map*. Mind maps are used to summarize the technical concepts presented and their relationships to one another. In addition, every chapter except the first and last contains a table summarizing the benefits of the technology addressed within it, along with industry experience and observations that support why this technology is worth considering.

Acknowledgments and Reflections

The writing of this book was a soulful endeavor, one not easily explained in terms of professional career goals or a desire for material gain. It expresses my strong passion for technology and for writing. I can confidently say that to complete this book I put forth every ounce of effort I had. Books like this one do not get completed in months. They demand years of ongoing sacrifice, in every aspect of your life.

I was not alone in this effort. First and foremost, I would like to thank Mary Treseler O'Brien of Addison Wesley Longman. The connection and work chemistry that Mary and I share are anything but common. From the first time we spoke and through every last painful, happy, and manic phase associated with completion of this project, Mary supported me and guided this book as if she and I had been preparing for its completion all our lives.

Working alongside of Mary was Elizabeth Spainhour, who put up with my incessant nagging and worry about every detail of the process. Elizabeth and Mary make a great team. "Two on one" was the minimum requirement to keep me under control at times. Thank goodness Elizabeth was there to keep me in my cage.

Given a large, unpolished manuscript, Addison Wesley produced a book. Providing form, consistency, color, and clarity, a talented group of production and marketing professionals were unleashed on this project. I'd like to thank Jean Peck for copyediting with such great care and skill. Jean has infinite patience and a talent for knowing what I intended to write but didn't. Maureen Willard orchestrated the production process, keeping me calm. Tracy Russ and Katherine Kwack led marketing, a difficult task because this book is different. Finally, John Fuller project-managed the effort to completion.

Addison Wesley Longman assembled a powerful and diverse team of reviewers for this book. Each one offered a unique perspective and style, and, as a whole, they complemented each other wonderfully.

Clem Cole brought deep insight, character, maturity, and a great sense of humor and understanding to the review process. He provided seasoned input into the history and content of the technologies presented in this book.

Peter J. Welcher reviewed the manuscript with the utmost in tenacity, completeness, and precision. We disagreed often, right to the end, and there are a few holes in the walls of my office with Peter's name underneath them. At the same time, this book is orders of magnitude better because of his involvement.

Thomas R. Amlicke, Jr., provided memorable kindness and understanding through his comments and guidance.

And then we have Lou Breit, Rich Sherman, Roger Snowden, and Ed Wax. While they acted independently, together they were great motivators. Rich, with the project from its beginning, was like a steady beacon, always reinforcing the premise of the book and encouraging me to move forward. Roger provided the greatest sound bites—if I hadn't slept in what seemed like days, and needed more energy, I'd just pickup one of Roger's reviews and I'd instantly be motivated once again. Likewise, Ed provided great input and memorable words. And rounding out the group was Lou Breit, who also lent his expertise to the review of this book.

Now for my friends and colleagues. First, I'd like to thank Judy Peck for noticing that the single guy living in the apartment below her didn't know how to keep anything but Diet Coke in his refrigerator. Judy brought me fruit salad every week and became a great friend.

And thanks to Tom McKnight, a friend of mine for years. He also happens to be the most brilliant person I know. Also thanks to Colleen, Tom's daughter, for putting up without her daddy while he helped me build a strategic consulting practice.

To my friends and former colleagues at Netscape, the Litronic crew, the Global SprintLink team, Simson Garfinkel, Susan Fitzgerald, Steve Petri, Cam, Leslie Aimone, Grace Adams, Chandra Shah, Jack Schiff, Sarah Gottlieb-Hecht, Jack Ziros, Larry Elfes, Don Williams, and Sami Mousa.

Thanks to Katie, Rachie, and Robbie Greenberg for putting up with Uncle Eric's writing over the holidays. Thanks to my brother, James, and sister-in-law, Lisa.

In memory of the late Phil Karlton and his wife, Jan.

I hope that this book is helpful, and I wish you great success in your professional endeavors. Please feel free to contact me directly with any comments, corrections, complaints, or kind words. My e-mail address is eric@seinedynamics.com.

Network
Application
Frameworks

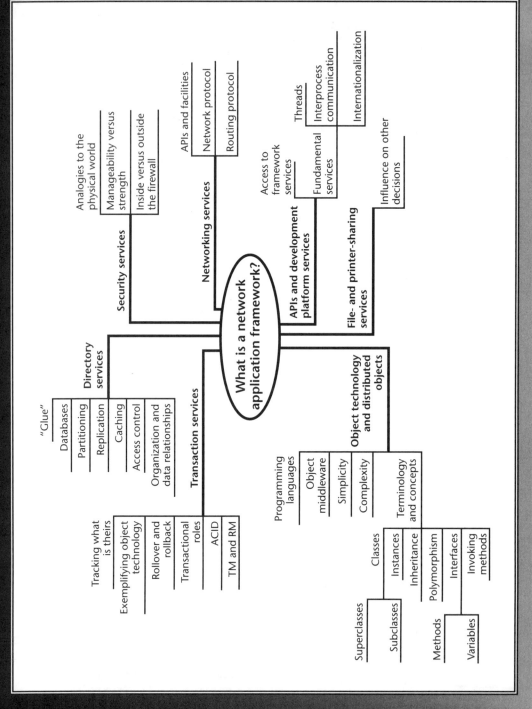

What is a network application framework?

- Security services
  - Analogies to the physical world
  - Manageability versus strength
  - Inside versus outside the firewall
- Networking services
  - APIs and facilities
  - Network protocol
  - Routing protocol
- APIs and development platform services
  - Access to framework services
    - Fundamental services
      - Threads
      - Interprocess communication
      - Internationalization
- File- and printer-sharing services
  - Influence on other decisions
- Directory services
  - "Glue"
    - Databases
    - Partitioning
    - Replication
    - Caching
    - Access control
    - Organization and data relationships
- Transaction services
  - Tracking what is theirs
    - Exemplifying object technology
  - Rollover and rollback
  - Transactional roles
    - ACID
    - TM and RM
- Object technology and distributed objects
  - Programming languages
    - Object middleware
    - Simplicity
    - Complexity
  - Terminology and concepts
    - Classes
      - Superclasses
      - Subclasses
    - Instances
    - Inheritance
    - Polymorphism
    - Interfaces
    - Invoking methods
      - Methods
      - Variables

CHAPTER 1

What Is a Network Application Framework?

1.1 Introduction

What is a *network application framework*? Glad you asked. The definition of the term *network application framework* is by no means universally agreed upon. In this book, the term is applied to the collection of interoperable technologies that, when combined, allow the network and its applications to operate seamlessly as one fully connected interdependent ecosystem. By studying these technologies as part of an overall framework, we are less likely to lose sight of their integrated nature.

With all the network and application advancements of our time, it is safe to say we are in an era of historical significance. The key technologies fueling this advancement are what comprise the network application framework. These include

- Object technology and distributed objects
- Directory services
- Transaction services
- Security services
- Networking services
- Application programming interfaces (APIs) and development plaform services
- File- and printer-sharing services

Each of these technologies will be introduced in this chapter and discussed throughout the book. We will explore key network application framework elements supported by IBM, Microsoft, Netscape, and Novell, and we will look at important core open standards.

1.2 Object Technology and Distributed Objects

We begin our study with a technical introduction to object technology. More and more, software is being developed according to the principles of object-oriented technology. Perhaps the single most distinguishing characteristic of object technology is its ability to provide a standard application-layer interface specification upon which all software components, be they local or remote, can agree. From the perspective of the software developer, this simplifies various aspects of the development process, enhances software interoperability, and allows for software reusability. From the perspective of the network, it sets the groundwork for a less centralized data flow by allowing remote objects to "chat" at will across the network, knowing there is a common application-layer language with which they can communicate.

Prior to object technology, it was more work for an application developer to arrange a chatty distributed traffic flow willy-nilly, so it happened less frequently, thereby producing a more predictable centralized traffic flow. Anyone who has designed a network for a large corporation knows that data has traditionally flowed through such networks in a rather centralized fashion, with either IBM mainframes or other high-powered servers operating at only a few "data centers" within the corporation. All the users (clients) in the network tend to communicate mainly with those data centers, and most network traffic flows to and from those centers. This arrangement is often called a *star topology* because data flows to and from the center of the star and is highly centralized. By allowing data and processing capability to be more conveniently spread among many computers, distributed object technology sets the stage for a reduction in centralized computing.

In fact, as we'll see when we take a look at directory services and the Common Object Request Broker Architecture (CORBA), these objects may dynamically learn of one another, allowing the physical locations of the communicating objects to change over time and thus potentially producing even less predictability in network traffic patterns. Also, some object technologies, such as Java and Microsoft ActiveX, allow remote objects to be dynamically downloaded onto the client machine and executed there. This on-demand transfer of object-executable content through the network can cause an additional network capacity burden.

One other point before we embark on our study of object technology—let's not overhype it. While revolutionary and quite beneficial, it does not do everything. Objects provide a common application interface, but they do *not* alleviate the need for the "worker-bee" hardware and software operating beneath the interface—an interface is an interface, not an implementation. By analogy, what good would the steering wheel of a car (an interface for the car) be without an engine, a transmission, an axle system, four wheels, and all its other parts (the implementation)? We can easily get carried away with defining objects and interfaces and forget that there must be an implementation beneath them. Without implementations, we have nothing.

1.2.1 The Study of Object-Oriented Concepts and Component Models

An *object* is anything—what could be simpler than that? The book you are holding is an object, a bookshelf is an object, and a person can be an object of another's desire. However, the study of object-oriented programming and distributed objects is anything but simple. We are thrown into a sea of abstract terminology and concepts. Newcomers to object technology can quickly be made to feel inadequate in a crowd of object-literate folks who speak in a language that is as good as encrypted to the uninitiated. Eyes glaze over as words like *polymorphism, instantiation, classes, methods,* and *metadata* fill the air. What happened here? Where did the simplicity go?

If I could answer that question, I would define a whole new language for describing object technology and would probably be elected president for having achieved such a feat. The problem is, I can't. The deeper our understanding of object technology, the greater our appreciation for the precision of its language and the purity of its science. With this depth of understanding comes a realization that this simple concept is enormously powerful.

In a later section, we will review object terminology and concepts in a simple and clear manner. Object terminology is an acquired taste for many, like spinach. And, like that green, leafy vegetable that made Popeye so strong, it can be good for your health.

1.2.2 Categories of Object Technology

In the world of objects, we generally speak of two categories of technologies:

1. Object-oriented programming languages
2. Distributed object frameworks and object middleware, also referred to as *component models*

It is very important to draw a distinction between the two categories. While there is overlap of concepts and terminology and there can be overlap of technologies between the two categories, they are not necessarily the same.

Object languages are designed to allow programmers to package collections of instructions into nice neat bundles (objects) and to reuse them. Popular object languages include C++ and Smalltalk. These languages allow programmers to leverage the object-oriented techniques that we'll discuss later in this section, which makes this bundling and reusability simple and efficient.

CORBA and Microsoft ActiveX/DCOM are examples of *component models. You are not required to use object-oriented languages with object component models.* Such is the beauty of object component models, and it is one of the most compelling arguments for their use. Component models allow you to take a computer program, be it a legacy one written in COBOL or FORTRAN or a newer one written in C++, and put a wrapper around it. This wrapper turns the program into a neat reusable bundle—an object. The component model framework then provides a whole suite of services and communication mechanisms that allow these objects (bundles) to communicate with one another either locally (on the same computer) or in a distributed fashion (across a network) using a commonly agreed-upon protocol (interface). The component model middleware shields the programmer from the details associated with whether another object to be communicated with is local or remotely located across the network. All objects can also leverage any component model middleware services using this same common protocol.

Java sits in between all of this, offering both an object-oriented language and also component model middleware. You can use Java with component model middleware such as CORBA and Microsoft ActiveX (COM and DCOM). That would be using Java as an object-oriented programming language only. However, you can also leverage the Java component model middleware by using the wide range of Java middleware APIs, Java Remote

Method Invocation (RMI), and the JavaBeans component technology. When combined with these APIs and component technology, Java couples the language directly with the component model middleware. This approach is different from, for example, that of C++, which is a language only.

And Java is One More Thing . . .

While we're at it, it is important to note the other fundamental characteristic of Java—that of platform independence.

Unlike other programming languages that, when compiled (made ready for the target computer), produce a stream of binary 1s and 0s that are interpretable only by a predefined target operating system and hardware platform, Java compiles into *byte code*. The byte code is platform-independent, so whatever the target computer's operating system is, be it UNIX, an IBM mainframe, Windows, the Macintosh, Linux, or what have you, the byte code is the same. At the destination, a Java *virtual machine* interprets the byte code into something that the specific local operating system and hardware platform can understand.

The advantage here is that, when you write applications using pure Java, they can run on every computer out there that supports Java—you do not need to be concerned with the operating system or hardware platform of the destination system when coding in Java. There is one possible exception: Microsoft has added Windows-specific extensions to Java as part of their software development offering, and these extensions may run only on Windows machines.

1.2.3 Object Terminology and Concepts

It was stated earlier that objects can be anything. So, for our study, let's choose an approachable, simple, familiar object—the motor vehicle.

In object terminology, objects have *interfaces*. We can't ask an object to do anything for us unless we understand its interface. Motor vehicles have a number of interface elements. These include

- A brake pedal
- An acceleration (gas) pedal
- A steering wheel
- An ignition to turn the vehicle on and off

The ability for a car to turn on and off, to brake, to accelerate, and to steer are all functions of a motor vehicle. In the world of objects, these are called *methods*.

When we use an object's methods, we typically must provide it with certain specific information that may change. For example, by turning the steering wheel of your car, you are telling the motor vehicle object to turn its wheels to the left a certain amount, to turn to the right some other specific amount, or to go straight. You might need to make a hard-left turn or simply merge into the next lane. This information—the specific amount to turn, accelerate, brake, or what have you—is stored in *variables*. The interface of an object can be completely described by its methods and variables.

Our world is comprised of objects. Your particular neighborhood is comprised of objects. Your house is full of objects. Parking lots are typically full of motor vehicle objects. With all this flexibility, we would be wise to come up with a way to organize and interrelate our objects. *Classes* allow us to do this.

There are many different kinds of motor vehicle objects. Let's consider the following motor vehicle classifications:

- Passenger car
- Pickup truck
- Bus

As shown in Figure 1.1, all three of these objects are still motor vehicles. They all steer, accelerate, brake, and turn on and off. They can all be said to *inherit* these methods from their parent class, Motor Vehicles. The passenger car, pickup truck, and bus are **subclasses** of the Motor Vehicles class. From the perspective of the subclasses, Motor Vehicles is a **superclass.**

Subclasses can add to and extend the methods of their parent class. In our example, subclasses add specific information about the body type of the vehicles, among other things. The pickup truck, for example, has a flatbed area into which we can load things and has a tailgate that can be opened and closed. Depending upon where you are in the United States, the pickup truck may even have a rifle-rack method that may or may not have a rifle installed.

An *instance* is an object with all its variables filled in. A red Ford Taurus traveling straight down the road at 10 miles per hour is an instance of the passenger car object class. An instance is nothing more than a specific run-time example of an object class. On the computer, an instance requires that memory be allocated and that the CPU be prepared to respond to object *invocations*. Invocation is what we're here for. We want to do something with

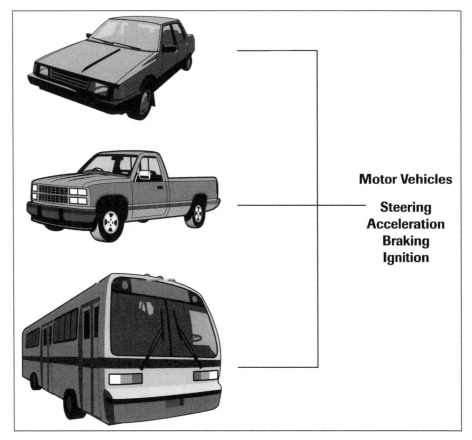

Figure 1.1 Object classes

this object, and the way we do that is by invoking its methods. For example, the steering method on the red Ford Taurus can be invoked, forcing the car to go round in circles.

Note that, in this entire discussion, we never mentioned exactly how the passenger car object moves its wheels and steers—we didn't talk about the design of the gas combustion mechanism in its engine, or its disc braking system design, or its power steering pump operation. The beauty of object technology is that we can separate the object's *implementation* (how the engine works, for example) from its interface. This feature allows us to, for example, change the engine and change the braking system—change the implementation—and not impact any other objects relying upon the

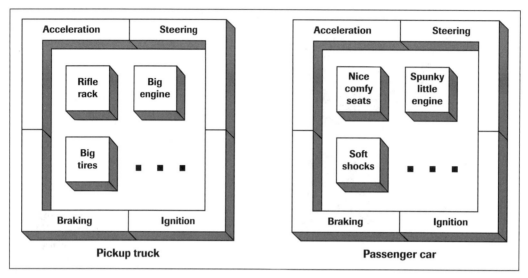

Figure 1.2 Polymorphism

passenger car object. Other objects know the passenger car object by its interface (method and variable definitions), not by its implementation. In fact, you can control any of the motor vehicles (car, pickup, or bus) with the same interface (steering, acceleration, etc.). This powerful aspect of object technology lets us localize changes in our software to only those places requiring change.

The ability for two or more objects to respond to the same interface definition is called *polymorphism.* Returning to our example, all vehicles (passenger car, pickup truck, and bus) respond to the same interface, yet they are different objects. Figure 1.2 illustrates the idea, showing that the interface (the outer rectangle in the figure) can be the same but that the object and the manner in which it responds can be different (in this case, moving a pickup truck versus a passenger car).

1.3 Directory Services

Directory services are distributed databases of information. They are specifically designed for data that does not change too frequently—data that is read mostly and written (changed) far less frequently. Directory servers are distributed across your network so that they are easily reachable by clients and servers.

Directory servers can hold a diverse collection of information, including

- E-mail addresses of your colleagues
- Permissions

For example, if you are using Netscape Messenger as your messaging client, you can choose to look up a person's e-mail address using the Lightweight Directory Access Protocol (LDAP), which we'll study in Chapter 2. For the case of Netscape's product, you merely select your address book, then select the directory service you might like to use, such as the Four11 Directory, and type in a name. The directory service will respond with e-mail addresses assigned to people having that name.

We'll see that, in using Microsoft's directory services, the directory service holds a user's username and password. When users wish to take advantage of NT file and print services, for example, they may be required to authenticate themselves to the NT directory service. Information stored in directory servers includes security-related data defining users of systems, groups of users, servers that clients might like to access, specific directories on those servers, and shared printers. Both end users and applications can send queries to directory servers and, if granted appropriate permissions, can edit information in the directory server.

Directory Services and Distributed Objects: Yes, They Are Related.

One bit of information that might be stored in the directory service but that is not frequently mentioned is that of the location of distributed objects (such as DCOM or CORBA objects) within the enterprise. For example, suppose you want to perform a search for an object capable of spell-checking in Italian. You might like to locate that object using the directory service. Object technology providers have been woefully inadequate in integrating their object frameworks with mainstream directory services offerings. To date, they either have invented their own, behaving as if they are in isolation, or have barely addressed the issue at all. We'll touch on this a few other times in this book. Start a trend and we might achieve the object Web discussed in the introduction to the CORBA section later in this book—ask your object technology providers how they integrate with your directory service!

1.3.1 Characteristics of Directory Services

Let's review a few of the common characteristics of directory services.

1.3.1.1 Data Relationships

General-purpose directories contain complex data relationships. In the case of *Domain Name Services* (DNS), a directory service standard traditionally deployed for address resolution and used extensively in the Internet, comprehensible, human-friendly address formats, such as www.whitehouse.gov, are mapped to unintuitive, computer-friendly numerical network addresses, such as 198.137.240.92.

1.3.1.2 Organization

The way data is organized within a directory service, often referred to as its *schema,* as well as the decision of where to place directory servers in the network, are popular topics of discussion because they can strongly impact network and application performance and manageability. By influencing where a client or server must go in the network to get directory service information, these organizational decisions directly affect network traffic patterns, user response times, and directory information manageability. Throughout this book, when the topic of directory services is addressed, we will look at these organizational principles.

Most advanced directory service offerings allow for directory service information to be organized in a treelike structure. The Microsoft NT 4 directory service, which we'll discuss in Chapter 8, is an exception and incorporates a flat architecture. Figure 1.3 illustrates a directory service information tree.

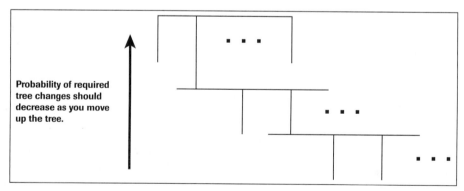

Figure 1.3 Directory service information tree

Information is typically organized in a hierarchy, with less frequently changing information placed near the top of the tree, such as company locations and departments, and frequently changing information, such as a particular user's privileges for access to a network file server, stored toward the bottom of the tree. We will look at these and other topics more closely when we study specific directory service implementations later in this book.

1.3.1.3 Replication

Directories are, as previously mentioned, distributed databases. The same information accessible, for example, to someone in McLean, Virginia, may also need to be accessible to an application in Osaka, Japan, or in Paris, France. How do we make this access efficient? If we keep all the data on one server, then everyone, from all around the world, must use the network to get to that faraway place where the data is stored. Given that this information can be frequently accessed, would we really want to centrally locate it at one place in the world? We deal with this situation through *replication* (also sometimes referred to as *shadowing*) of the directory service database. In our example, we would place a copy of the directory service database in Osaka and another in Paris.

Replication breeds the need for *synchronization*. When data changes, the change must be propagated to all replicas of the data, which, in our example, are located in Japan and in France. In order to synchronize the replicas, directory servers implement a reliable transaction-oriented database update protocol. From the perspective of the network, this translates to data traffic across the network. Every time there is an update to the portion of the directory service that has been replicated, synchronization update packets are sent across the network to all the replicated directory servers. Sometimes, data will get out of control and oscillate, changing from one value to another, perhaps due to a malfunction in one of your programs. A *synchronization traffic storm* can result. Such a storm has been known to bring down the network of one of the largest private corporate networks in the world.

You are not required to replicate the entire directory database. You can usually choose exactly which portions of the directory service database you would like to replicate. This process is referred to as *selective* replication. The general rule is that you should replicate no more than is necessary. By doing so, you will minimize the synchronization traffic on the network and reduce the processing burden within the directory servers.

There are two fundamental approaches to replicating directory service databases:

1. With the *master/slave* approach, changes to the directory service database must first be made at a predesignated master version of the database. After the master is updated, then all the slaves (the replicas) are updated. If the master is not updated, then the slaves are not updated, which makes the master a single point of failure. So, in this case, we have a single point of administration—the master—and it had better be fully operational when it comes time for an update.

2. With the *peer-to-peer* approach, changes can be made on any directory server, and that particular directory server then begins the process of updating other directory servers in a distributed transaction-oriented fashion. The key distinction here is that no concept of master/slave exists in the peer-to-peer approach. You make an update at any of the directory servers (typically a convenient option to have), and the system goes through a series of update transactions to spread the change across the network of directory servers. With the peer-to-peer approach, the master is *not* a single point of failure.

1.3.1.4 Caching

Caching can be thought of as on-demand selective replication. When caching data, the directory server will save a copy of frequently requested directory service information locally, rather than constantly fetching this information from the source directory server, which may be located remotely across the network, each time it is requested. Cached information must be kept up-to-date by the directory service infrastructure since the information stored there could change at the source. Your particular directory server product will implement some proprietary mechanism to achieve this. By enabling caching, you may reduce network traffic attributable to directory service queries and also reduce the processing burden on the source of frequently requested directory service information.

1.3.1.5 Partitioning

Another approach to controlling synchronization traffic and enhancing manageability is through *partitioning* of the directory service database. Partitioning allows you to designate exactly which portions of the directory database a particular directory server must store. For example, if your company has two divisions and there are certain portions of the directory service database that are not typically shared between these two divisions, then you might partition the database accordingly.

1.3.1.6 Access Control Lists (ACLs)

Access to particular information (data) within the directory service may, depending upon the design of the directory service, be controlled by *access control lists* (ACLs). ACLs express the privileges assigned for access to a given directory service information element. The most obvious ACL requirement is for permission to change the directory service database—that is, certain administrators are allowed to change some directory service entries but not others. Here are two other examples of common ACLs:

1. To provide file access privileges (e.g., user Alice can read user Bob's e-mail).
2. To provide administrative privileges (e.g., user Beth can delete users in the engineering group).

The directory service will increasingly become the lifeline of the enterprise network. It will contain information needed to make addressing more and more user-friendly; to locate value-added services available within the network; to bind disparate distributed objects (such as CORBA and DCOM) together, thus forming the backbone of the distributed computing environment; plus a million other things not mentioned here. The directory service is the "glue" that will bind applications to one another and the network to the applications.

1.3.2 Directory Services and the Network

Directory servers use the network to communicate with one another, synchronizing data, replicating data, and referring queries back and forth. Clients use the network to communicate with directory servers to issue queries and update information. Likewise, servers may also query the directory service and update information.

In some cases, as in the case of DNS, directory services are a required part of the network—without them, the network can become unusable to clients and servers. This trend is likely to continue, wherein the network and directory services will become increasingly codependent.

Because of their importance, directory servers should be placed in highly available portions of the network—areas reachable by more than one communications link and typically with redundant router communications equipment. Since they are often combined with the fundamental authentication scheme used within a corporation (we'll learn more about this throughout the book), it is likely that clients will need to access the directory service successfully at least once upon start-up or, more likely, multiple times, if they are to do anything productive.

As you learn about the functional operations of directory services in this book, think about how your corporation might leverage these services, about the flow of traffic, and about the importance of that traffic. Combine that knowledge with an understanding of your organization's network protocols and routing infrastructure to derive designs that meet your requirements.

1.4 Transaction Services

As Jim Gray and Andreas Reuter point out in the opening of their classic book entitled *Transaction Processing: Concepts and Techniques,* the concept of transaction processing has been around for a while: "Six thousand years ago, the Sumerians invented writing for transaction processing. The earliest known writing is found on clay tablets recording the royal inventory of taxes, land, grain, cattle, and gold; scribes evidently kept records of each transaction." Consistent with meeting humankind's desire to keep track of what is theirs, most network application frameworks offer services that make transactions easier to perform and manage. Note, however, that transactions are useful for more than keeping track of what is yours and theirs. Any interaction between two computers that must be guaranteed either to complete successfully or to return to exactly the state things were in before the transaction was attempted benefit from transaction processing services.

Transactions are complicated. Think of all that can go wrong from the time you give money to a bank teller or ATM machine for deposit to the time the money is registered in all of the bank's systems. Imagine all the steps involved in fulfilling an order you place by phone or over the Internet. Figure 1.4 illustrates the highest-level transactional roles involved in placing an order. Clearly, this figure shows only the three highest-level steps. Many more are not shown, such as how refunds are handled.

Most transaction processing systems are built around a *three-tier* architecture, which means that the following three components are separate:

1. The client, which offers a user interface and the ability to perform some amount of processing.
2. The application, which houses the so-called business logic. Business logic is nothing more than the steps an application must follow to complete a transaction, like getting approvals and checking inventories and account balances.
3. The *Resource Manager (RM)/data store,* which is the database holding the long-term information associated with the transaction—information such as your bank account balance.

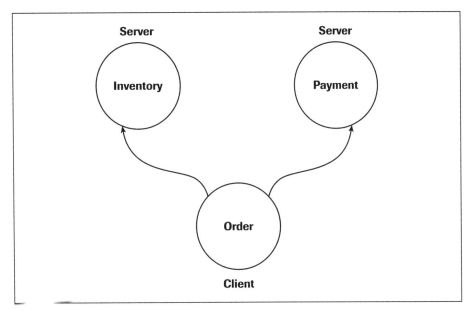

Figure 1.4 Transactions

Database Management System (DBMS) and Transaction Processing

In their early days, transaction processing systems were sometimes referred to as *Database-Data Communications* (DB-DC) systems. This term helps to accentuate the importance of database technology in the world of transaction processing. A *Database Management System* (DBMS) typically stores the fundamental information associated with a transaction, such as bank account balances, a history of deposits and withdrawals, and so forth. Furthermore, the DBMS can hold *stored procedures*, which are sets of instructions stored *in the server* that can be used to synthesize information in the DBMS, such as to summarize a bank account balance based on a sequence of deposits and withdrawals for use as part of some larger transaction. Stored procedures have the benefit of minimizing the need to analyze and collect information on the client-side by summarizing the result of a series of database operations on the server-side and sharing only the summarized result with the client. This can reduce the network burden by decreasing the amount of data needed by the client to get what it is after (the balance instead of all deposits and withdrawals). There can be drawbacks here as well. Some DBMS stored-procedure implementations do not utilize standard programming languages and APIs, which can therefore tie you into a particular vendor's proprietary programming environment.

Transaction processing services cater to the processing needs associated with entry, query, and update of data spread across multiple systems, such as a credit card approval system, an inventory system, and an order entry system. These systems are usually interconnected by a communications network.

A transaction is one complete thing. If everything within a transaction isn't completed successfully, then the transaction itself hasn't completed successfully. If, in the middle of a transaction, something is modified (for example, your credit card is charged) but the transaction never completes (that is, your order can't be satisfied), then a *rollback* must be performed—the transaction processor must be able to undo any changes (your credit card would therefore be credited). If all elements of a transaction complete successfully, then it is said to be *committed.* Excessive transaction rollbacks may be due to intermittent problems within the network itself. Such problems can be caused by network congestion, excessive bit errors, router instability, or, as discussed in Chapter 4, route flapping.

Transaction processors (TPs) become involved with performance challenges such as load sharing, in which individual elements of a transaction are farmed out to multiple systems, thus distributing the processing burden.

When learning about transactions, you will often see the term *ACID.* Originally introduced by Gray and Reuter, the term is intended to serve as an easy way to remember the four key ingredients of a successful transaction processing implementation:

Atomicity   Consistency   Isolation   Durability

1. *Atomicity* indicates that a transaction needs to be treated as a single unit of work—as a whole. If any one of the elements that comprise it fail, then the entire transaction fails.

2. *Consistency* demands that the implementation leave everything in a known and correct state. If the transaction fails, the databases and all other resources must be rolled back to a known and correct state. For example, you can't have half the data updated and the other half not.

3. *Isolation* requires that transactions running concurrently do not disrupt one another, haphazardly updating shared resources without regard for other transactions that may be executing. So, for a transaction to complete successfully, it must do so without disrupting others.

4. *Durability* is a rather strange term here. (You may also sometimes hear the term *durable data*, which sounds impressive.) Within

this discussion, durability refers to the permanence of the data. Specifically, what it means is that, before the transaction is committed, all of the data elements associated with it must be stored safely in a *persistent* storage mechanism, one that won't lose its record of the data, for example, if the computer system is shut down for maintenance or if the computer's processor decides to crash.

One example of a nonpersistent storage mechanism is a *cache*. Most computers have a cache that acts like a hard drive but really is information held in volatile memory (that is, RAM), thus speeding up file access requests so that information requests need not wait for the hard drive to search for the information but instead can be more quickly satisfied by querying information temporarily stored in system RAM (the cache). Changes made to the cache are typically written to the hard drive on a timed basis unless specific instructions are given to perform the write to the hard drive directly. Instructing the cache to write information changes down to the hard drive is called *flushing* the cache. What durability means, for this example, is that these changes are written down to the hard drive, not just to the cache (that is, flushed), *before* the transaction is committed. Hard drive caches are not the only caches that may need to be flushed before the transaction can be committed. For example, directory servers contain caches, and, in the event they contain data that changes as a result of a transaction, their caches may also require flushing.

In the world of transaction processing, we often refer to the *Resource Manager* (RM) and the *Transaction Manager* (TM). The RM manages databases and other similar resources for the transaction. The TM coordinates the sequence of events of the transaction until it is committed. Examples of commands between the TM and the RM might be Prepare, Commit, or Abort.

From this discussion of transactions, you may have correctly concluded that transaction elements do indeed exemplify objects. The combination of object technology and transaction processing is very powerful. To the extent that elements of the transaction can be treated as nicely encapsulated objects, the implementation and the management of the transaction are simplified. For example, the Microsoft Transaction Server (MTS), a product we'll study in Chapter 7, relies heavily on Microsoft's object component model, COM and DCOM.

1.5 Security Services

Security is not really a stand-alone topic. It is better viewed as a systemic one, integrated with everything. Our universally connected society demands greater security. Once you connect it to the meganetworks of our day, you need to be concerned with the world of people that can now attempt to access it. Also, when you transmit data across public networks, you must understand that your information can be read by others unless you employ techniques to keep your data private. Privacy, tampering, impersonation, traceability—all the concerns of our physical world translate to our electronic world. Our worldwide, fully connected, distributed data and processing environment makes security a number one concern.

As we get more comfortable with the security topic and analogize it to our physical world, we begin to associate different levels of safety with where we are in the network, just as human beings feel safer in some physical locations more than in others. In our networks, we construct protective *firewalls* between our private networks and public ones. Firewalls are good examples of combined network and application devices because they examine both the network and application-layer implications for information passing through them, looking out for events considered to be suspicious relative to the security policies of the firewall administrator. It is not uncommon for applications operating behind a firewall to employ fewer security mechanisms than those that reach beyond it. This is directly analogous to how we feel when we are sitting in our living rooms at home versus walking down a busy city street. In one case, we construct various defenses, including locks on doors and windows, that allow us to let down our guard and employ fewer security mechanisms while watching television or eating dinner. In the other case, however, we know to watch out since the standard protection mechanisms of our homes are not in place on busy city streets.

Let's continue this physical analogy. Depending upon the desirability of whatever it is we are carrying, we may also take special precautions. Therefore, the security measures we employ not only are a function of where we are but also relate to the value of what we have. For example, valuable items you keep at home might be hidden, whereas less valuable items appear out in the open. If you walk down a busy city street with something valuable, you often conceal it, whereas you don't bother to conceal the soda you brought with you from lunch. Likewise, with networking and computing—if the data is very sensitive and desirable, we take more precautions to protect it, sometimes independent of where the data is (inside or outside of the firewall, for example).

All this talk about letting down our guard relates to manageability and convenience—to comfort. Too often, people working in security forget about comfort and believe they earn their salary by simply offering solutions that seem to them to be unbreakable. They are unrealistic. They forget that we live in a world of human beings who have finite time, resources, and patience. Forgetting fundamentals like this is the stuff disasters are made of. Here's an axiom that emphasizes the point:

> If the security mechanisms are not easy enough to use and administer, then people won't use them, or they will use or administer them incorrectly, or the security mechanism may excessively impede day-to-day business operations by making simple tasks too difficult. In such cases, having found a less robust security mechanism that is more easily administered and used might have been a better solution. What is usable and administerable depends on the particular people, networks, and computers involved.

In other words and by following our earlier analogy, if the only two options you have left yourself for securing your home are (1) to arm yourself with a machine gun and not worry about the locks on the doors and windows since they can't keep really bad people out because they'll just break a window or pick a lock or (2) to leave everything unlocked and unsecured, then you have not done a good job.

In this book, we'll explore a wide range of security mechanisms and concerns. Some, such as the Secure Sockets Layer (SSL) protocol, offer a very high grade of security, and others, such as the username/passwords used for certain TCP/IP applications, offer considerably less. We'll look at the manageability, strength, and ability to integrate leading security mechanisms into the network application framework.

1.6 Networking Services

This book covers the network protocol layer (for example, TCP/IP and Novell IPX) and the routing-layer networking technologies (for example, RIP, OSPF, and BGP-4) in considerable detail, along with how applications leverage them. Figure 1.5 summarizes the networking technology covered in this book and its relation to application development.

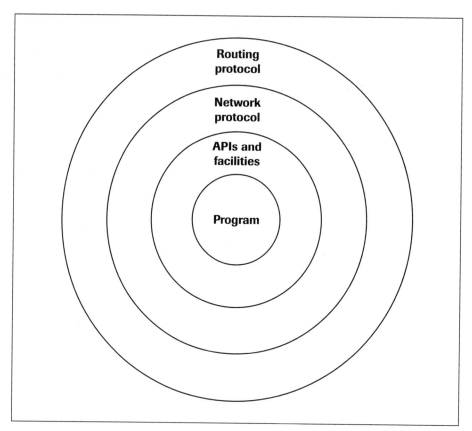

Figure 1.5 Networking

    The network protocol and routing interactions offer, based on my experience, the most likely design and architecture challenges. Most of the problems and issues I have faced when designing and analyzing worldwide applications and networks have, from a communications perspective, been related to operation of the network protocol, behavior of the routing protocols, and the manner in which the application responds to and burdens the network. Whether or not a specific communications link is experiencing high utilization and may require an increase in capacity is often not the first question to ask—these links often become overloaded, as we'll discuss, due to inefficiencies, poor designs, and malfunctions within the applications, routing infrastructure, network protocols, or all of the above. Seeing high utilization along communications links in your network or poor performance

should not immediately trigger a call for increased network capacity. I dare
say that, in the majority of private enterprise (corporate) network cases I have
worked with, unexpected demands for increased capacity within the network
are not due to a genuine increase in customer usage but instead to
inefficiency and malfunction. And, even in the case of portions of the public
Internet, it is not uncommon to discover that the routing infrastructure could
be better leveraged to distribute traffic across less heavily utilized links.

In studying the performance and efficiency of a given network protocol
and associated application, we will consider these aspects:

- Retransmission and flow control
- Byte overhead
- Character echo
- Packet size and queuing

1.6.1 Retransmission and Flow Control

Networks and computers can introduce data errors and can overrun one
another by sending data at a rate faster than the destination can process. In
order to deal with data errors and potential data overruns, protocols are used
to request data retransmission and to control the sender of data so that it
does not overrun the buffers of a slower receiving computer. We will examine
a number of these protocols in this book. The efficiency of these protocols
will greatly impact the performance of your combined network and application. For example, we'll study a protocol called *Novell NetWare IPX nonburst
mode.* We'll see that, when using this protocol over a wide area network
(WAN), the speed at which two computers can share data may be reduced to
a small fraction of what the network itself is capable of. We'll look at one
example where it is reduced to approximately 11% of the available network
capacity, which is dramatic and roughly equivalent to converting your
64-Kbps link to a 7.3-Kbps link. Fortunately, NetWare burst mode exists to
deal with this problem and improve efficiency. However, plenty of nonburst
mode configurations are still deployed.

1.6.2 Byte Overhead

Network and application protocols require *headers,* also sometimes called
control fields, in order to signal protocol commands to the network and/or

receiving application. These headers add significant overhead to each and every data packet sent through the network. The overhead is substantial and, for most corporate networks, cannot be ignored. For example, the IPv4 and TCP headers together add 40 bytes to every packet, and Novell IPX and NCP similarly add 40 bytes. If you have 128 bytes of data to send, for example, then the TCP/IP header adds approximately a 30% overhead factor. For network design purposes, the required capacity is often determined by analysis of data transmission requirements. An important theme of this book is that, when doing so, it is wise to include the byte overhead added by protocols, as well as to consider their other efficiency characteristics.

1.6.3 Character Echo

As we'll see in Chapter 3, it is not uncommon for legacy applications to be based on *VT-100* terminal emulation and for application developers to utilize a TCP/IP protocol called *TELNET*, in *remote character echo mode*, to perform a simple port of this application for use over a local area network (LAN). Furthermore, many new applications are still being developed that utilize TELNET. TELNET remote character echo mode is a perfect example of something that application developers probably would not use if they understood the networking impact. As we'll see later, each character typed by the user (that would typically be 1 byte) is appended with a 40-byte TCP/IP header, sent across the network, echoed by the remote computer, transmitted back across the network to the client, and then displayed. Can you imagine anything more inefficient than this? Guess what? A medium-to-large-sized corporation is likely to have one or more of this style of application running across its network.

1.6.4 Packet Size and Queuing

With all the byte overhead added by today's protocols, it seems natural to argue that we should make data packets as large as possible so that we require the transmission of fewer protocol overhead bytes. For example, if you have 5,000 bytes to send and have 100-byte packets and are using TCP/IP, then every 100-byte packet requires a 40-byte header. That would be 40 bytes/packet × (5,000 bytes to send ÷ 100 bytes/packet)= 2,000 bytes of overhead. If, on the other hand, you utilize 1,000-byte packets, there would be only 40 bytes/packet × (5,000 bytes to send ÷ 1,000 bytes/packet) = 200 bytes of overhead. That is 10 times less overhead. Plus, as we'll see, by having fewer packets, we are less likely to incur a penalty for efficiency losses caused by our error recovery and flow control mechanisms (unless, of course, we have error-prone links).

Why not always use larger packets? Let's return to our earlier TELNET discussion to answer this. If you just typed a character and are waiting for it to be echoed back from the destination, you will get a quicker response if it is queued behind a small 100-byte packet versus a 1,000-byte packet. In other words, these bigger packets can become "bullies," relative to the available network capacity, by sitting in the queue and taking large amounts of time to transmit before other packets get onto the network. For those familiar with the ATM protocol, this is one reason a small fixed packet (cell) size was chosen—to reduce delay variation caused by large packets. Because the benefit of larger packets can be significant for large data transfers, modern network routers provide mechanisms, which we'll touch briefly upon, to prioritize traffic so that these small packets can get prioritized ahead of larger packets over the network, thus helping to alleviate the bully phenomenon.

1.7 Application Programming Interfaces (APIs) and Development Platform Services

Application programming interfaces (APIs) and development platform services are required in order to allow an application to leverage services offered by the network application framework, including networking services, security, and so forth. These interfaces and services also provide fundamental capabilities such as *interprocess communication* and *threading*, terms that we'll be defining later. As another example, standardized mechanisms to internationalize an application so that it can support multiple spoken languages would be part of the API and development platform services. Certainly, the more global our network, the greater our internationalization challenge. The open versus proprietary debate for these services is especially important because the APIs and services your developers directly leverage and program to clearly affect your dependence on a single vendor and ability to choose.

1.8 File- and Printer-Sharing Services

File- and printer-sharing services are relatively self-evident to most folks. Our ability to access files located remotely on a server or a printer across the network is provided by these services. Most of us take them for granted, but it is important to recognize that whomever you go to for these services tends to influence other network application framework components you choose.

1.9 Conclusions

The remainder of this book explores the elements of this technical revolution, old and new. In Chapter 2, we'll examine important open standards-based core network application framework technologies that are being rapidly deployed across public and private networks worldwide.

FOR FURTHER STUDY

1. W. R. Cheswick and S. M. Bellovin. *Firewalls and Internet Security: Repelling the Wily Hacker.* Reading, Mass.: Addison-Wesley, 1994.

2. S. Garfinkel and G. Spafford. *Web Security and Commerce.* Sebastopol, Calif.: O'Reilly, 1997.

3. J. Gray and A. Reuter. *Transaction Processing: Concepts and Techniques.* San Mateo, Calif.: Morgan Kaufmann Publishers, 1993.

4. J. M. Hart and B. Rosenberg. *Client/Server Computing for Technical Professionals: Concepts and Solutions.* Reading, Mass.: Addison-Wesley, 1995.

5. T. Howes and M. Smith. *LDAP: Programming Directory-Enabled Applications with Lightweight Directory Access Protocol.* Indianapolis, Ind.: Macmillan Technical Publishing, 1997.

6. R. Orfali, D. Harkey, and J. Edwards. *Essential Client/Server Survival Guide.* New York: Van Nostrand Reinhold, 1994.

7. R. Orfali, D. Harkey, and J. Edwards. *The Essential Distributed Objects Survival Guide.* New York: Wiley, 1996.

8. A. S. Tanenbaum. *Computer Networks*, 3d ed. Upper Saddle River, N.J.: Prentice-Hall, 1996.

9. D. Taylor. *Object-Oriented Technology: A Manager's Guide*, 2d ed. Reading, Mass.: Addison-Wesley, 1998.

10. W. Richard Stevens. *TCP/IP Illustrated Version 3.* Reading, Mass.: Addison-Wesley, 1994.

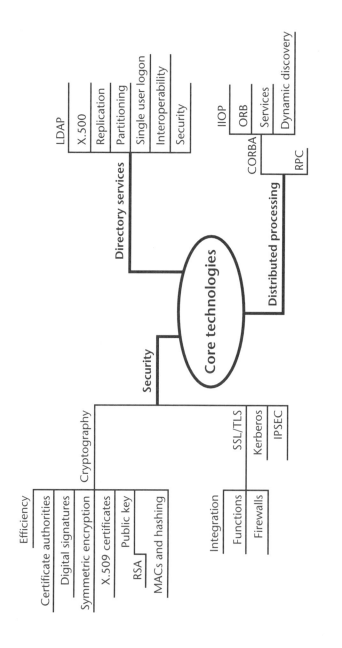

CHAPTER 2

Core Network Application Framework Technologies

CHAPTER HIGHLIGHTS		
Topic	**Benefits**	**Experience**
Common Object Request Broker Architecture (CORBA)	CORBA allows for open multiplatform object-oriented distributed application development. What more could you ask for?	CORBA has been rapidly adopted by enterprise software providers, including Netscape, Oracle, and Novell.
Remote Procedure Call (RPC)	RPC provides a procedural mechanism for a client and server to communicate across the network.	RPC has received widespread adoption. For example, Microsoft DCOM uses RPC.
Security and cryptography	Cryptography provides the strength of security demanded by our now fully connected world. It provides a means to address the security fundamentals, including authentication, authorization, privacy, integrity, and nonrepudiation.	Cryptography plays a role in just about every well-designed security protocol in use today. Cryptography is the backbone of protocols such as SSL/TLS, Pretty Good Privacy (PGP), Secure MIME (S/MIME), IP-level security (IPSEC), and Kerberos.

CHAPTER HIGHLIGHTS		
Topic	**Benefits**	**Experience**
Secure Sockets Layer (SSL) and Transport Layer Security (TLS) protocols	SSL is a robust security protocol that has been held to the scrutiny of the world's finest hackers, via the Internet, thereby making it one of the most tested security protocols of our time. TLS is an IETF standard based on SSL.	SSL/TLS is perhaps one of the most widely available security protocols available today, having been implemented on all major Web browser and server products.
Kerberos	Kerberos provides a viable framework for achieving enterprisewide authentication and single-user logon.	Kerberos is being adopted by Microsoft as part of NT server version 5.0 and is used by the DCE application framework. A number of public domain and commercial Kerberos implementations are available.
X.500	X.500 offers a comprehensive, but complex, standards framework for directory services. Directory services are fundamental to the exchange of service availability information, security attributes, and other fundamental distributed information required by clients and servers.	X.500 has been widely adopted in Europe, and many directory services products and standards borrow from it, including Novell NDS and LDAP.
Lightweight Directory Access Protocol (LDAP)	LDAP provides a lightweight implementable directory services protocol that runs over TCP/IP and leverages important elements of the X.500 architecture.	LDAP has been widely adopted by just about every major network application framework provider, including Netscape, Microsoft, and Novell.

2.1 Introduction

In this chapter, we will discuss fundamental technologies that can play a part, in one way or another, in every network application framework we will study in this book. All are important open standards-based (nonproprietary) technologies that have been broadly adopted. We will focus our discussion on three basic areas:

1. Security
2. Distributed processing
3. Directory services

First, we will discuss the key elements of security that have become staples of Internet, Extranet, and enterprise communication. These include public key cryptography, SSL/TLS, IPSEC, and Kerberos, which is being adopted by Microsoft as part of NT version 5.0. Note that security is discussed throughout the book, not just in this chapter. Here, we merely lay further groundwork for the rest of the book, as the topic of security is woven throughout it.

Why Should You Care about SSL?

Let's make one thing clear about SSL right away—it is everywhere. Just about every site on the Internet doing any kind of money transaction uses SSL. Corporations use it extensively to secure proprietary and confidential information. It is so easy to use, as we'll see, that Web administrators need only enable it on their Web server and obtain something called a *certificate*. Furthermore, as we'll see, IPSEC in no way displaces SSL's role but at best complements it by providing focused network-layer security. If you want to understand how SSL, IPSEC, and other public key cryptography-based protocols operate, then the discussion of public key cryptography in this chapter is for you.

Next, we will look at Remote Procedure Call (RPC), a fundamental means for a client and server to communicate with each other in a distributed environment. We will study Common Object Request Broker Architecture (CORBA), which also provides a means for the client and server to communicate, but within a much broader feature-rich environment—one that offers the promise of changing the face of computing as we now know it, transforming us from the procedural model, such as that supported by RPC, to a fully distributed object-oriented world.

Finally, we will examine directory services. They provide the means to share information such as security rights, e-mail addresses, and server and service availability with clients and servers. In short, directory services are becoming an absolute requirement for the networked enterprise. LDAP, a recent directory services standards advancement, has brought directory services to the masses by providing a practical means for its integration within the Web environment and anywhere else you choose. Its predecessors, including X.500, offer more complexity but also, in some cases, more functionality. We'll discuss both X.500 and LDAP, and, later in the book, we'll talk about Novell NetWare Directory Services (NDS) as well as directory service products offered by Microsoft.

2.2 Core Security Technologies

In this section, we will study fundamental security framework components, including public key cryptography, SSL/TLS, IPSEC, and Kerberos. All of these technologies aspire to provide one or more of the following functions:

- Authentication
- Authorization
- Privacy
- Integrity
- Nonrepudiation

Authentication answers the question, who are you? To answer this question, you generally need to provide some kind of proof, such as knowledge of a password or, in the case of public key cryptography, ownership of a private (secret) key and elements associated with it, such as an X.509 certificate, which we'll examine later. When a server authenticates a client, we refer to the function as *client authentication*. When both the client and the server prove their identities to each other, we refer to it as *mutual authentication*.

Once you know to whom you are speaking, generally the next question to answer, if you are a server, is, what resources is this client allowed to access? This leads us to the topic of *authorization*. Authorization information is typically stored on a server inside an access control list (ACL). ACLs are defined for resources that are controlled by the server and require protection such as files. They may be used to limit resource access to individual users or to users that have been configured to be part of a group. For example, the HR (human resources) group may get access to employee salary history, but the group representing the sales department may not.

Privacy is a critical issue. The client and the server often require that their information exchange be private. For example, if you are doing an online banking transaction or giving your credit card number online, you want that information to be shared only with the bank or merchant you have chosen to do business with, not with anyone else. Within the world of cryptography, we hide data by mathematically scrambling it so that only the two endpoints know how to read it. This process is called *encryption*.

Integrity means incorruptibility. Suppose you decide to purchase something online. For example, maybe you want to buy 10 pairs of socks from a retailer selling socks on the Internet. To your dismay, you receive a box containing 1,000 socks a few days later. What happened? One explanation is that your order (your data) could have been tampered with so that the integrity of your data was corrupted and now you have far too many socks. Later, we'll learn about a technology based on *hash functions* that allows security protocols such as SSL/TLS to detect whether data has been tampered with.

Nonrepudiation occurs when you write a check, sign a letter, or sign a contract. In so doing you are providing a means to prove that you agreed to a certain transaction or sent a certain message. Nonrepudiation is the ability to prove that one party actually agreed to a transaction.

Note that, as you learn about security technology and other technologies in this book, you are going to get help from three folks who are experts at playing various roles in textbooks such as this one: Alice, Bob, and Bad Guy. Alice and Bob will typically play the roles of client/server as we look at various technologies. We presume Alice and Bob to be fine upstanding folks. Bad Guy, on the other hand, is up to no good. Many of you, over the years, may have wondered what Alice and Bob look like, perhaps having read about their experiences but never having seen them. The wait is over. Alice and Bob posed for the pictures provided in Figure 2.1. Bad Guy, however, refused to cooperate—he is, after all, a fugitive of sorts.

Figure 2.1 Pictures of two fine folks

2.2.1 Public Key Cryptography

In this section, we will study public key cryptography, symmetric encryption, and hash functions. All of this technology plays an important role in modern security technologies, including SSL/TLS as well as secure e-mail based on standards such as S/MIME and Pretty Good Privacy (PGP).

In the world of *public key cryptography,* everyone has his or her own unique public key and private key: Your public key is *public,* meaning it is OK to let anyone, even Bad Guy, know it; your private key is *private,* meaning you don't share it (your private key is a secret). If Bad Guy gets your private key, then the public key cryptography framework has been compromised and, consequently, so has your security.

Our discussion will focus on *RSA* public key cryptography since it is widely deployed across the Internet and Intranet. RSA public key cryptography is based on a mathematical cryptographic algorithm developed by the three people after whom it is named: Rivest, Shamir, and Adleman. RSA Data Security is the company, acquired by Security Dynamics, that has historically owned the patents relating to the RSA algorithms and that supplies software development toolkits and standards that further its adoption.

RSA makes use of two keys, the public key and the private key, and special relationships that can be made to exist between them, which we'll discuss. The RSA algorithm is based on prime numbers, exponentiation, and other mathematical operations, but we'll focus on a functional understanding of how the algorithm works and its relationship to enterprise security, as opposed to its implementation.

The public/private key pair can be of different lengths. The longer the keys, the harder it is for a hacker to crack RSA. As of this writing, it is generally believed that 1,024-bit keys provide more than adequate security for the networked enterprise and for electronic commerce. The U.S. government agrees and, in fact, sees them as so powerful that it has historically export-controlled them like a munition—like a sidewinder missile if you will. Right now, 512-bit keys are freely exportable, but 1,024-bit keys require special export approval when used for encryption.

All this is changing at a rapid pace, with different mechanisms being agreed upon with the government that potentially ease export restrictions based on the recipient's country (government) and industry.

The U.S. government's export law is vague in many areas yet somewhat specific with regard to the types of industries and countries the government sees as a threat. A separate book could be written on U.S. export law, but, before we close the topic there, it is important to stress that, for the enterprise, you typically must work in partnership with your vendor to get government approvals, as needed, to export strong cryptography to offices you have outside of the United States.

Two Sides in the Export Debate

In the opinion of many, U.S. export controls hamper U.S. competitiveness, and they're a big problem as now written for industry. We're in a new era where ubiquitous connectivity demands ubiquitous security—we can't assume that people and businesses can or should do without it. To understand the flip side in this debate, we need to realize that eavesdropping and the ability to use stronger unreadable codes and to crack enemy codes have played a strategic role in the military and in the outcome of wars, especially World Wars I and II, in monitoring hostile nations and terrorist activities, as well as in domestic and international law enforcement. People involved in these areas have history behind them to support the impact of cryptography on all of our lives. They take the matter seriously, and understandably so. We need to make sure, however, that we don't produce economic threats that, over time, are commensurate with those we are trying to avoid by limiting cryptographic technology export.

2.2.1.1 Fundamentals of Secure Information Exchange Using Public Key Cryptography

The best way to understand the concepts of public key cryptography and secure information exchange is to work through an example of various information exchanges that leverage increasing dosages of this fascinating and useful technology. So, in this section, let's track Alice and Bob in their unwavering pursuit of a reliable and private exchange of information—in this case, love letters.

2.2.1.1.1 Information Exchange Terminology   Before we begin, let's agree to some notation:

- Alice has a public key, which we'll call *Alice-Pub*, and a private key, which we'll call *Alice-Priv*.
- Likewise, Bob has *Bob-Pub* and *Bob-Priv*.

When Alice runs some data through the RSA algorithm and feeds the algorithm her public key, we'll denote that as *Alice-Pub(data)*. What this means is that her data is all jumbled up because her public key was used as input into the RSA algorithm and out came a seemingly crazy string of 1s and 0s, at least from the perspective of the human eye. This RSA algorithm is illustrated in Figure 2.2. If Alice instead applies her private key to data using the RSA algorithm, then we'll denote that as *Alice-Priv(data)*.

2.2.1.1.2 Public and Private Key Reciprocity   Let's look at an interesting property of the RSA algorithm. If we apply Alice's public key to some data

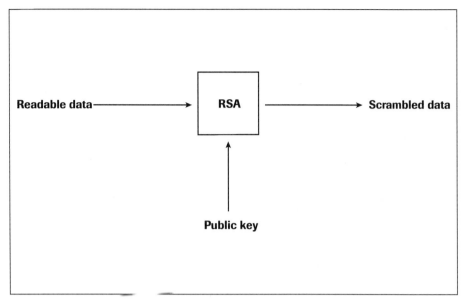

Figure 2.2 RSA algorithm

like, for example, her bank balance, the result is a bunch of 1s and 0s that, if we just looked at, we wouldn't recognize as her bank balance. But, if we then apply her private key onto this jumbled string of 1s and 0s, we get her bank balance back, and we will read it and understand it. Public and private key reciprocity is illustrated in Figure 2.3. One explanation of this concept is to describe the public and the private keys as canceling each other out, which is a distasteful oversimplification for some experienced cryptographers. Nonetheless, it's true—from a functional perspective, they *do* cancel each other out.

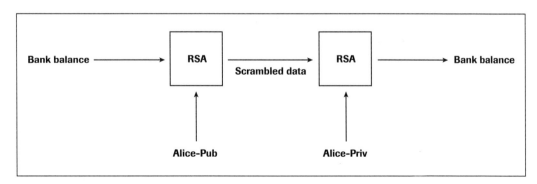

Figure 2.3 Public and private key reciprocity

2.2.1.1.3 Public Key Encryption and Digital Signing   The preceding discussion was interesting, perhaps, but it still doesn't explain why we're interested in public and private keys from a security perspective. Let's take a closer look, remembering the properties and ideas we just considered.

Recall that the public key is public—anyone can get it. Public keys are stored in X.509 *certificates* so that they can be easily shared. X.509 is a standard that defines the format of the certificate. Within the certificate are fields (sometimes referred to as *attributes*) that provide information about the person (or entity, server, etc.) for whom it was generated. One such field is called the *Distinguished Name* (DN). Alice's certificate would, for example, contain a DN uniquely identifying her.

The certificate can also hold other descriptive information about the person for whom it was issued, such as his or her role within a company. For now, just remember that the certificate contains Alice's public key and also other public information about Alice.

Both Alice and Bob have X.509 certificates. Furthermore, Alice can freely get a copy of Bob's certificate and Bob can freely get a copy of Alice's. So, from this point forward, assume that Alice has a copy of Bob's public key and Bob has a copy of Alice's.

Now, suppose Bob decides to send private data, like a love letter, to Alice and wants to make sure that nobody can read it except Alice. Bob uses Alice's public key and applies it to the data like this:

Alice-Pub(Love Letter)

Note that, after Alice's public key is applied to the data (the love letter), *only Alice* can read it because *only Alice* has the corresponding *private* key required to make the love letter intelligible. To repeat, *only Alice*—nobody else—has Alice's private key. In order to read data that has Alice's public key applied to it, the RSA algorithm demands that you have Alice's private key. By applying Alice's public key to the data, Bob has *encrypted* the data—to be exact, he has utilized *public key encryption.* Cryptographers also refer to this as *asymmetric encryption,* the term *asymmetric* coming from the fact that there are two different keys required to lock and unlock the data, not just one key.

So, public key cryptography allows us to encrypt data—to hide data and to offer privacy. Continuing with the love letter example, let's look at another one of this technology's capabilities.

It turns out that Bad Guy also has a crush on Alice. He's angry about Alice and Bob's relationship and wants to make Alice angry at Bob. So, Bad Guy sends Alice a nasty love letter but makes it look as though it came from

Bob. Bad Guy even encrypts the letter with Alice's public key since he has a copy of it, so there is no way for Bob to see what means and nasty things Bad Guy has written.

Alice naturally gets angry at Bob. Bob denies he sent the letter and decides to set the record straight. He believes that he can use public key cryptography to save his relationship with Alice. Bob figures out that if he takes his love letter and applies his private key to it, then Alice can read it since she has his public key. So, he sends it like this:

Bob-Priv(Love Letter)

If, after receiving Bob-Priv(Love Letter) and after having applied Bob's public key to it, Alice finds an intelligible, readable letter, then Alice knows that it must have been sent by Bob since *only Bob*—nobody else—has Bob's private key. She knows that Bad Guy couldn't have sent this letter. If Bad Guy had sent it, then, after applying Bob's public key to what Alice received, she wouldn't have had an intelligible, readable letter; it would have been an unintelligible collection of 1s and 0s.

What Bob has done here is called *digital signing*. By digitally signing the love letter, Bob has performed the equivalent of signing a piece of paper. Through digital signing, we achieve the security property of nonrepudiation.

The Alice/Bob saga is not over just yet. While Bob may have sent Alice a *digitally signed* message, he did not *encrypt* it. So, Bad Guy read the message by applying Bob-Pub to it, and he has been teasing Bob about the letter regularly, telling him how Alice has him wrapped around his finger and that Bob isn't a real man. Enough of this, says Bob. I must get Bad Guy out of my love letter life altogether. So, Bob decides to combine digital signing and encryption when sending his next love letter to Alice, like this:

Bob-Priv(Alice-Pub(Love Letter))

When Alice receives the message, she first applies Bob's public key to it and verifies that it came from Bob. She then applies her private key to it so that she can read the letter. Best of all, Bad Guy can neither read the letter nor pretend he is Bob. But, alas, things are not that simple. One thing you'll learn about Bad Guy and folks like him is that they'll stop at nothing; they'll work day and night to foil your security strategy. Unfortunately, Bad Guy figured out that, if he could construct an X.509 certificate that stated it belonged to Bob but put his own (Bad Guy's) public key into it, he could fool Alice into accepting the public key as Bob's and then continue to send her false love letters and do other mean things.

2.2.1.1.4 Certificate Authorities (CAs)   How does Alice know whether
or not she has a valid certificate for Bob? She doesn't unless the certificate
itself is digitally signed by someone or some organization she trusts. In order
for Alice and Bob to trust each other's certificate, they could make use of a
third party that they both trust to digitally sign their certificates and certify,
in an electronic (public key cryptographic) sense, that Alice is Alice and Bob
is Bob. These trusted third parties are called *certificate authorities* (CAs).

Let's say that Alice and Bob both trust a CA by the name of HappySign.
HappySign is in the business of verifying people's identities and issuing them
signed certificates. Here are a few of the responsibilities that HappySign has
in doing its job:

- HappySign itself must heavily secure its own private key. If its private
  key is compromised, then any certificates it issues with that private
  key are suspect.

- HappySign must do background checks on Alice and Bob. It must
  ensure that, when Alice and Bob contact HappySign for a certificate,
  it is really them and not someone else like Bad Guy. This certification
  may involve phone calls and the passing of various credentials, proof
  of residence, and so forth. HappySign needs to make it difficult or
  impossible for Bad Guy to approach and pretend he is someone else.

- HappySign must work with whomever it is issuing a certificate to—
  Bob, for example—so that it reliably and securely receives Bob's public key (and not Bad Guy's public key) and that Bob understands that
  he must keep his associated private key secret.

Alice and Bob discover that HappySign performs these responsibilities
to their satisfaction but only for a certain basic grade of certificate. It turns
out that HappySign gives out various grades of certificates, some being much
easier to get (and easier to use to pretend you are someone else) than others.
A higher-grade certificate is harder to get, meaning that Alice and Bob need
to do more work to prove they are who they say they are. Alice and Bob decide
they want the premium-grade HappySign certificate, which means more work
for them, but, since their relationship is on the line here, more work is a small
price to pay. "Bad Guy, go away," yell Alice and Bob, as they together walk
through the paces of getting certificates digitally signed by HappySign.

Mission accomplished, Alice and Bob receive their HappySign certificates. Alice receives an e-mail from Bob that says, "Here's my HappySign
certificate. Please use the public key inside when sending me love letters."

Alice decides to check and make sure that this certificate was signed by HappySign. She uses HappySign's public key (which she was given during the certificate registration process in a secure way) and applies it to the certificate she just received. "Eeek," screams Alice. "This certificate wasn't signed by HappySign!" She knows because, after applying HappySign's public key to the certificate, it doesn't say anything about coming from Bob—in fact, it is unreadable. Bad Guy is up to his dirty deeds again. Later, the real Bob sends Alice his certificate. Alice knows it came from Bob because, after applying HappySign's public key to the certificate, out comes a well-formed X.509 certificate that states it is owned by Bob. Plus, in one of the certificate's attribute fields is written the phrase "Bob loves Alice," and Alice knows that only Bob could be sweet enough to pronounce their love in his certificate like a digital tattoo of sorts.

2.2.1.2 Efficient Use of Public Key Cryptography: MACs, Hashing, and Symmetric Encryption

Public key operations can be processor-intensive, and, for security reasons as noted later, you should digitally sign the smallest amount of data necessary to achieve your goals. So, when we design security protocols that leverage public key cryptography, it is important that we consider these issues. There are two additional technologies that we use to assist us in this area and to enhance security:

1. Message authentication codes (MACs) based on hash functions
2. Symmetric encryption

2.2.1.2.1 Message Authentication Codes (MACs) A *message authentication code* (MAC) is produced through the use of a *hash function,* which produces a unique number, a pattern of 1s and 0s, based on data we provide to the hash function. The probability of getting the same unique number produced for two different data inputs to a properly designed hash function is approximately zero—this is the fundamental property of a well-designed hash function.

Why might we want to do this? Let's return to Alice and Bob's love letter for explanation. We could run the love letter through a hash function, returning the MAC illustrated in Figure 2.4. Note that, while the love letter may be comprised of many bytes of data, the MAC could be much shorter, maybe 16 or 32 bytes, for example. Here's how the MAC helps us out.

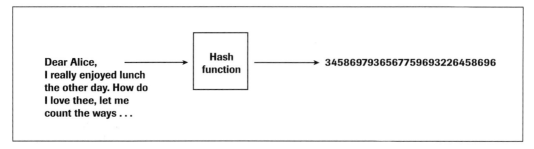

Figure 2.4 Hashing a love letter

Assume that Bob writes long, wordy love letters, but that he is aware of the efficiency issues we raised. So, what is Bob to do here? Stop signing his love letters to Alice? Start writing love letters only a few sentences long? No, none of this will do. Instead, Bob just needs to append a digitally signed MAC to his love letter. There is no need to sign the whole letter, just the MAC. Here's why.

Bob computes the MAC of his love letter, a quick and easy task for his computer, and then digitally signs just the MAC, not the whole love letter. He then appends the digitally signed MAC to his love letter and sends it on its way. This time, for the sake of our example, Bob does not choose to encrypt the love letter. Maybe he wants to make Bad Guy jealous—who knows. He just sends the love letter, unencrypted, along with the digitally signed MAC.

Bad Guy intercepts this love letter as always. With excitement he can hardly contain, he proceeds to modify Bob's love letter, changing it to a mean and nasty one. He then sends it on its way to Alice.

Alice gets the love letter, but, since she is hip to this new MAC thing, the first thing she does it compute a new MAC for the love letter all on her own. She then looks at the digitally signed MAC attached to the love letter. She applies Bob's public key to the MAC so that she can read it and verify that it came from Bob. She then compares this MAC to the one she computed on her own. They are not the same. Alice knows this message has been tampered with. The MACs must be equal, but they are not, as illustrated in Figure 2.5.

Alice asks Bob to send the love letter again. This time, Bad Guy is busy doing something else and doesn't intercept the love letter. Alice gets it and repeats the procedure: She computes her own MAC, applies Bob's public key to the digitally signed MAC attached to the message, and compares the

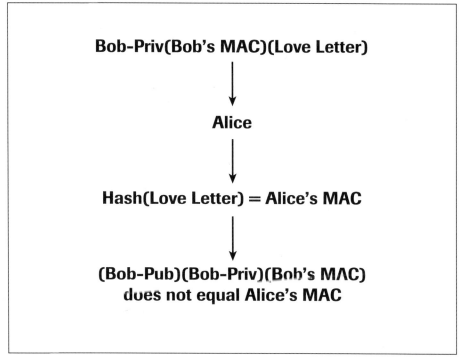

Figure 2.5 Verifying a love letter

MACs. This time, they are the same. Alice knows that (1) this message came from Bob because the MAC is signed and, because the MACs are equal, that (2) the message has not been tampered with.

OK, now Bob has figured out a way to prove to Alice he sent her love letters—by appending a digitally signed MAC. For all intents and purposes, this is as good as his having signed the entire love letter. It turns out that it is safer for Bob to sign this smaller hash than to sign the larger love letters because, over time, Bad Guy's probability of cracking Bob's private key increases with the amount of Bob's digitally signed data that he can archive offline and scrutinize (through intense Bad Guy number-crunching techniques). By signing a hash, a much smaller data quantity, there is less data for Bad Guy to archive and analyze.

Examples of hash functions in use today include MD5 and SHA. SSL version 3 makes use of these two hash functions.

2.2.1.2.2 Symmetric Encryption   We still have a slight problem here.
Public key encryption is processor-intensive. Bob must find a way to encrypt
his love letter to Alice while not bringing his computer to its knees.

Bob has an idea. He has been correctly told that *symmetric encryption*
is less CPU-intensive than public key encryption. He decides he'll try to
make use of symmetric encryption to reduce the burden on his computer.

Recall that we earlier referred to public key encryption as *asymmetric*
because it relied on *two* keys, one public and the other private. *Symmetric
encryption relies on only one* key and is the kind of encryption with which
we are more familiar. It relies on a *shared secret,* one Alice and Bob both
know but Bad Guy does not know. Bob encrypts data using the secret, and
Alice, who knows the same secret, uses it to decrypt the data. Symmetric

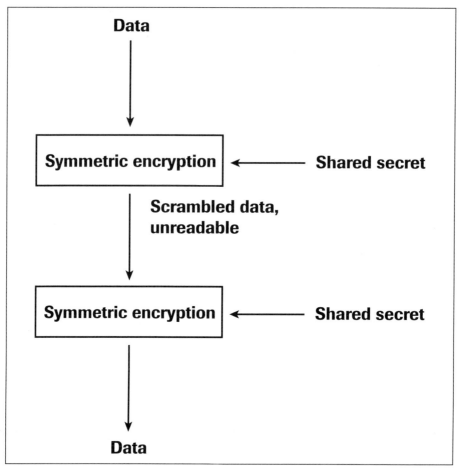

Figure 2.6 Symmetric encryption

encryption is illustrated in Figure 2.6. Popular symmetric encryption algorithms include RC4 and DES.

Bob decides that each time he wants to send Alice a private message, he'll choose a really hard-to-guess secret by using his computer to randomly generate one that will take Bad Guy virtually forever to guess. He'll use public key encryption (Alice-Pub) to encrypt that secret and send it to Alice before sending her the love letter so that they both share the secret. He'll also digitally sign the secret so that Alice knows it came from Bob.

Now, both Alice and Bob know the same secret (it's now a shared secret), and Bad Guy does not know it since Bad Guy can't read anything that is public-key-encrypted with Alice's public key. Also, the secret is digitally signed by Bob, so Bad Guy can't swap it out with his own. Instead of public key encrypting the entire love letter, Bob can now use symmetric encryption to encrypt the love letter, which is much faster and more efficient for his computer.

2.2.1.3 Public Key Cryptography Wrap-Up: Alice, Bob, and Secure Love Letters

Let's summarize the important points so far, with a corresponding wrap-up of how they impact Alice and Bob:

- *Information must be securely exchanged.* Bob has a love letter for Alice.

- *There are hackers out there.* Bad Guy wants to read it, modify it, or otherwise aggravate Alice and Bob's love letter exchange. Alice and Bob are intent on not letting this happen.

- *Clients and servers need trusted credentials like X.509 digital certificates.* Alice has a digitally signed X.509 certificate. Bob has one also. Alice has Bob's certificate, and Bob has Alice's.

- *Clients and servers must protect their private keys.* Alice and Bob both have private keys, which they share with nobody, not even with each other.

- *For efficiency, we combine symmetric encryption with public key encryption.* Bob chooses a shared secret so that he can symmetrically encrypt his love letter to Alice.

- *Digital signing can prove authenticity.* Bob digitally signs the public-key-encrypted shared secret and sends it to Alice, who checks the signature, verifying it is from Bob, decrypts it, and records the shared secret.

■ *Hash functions/MACs can detect tampering and improve efficiency, and techniques we have learned can be combined.* Bob completes the following steps:

1. Computes a MAC for the love letter.
2. Digitally signs the MAC.
3. Appends the MAC to the love letter.
4. Symmetrically encrypts the whole thing with the shared secret.

Alice, upon receiving the message, follows these steps:

1. Receives the glob of 1s and 0s that was once a love letter.
2. Applies the shared secret to the glob, decrypting it.
3. Strips off the appended MAC and applies Bob's public key to it.
4. Computes her own MAC on the love letter itself.
5. Compares the MAC she received from Bob with her own computed MAC of the love letter. If the MACs are equal, then this love letter is from Bob. If not, then Alice knows something happened to this love letter and, whatever it was, it wasn't what was intended by Bob.

Such are the fundamentals of public key cryptography, symmetric encryption, and hash functions. The SSL/TLS protocols, which we'll examine next, use all the principles we just studied.

2.2.2 Secure Sockets Layer (SSL) and Transport Layer Security (TLS) Protocols

The *Secure Sockets Layer* (SSL) protocol was specified and first implemented by Netscape. Other implementors followed, including Microsoft. Microsoft's competing standard, PCT, never gained widespread deployment and usage. Today, SSL is heavily deployed within the Internet and the networked enterprise. It is at the heart of the majority of available electronic commerce solutions and is heavily integrated into the network application frameworks we discuss in this book. Go to any Web site doing commerce, to any of your favorite merchants, or perhaps the online service offered by your bank—chances are very high that you'll encounter SSL. Also, corporations use SSL extensively internally to protect important information.

Early on, Netscape recognized that, in order for the Internet to reach its potential, it needed far more advanced security than what was typically employed across networks at the time. The development and product management teams set out a path, from SSL version 1.0 to the current 3.0, to evolve this protocol to meet the needs of the enterprise and of electronic commerce.

One of my responsibilities while I was at Netscape was to bring SSL into the Internet Engineering Task Force (IETF) standards process in the form of the *Transport Layer Security* (TLS) protocol. As of this writing, the TLS specification is in final draft stages. It is based entirely on SSL version 3.0, with relatively few changes. TLS-compliant applications will, if following the current specification, be able to communicate with other TLS devices as well as systems compliant with SSL version 3.0.

Note that hereafter throughout the book, any reference to *SSL/TLS* means SSL version 3.0 or TLS version 1.0. Where a specific reference to one or the other is intended, one or the other will be written by itself—that is, just *TLS* or just *SSL*.

SSL is integrated with Netscape and Microsoft's Web browsers and servers. The specification is relatively unambiguous, and therefore it is unusual to experience interoperability issues among products from different vendors implementing SSL.

SSL is a transport-layer protocol, a pipe if you will, that is established between a client and a server. SSL is typically integrated directly with an underlying application protocol. For example, HyperText Transfer Protocol (HTTP), the protocol used to attach to Web sites, is integrated with SSL. HTTP packets are encapsulated in SSL packets and are then sent over TCP/IP. HTTP integrated with SSL is commonly referred to as *HTTPS*. Other protocols integrated with SSL by various vendors include LDAP, IMAP (for e-mail), and NNTP (for collaboration and news).

2.2.2.1 How SSL Works

SSL is intended to provide a secure pipe between a client and a server. It is session-oriented, so it is able to maintain state, even when running over protocols such as HTTP that are themselves stateless (more on this later). SSL provides privacy through encryption, authentication based on certificates, a vehicle for authorization through its support for certificates, integrity by incorporating hash functions, and it incorporates digital signing as part of the transport protocol.

In this section, we will look at how SSL works and also consider its performance impact on Web servers running it. A summary of how SSL performs functionally will be given at a level of detail greater than a number of textbook discussions but at one not great enough to satisfy a cryptographer. So, purists, please stand back for broad brush strokes. The objective here is to communicate the look-and-feel and high-level functional methodologies of SSL.

Before we walk through SSL session establishment, however, let's consider the issue of certificates on the client-side and sever-side. A client, such as you and your Web browser, may *optionally* have an X.509 certificate. If you do not have a certificate, then the server is unable to authenticate you via SSL and, if needed, will have to rely on some other means such as HTTP Basic Authentication, which we'll discuss in Chapter 3. On the other hand, a server is always *required* to have an X.509 certificate. The server must have a certificate and associated public and private keys in order for SSL to work.

We are now ready to walk through session establishment based on SSL and the HTTP protocol (HTTPS):

1. *Client selects SSL-protected Web page.* The client selects a uniform resource locator (URL) referencing HTTPS, such as https://www.spendmymoney.com.

2. *Client verifies server certificate.* The server delivers its certificate to the client. The client looks at it. If the certificate is not signed by a certificate authority that the client trusts (this is configured within the Web browser), then the user sees a warning dialogue box stating that the host's certificate is signed by an untrusted certificate authority. The client may choose to proceed or not in communicating with the host, www.spendmymoney.com. If the client chooses to continue, then a few more things happen.

3. *Server performs optional client authentication.* The server may, if so configured by the Web site administrator, choose to request a certificate from the client. The client, if the client has one, will deliver it. This action is called *client authentication.* If the server trusts the signer of the client's certificate and also trusts the holder of the certificate, as indicated by the Distinguished Name (DN) within the certificate and any other attributes, then the SSL session continues. Otherwise, the session is ended.

4. *Possession of private key is verified.* The client generates a random string of data, encrypts it with the server's public key, and then asks the server to deliver the data back. This operation is called a *challenge.* In order for the server to send the data string back in an intelligible fashion, the server would have to have the private key associated with the public key associated with the public key contained in the trusted certificate the client received from this server.

The client issues this challenge to determine whether the server truly possesses the private key associated with the public key contained in the certificate it presented. If the server doesn't have this key, then it could be Bad Guy, for example, who picked up the certificate from www.spendmymoney.com but doesn't have its private key. Note that the server may perform the same challenge operation in reverse, with the client, if the server is required to authenticate the client. Note also that if the session has gone this far successfully, it means that the client has authenticated the server and that, optionally, the server has successfully authenticated the client.

5. *Client and server agree to a shared secret for symmetric encryption.* The client and server will agree upon a shared secret known only by them for use with a symmetric encryption algorithm so that all data sent back and forth can be symmetrically encrypted. The client will select a secret and encrypt it with the server's public key. The client sends that to the server so that both the client and the server then share a common secret.

6. *Session ID is agreed upon.* Note that steps 4 and 5, client/sever challenge and shared secret exchange, represent processor-intensive steps from the perspective of your Web server since they are based on public key operations. In order to improve performance, the objective is to reduce the number of these kinds of operations. SSL is designed to do just that and achieves this objective through use of an identifier that is securely exchanged between the client and the server. This SSL *session identifier* (ID) is agreed upon between the client and the server. The session ID along with agreed-upon shared secrets between the client and the server are stored on the server in a cache. The next time this client attaches to the host via HTTP, the client can present its session ID to the server. If the server still has it in its cache, then it is not necessary for the client and the server to reauthenticate themselves to each other, and they may resume their SSL session wherever they left off, using their previously agreed-upon shared secrets. The ability to reuse a session means that the server performs less processing. Bad Guy might try to guess what session IDs are in the server's cache, but trying to guess the session ID along with other secrets associated with the session and its state known only by the client and the server should prove to be far too

much work. There is no requirement for the underlying protocol—in this case, HTTP—to maintain state information.

In early versions of Netscape products and those from other vendors, the server would cache the session ID for very short periods of time, such as 30 seconds. Consequently, every 30 seconds, if the same client returned to the server, public key operations had to be performed again, which slowed things down. In later software releases, this timer was extended to as long as 24 hours and was made configurable by the server administrator. This timer is a good variable to consider in trying to reduce the processor overhead produced by SSL for servers performing heavy SSL processing.

7. *Data transfer occurs.* The client and server can exchange data after the preceding basic steps have been carried out. Note that data is protected via hash functions for integrity and is symmetrically encrypted. Relative to encryption, the U.S. version of Netscape Communicator utilizes 128-bit encryption keys, whereas the international version, when communicating with nonexport-approved sites, utilizes 40-bit encryption keys.

2.2.2.2 How to Integrate SSL into Your Applications

In the preceding SSL discussion, HTTP was used as the example protocol with which SSL was integrated. That was a good example because HTTP and HTML (Hypertext Markup Language) combined represent a very popular user interface for many of today's applications. If you want to integrate SSL security with your application, then you can utilize HTTPS, which is built into most Web browsers, such as those from Netscape and Microsoft, and you can enable it on your Web server since most Web servers also support it.

You can assign access control to information on the Web server or to information that you gather through external systems and present through the Web server (an example is IBM mainframe CICS and Web integration as discussed in Chapter 11). You can control access to this data so that only users who have certificates signed by a trusted CA and who have required attributes in their certificates gain access to it. Later, in the section on LDAP, an example is given showing how LDAP is combined with X.509 certificates, which can be presented through SSL, to achieve single-sign-on access control.

2.2.2.3 SSL and Firewalls

One of the challenges with SSL is that it is perhaps too good at what it does. As a two-way protocol, it is specifically designed to prevent a third party, such as Bad Guy or a well-intentioned network administrator, from seeing what is going on between the two endpoints of the SSL session. In addition to being a security benefit, it can also present itself as a problem since that is exactly what well-intentioned Internet firewalls are designed to do—to peek inside the packets and see whether something fishy is going on.

Later, we'll talk about the TCP/IP protocol suite and about TCP port numbers. SSL with HTTP uses TCP port number 443. Firewall administrators have only a few approaches when dealing with HTTPS coming in over the Internet:

1. They can punch a hole straight through the firewall on TCP port 443 and let SSL sessions come through, perhaps restricting on destination IP address and so forth. The disadvantage here is that the firewall can't be used to look at the information being transferred because it has been encrypted.

2. They can block all SSL traffic through the firewall altogether. The problem here is that they then prevent users from accessing SSL-enabled sites on the Internet.

3. If the problem is that they need to allow access from the public Internet to certain enterprise data via SSL, then they can move all SSL systems that need to be accessed from the Internet outside the firewall and use some other secure communication mechanism or a heavily controlled second SSL connection for data transferred between that system outside the firewall and any systems inside the firewall, if needed.

For enterprise users reaching out into the Internet from behind the firewall and wanting to utilize SSL, one approach is to use a *proxy server,* as illustrated in Figure 2.7. It will terminate Internet SSL sessions at the firewall, where the proxy server is located, allowing the firewall to monitor traffic for these connections. This means, however, that there is no SSL running within the enterprise up to the firewall, which is not all that much fun. This also means that client authentication can't be used since the proxy server would need to hold the client's private key to authenticate on its behalf, and

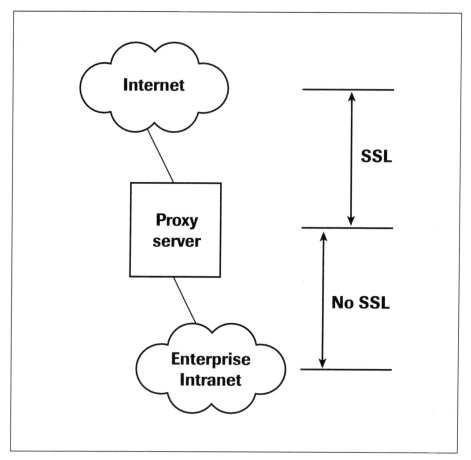

Figure 2.7 SSL and a proxy server

that, generally speaking, is a no-no unless you choose to escrow away client keys at the proxy server (and, of course, the proxy server product would need to support that function).

What is the solution? There is none yet. The preceding approach or some other creative ones not mentioned here will continue to be deployed until perhaps a three-way protocol is developed that allows the firewall to act as a trusted third party capable of receiving and decrypting data as needed. Some argue that IPSEC, the next protocol that we'll discuss, could help in this area. IPSEC offers more of a router-by-router network security mechanism as currently specified and is less of an end-to-end session-level application-oriented protocol.

2.2.3 IP-Level Security (IPSEC)

IPSEC is a connectionless security mechanism that has been retrofitted to work with IPv4 and is directly integrated with IPv6. IPSEC has received support from networking equipment vendors since it provides a vehicle for them to add value, in the form of security, to their products. IPSEC is evolving as more of a network-layer security protocol, as opposed to an application-level one such as SSL/TLS.

Unlike SSL, which is a transport protocol operating at a layer above IP, IPSEC integrates with the IP protocol—it is, if you will, *IP-centric.* In contrast, SSL is not tied to the underlying network protocol. In fact, SSL could be implemented over any network protocol, IP being only one of them. Also, while SSL is connection-oriented, IPSEC is connectionless.

IPSEC can be used to provide authentication, for example, between two network routers or, as another example, between a router and a firewall. It can also provide encryption. Authentication is provided by the IPSEC *Authentication Header* (AH), and encryption and data integrity are provided by the IPSEC *Encapsulating Security Payload* (ESP) header.

We previously discussed how SSL utilizes public key cryptography, symmetric encryption, and hash functions to achieve various objectives. IPSEC may utilize one or more similar functions depending upon what options have been implemented by the IPSEC network administrators. IPSEC supports a number of different mechanisms for exchanging secrets and selecting cryptographic operations, including the following:

- Shared secrets that can be manually configured between the two endpoints running IPSEC.
- The Simple Key Interchange Protocol (SKIP), which allows for keys to be dynamically shared.
- The full-fledged Internet Security Association and Key Management Protocol (ISAKMP), which allows for the negotiation of various authentication and security association mechanisms. ISAKMP is a complex protocol, and its combination with IPSEC aspires to bring it to more of an application-level security mechansim.

SSL is widely deployed, and IPSEC is the new kid on the block. Since applications require application-level security, whatever IPSEC does at the network layer is only of added value; it cannot replace application-level security functionality, such as that offered by protocols including SSL and, as we'll discuss in a moment, Kerberos, unless it is extended. Either IPSEC's role will need to be continually expanded to the application layer, or two classes of security protocols, one network (such as IPSEC) and the other application (such as SSL/TLS), will coexist within the overall network application framework. And, to the degree that this enhances security overall, that is a very good thing.

2.2.4 Kerberos

Kerberos is a security protocol capable of providing authentication and facilitating authorization within the enterprise. It provides a platform upon which single-user logon (single sign-on) can be implemented, requiring the user to enter his or her username and password only once, as opposed to *N* times, or once for each of *N* servers the user chooses to access. Microsoft NT version 5 incorporates Kerberos version 5 as part of its single-user logon architecture, which includes Active Directory. The Distributed Computing Environment (DCE) network application framework makes use of Kerberos version 5, the Andrews File System (AFS) uses Kerberos version 4, and a version of Kerberos is available for most flavors of UNIX.

Kerberos has received considerable attention since Microsoft decided to adopt it and because it offers a viable and manageable solution for authentication within the enterprise without the overhead of maintaining a public key infrastructure. Critics of public key cryptography point out that the maintenance of certificate authorities as well as the administrative overhead of making sure that everyone secures their private keys and has a means to take them with them, wherever they are, is overwhelming.

With regard to private key portability, one of the criticisms of public key cryptography is that the private key, 1,024 bits in length for the U.S. version of popular Web browsers, is not something human beings can easily remember, as they can a password. That translates to a need for people either to carry devices such as smartcards (credit-card-like computing devices) to carry their private keys or to use floppy disks or some other private key transport mechanism. Some view Kerberos as offering simpler administration by not requiring that users' private keys and associated portability mechanisms be managed along with the rest of the public key infrastructure.

The argument that Kerberos security might not be as strong as that offered by public key cryptography is not relevant to those who are concerned with the trade-off between security and manageability. For them, it is the ability Kerberos has to leverage usernames and passwords and to not require the immediate deployment of a public key infrastructure that makes it attractive. However, for generalized Extranet access, whereby business partners and others are being given access to resources within the enterprise from the Internet, it can be strongly argued that all the capabilities and strengths that SSL/TLS has to offer are required.

Kerberos was developed by members of MIT's Project Athena. The name *Kerberos* is derived from Greek mythology, wherein a three-headed dog named Kerberos stood guard over the gates of Hades and you had to be truthful and of high moral character to make it past that particular dog. The Project Athena team developed the Kerberos technology to protect networking and computing services being offered as part of their project.

Kerberos has evolved over time but only two versions are widely deployed: versions 4 and 5. Version 5, while based on roughly the same functional principles as version 4, offers more flexibility, improved security, and, yes, more complexity.

Kerberos does not directly define a data privacy or integrity implementation as does SSL/TLS. Therefore, if you must guarantee data privacy and integrity, you might either combine it with SSL/TLS or just use SSL/TLS entirely. We'll talk more about the integration of Kerberos and SSL/TLS later.

2.2.4.1 Kerberos Architectural Overview

In this section, we will look at the Kerberos architecture. Where helpful, Alice and Bob will represent the client and the server.

Users, servers, and computing resources can be administratively grouped into *realms* in Kerberos. Realms correlate to *cells* in DCE and to *domains* in NT. Each realm contains one master *key distribution center* (KDC). The KDC acts as a trusted third party between the client (user) and the server or resource for which authentication is being requested. KDCs may be replicated within a realm, enhancing reliability by allowing the replicated KDCs to act as backup servers and also by allowing load to be shared across multiple KDCs. The KDC holds all client and server secret keys within the realm, and, therefore, it must be heavily secured. If the KDC is compromised, then the entire Kerberos security framework is threatened.

The KDC can be thought of as comprised of three functional components that typically reside on the same physical server:

1. The *authentication server* (AS) is responsible for authenticating the user.
2. The *ticket granting server* (TGS) is used by authenticated users to gain access to specific servers.
3. Both the AS and the TGS have access to the *secret key database*.

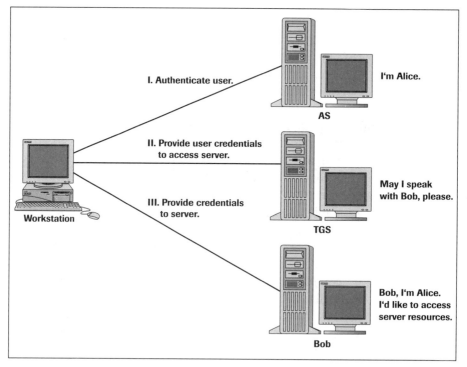

Figure 2.8 The three phases of Kerberos

The Kerberos authentication process can be viewed as having three phases, as illustrated in Figure 2.8. The explanation that follows is organized according to these phases.

- *Phase I. Authenticate the user.*

    1. Alice walks up to a workstation and enters her login name. This login name is sent in the clear over the network to the AS; however, her password, which she will enter in a moment, is not sent over the network. In fact, as we'll see, neither the client nor the server's password is *ever* sent over the network directly with Kerberos.

    2. The AS returns a *ticket granting ticket* (TGT). The TGT doesn't say anything about whether or not Alice wants to speak with Bob, Tom, Joe, or whomever. It is merely used as part of the authentication process to prove the user of the workstation claiming to be Alice is truly Alice.

The TGT is encrypted by the AS with a *secret key* that is cryptographically based on Alice's secret password. The AS selects this secret key from the secret key database based on the login name entered by Alice. In order for Alice's workstation to interpret and make use of the TGT, it must have Alice's secret password. So, if Bad Guy has a TGT but doesn't have Alice's password, he can't make use of it.

Bad Guy's Password Cracking

Note that, in order for Bad Guy to decrypt the TGT and make use of it, he must have Alice's secret password, which he doesn't have. If he can guess the password, then he can read the TGT. Therefore, Kerberos is vulnerable to standard password-cracking attacks. Kerberos version 5 adds some features here that make it more difficult for a hacker to gather a collection of TGTs that he or she can later perform offline password cracking on.

3. The workstation where Alice is sitting now requests that she enter her secret password. The workstation then attempts to decrypt the TGT using this password. If the password is correct, then the TGT is successfully decrypted.

   The TGT contains an important *session key*. Alice is able to read this session key since she is capable of decrypting the TGT. Note that the TGS, which we'll talk about next, is also capable of decrypting the TGT and reading the session key.

■ *Phase II. Provide the user credentials to access the server.*

4. Alice now instructs the workstation that she would like to connect to Bob. The workstation, in response to Alice's request, sends an encrypted message to the TGS in order to obtain a server-specific ticket—in this case, one for Bob. This message includes the name of the requested server (Bob), the TGT, and an *authenticator.* The authenticator can include a time stamp, the user's name (Alice), and the workstation's network address. Alice encrypts the authenticator with the session key she extracted from the TGT.

   The TGS attempts to decrypt the authenticator received from Alice by using the session key. If the resulting output contains an authenticator that makes sense, then the TGS assumes that Alice is who she says she is. The TGS then issues Alice a TGS-issued ticket, called a *service ticket,* which she can use to access Bob.

Tickets and Time Stamps

Kerberos tickets include a time stamp that helps prevent old tickets from being replayed by hackers at some later time, after they have had a chance to crack their encryption. This time stamp mechanism produces a cycle in which tickets expire and must therefore be reissued as required. Kerberos version 4 supports a maximum lifetime of approximately 21 hours. Kerberos version 5 offers various other features augmenting this, including renewable timers, and virtually unlimited maximum lifetimes. However, remember that the longer the life of the ticket, the more vulnerable to replay attacks.

■ *Phase III. Present the credentials to the server.*

5. The workstation decrypts the TGS-issued ticket and extracts two encrypted versions of a new session key. This new session key will be shared by Alice and Bob. One of the two encrypted versions of this new session key is encrypted with Alice's secret key (based on her secret password) so that Alice can read it. The other encrypted version of this new session key is encrypted with Bob's secret key so that Bob can read it. Alice then creates a new authenticator and encrypts it with the new session key. She then sends this new authenticator to Bob, along with the session key encrypted with Bob's secret key (the one she just received from the TGS). Bob decrypts the session key using his secret key and then uses the session key to read the authenticator he just received from Alice. If everything looks reasonable with the authenticator, then Bob trusts that he is communicating with Alice. Bob then determines what rights Alice has to files and any other resources he controls.

Note that Alice can also require Bob to prove he is Bob (mutual authentication) by requesting a response based on the session key. If it is truly Bob to whom Alice is talking, then Bob should have access to the session key.

In the future, if Alice needs to communicate with another server within the same realm—say, Tom, for example—then, assuming her TGT has not expired, she need only connect with the

TGS and follow the same basic process just outlined. For as long as the TGT does not expire, Alice need not reenter her password.

2.2.4.2 Kerberos and Authorization

Kerberos does not specify details with regard to how authorization is achieved. However, there is a field within the Kerberos ticket that can be used to communicate authorization information. Many implementations use this field to signal user and group identifiers. For example, Microsoft NT 5 uses the authorization data field within the Kerberos ticket to carry Windows NT security IDs, indicating user and group membership. The NT server then uses this user/group membership information along with access control lists (ACLs) defined for its resources to determine what the user has rights to. See Chapters 8 and 9 for more on NT users, groups, and authorization. Note that DCE, discussed in Chapter 6, makes use of a separate server to provide access control information.

2.2.4.3 Kerberos, X.509 Certificates, and Public Key Cryptography

Suppose a business partner is issued a certificate by a certificate authority (CA) that your company trusts. The current Internet draft entitled "Public Key Cryptography for Initial Authentication in Kerberos" is designed to allow this business partner to use the certificate and public key cryptography for authentication purposes and to obtain a Kerberos server ticket from your company by proving ownership of the private key and by possessing a certificate signed by an authority you trust. This is in lieu of a username/password.

Microsoft has stated that it intends to support Kerberos extensions supporting public key cryptography. Other companies have been working on this for quite some time and have been delivering public key crypto-integrated Kerberos solutions. For example, Gradient Technologies has integrated Kerberos with public key cryptography and also smartcards through its partnership with Litronic. Gradient's products provide an excellent example of how Kerberos can be used to integrate a variety of security mechanisms.

2.2.4.4 Kerberos Criticisms and Challenges

Kerberos has received criticism on the basis of two aspects of its architecture. First, servers must be time-synchronized since the Kerberos tickets utilize time stamps to guard against replay attacks. That means that you would need either to run a time-synchronization protocol such as the Network Time Protocol (NTP) within your network in order to keep all servers synchronized to the same time of day or to provide some other solid mechanism to synchronize clocks on each server. The counterargument is that it is not unusual for other distributed processing systems within the enterprise to also require time synchronization, so, in such cases, Kerberos does not add a new time-synchronization requirement.

Second, all passwords within the realm are maintained on a single server, the KDC. If that server is compromised, then the password of every user and server within the realm is compromised.

2.2.4.5 Kerberos and the Network

Based on our understanding of how Kerberos operates, let's make a few simple observations about its relationship with the network with regard to traffic flow, reliability, and security.

All users in the network will authenticate themselves once to the AS at least once per day. Since users do not like to wait long periods of time when they are being authenticated, the network should be prepared to handle this flow of authentication traffic quickly. Also, for each server the user wishes to access, there will be an exchange with the TGS. Access to the TGS must likewise be relatively quick. Typically, there will be some average number of TGS "hits" per user per day based on typical server usage.

The AS and TGS should be highly available to all client workstations. If they become unreachable, then pretty much all work can stop for users since servers in the network, even if they are themselves reachable, will not allow users to access resources unless they are authenticated. High availability from a networking perspective may imply multiple physical links to the site housing the Kerberos servers as well as redundant router hardware configurations.

One obvious place to *not* put your Kerberos server is outside the company firewall. In other words, guard your Kerberos servers heavily and provide no more access to them than necessary. In fact, by placing routers and firewalling devices in front of your Kerberos servers, you can filter away all protocol interactions, only allowing Kerberos requests and replies. There is no need to allow a whole range of traffic to pass by your Kerberos servers. Instead, only Kerberos protocol interactions need exist.

2.3 Remote Procedure Call (RPC)

As the name implies, *Remote Procedure Call* (RPC) is a method for a client to execute and communicate with a remote computer program (a procedure) on a remote server. Using RPC, the computing responsibilities for a given application can be distributed among multiple networked computers. RPC allows the programmer to call procedures on a remote computer as if they are being executed locally.

By defining a common API and computer-to-computer interaction, RPC provides a vehicle for computers from different manufacturers, running different operating systems, to communicate with one another. However, there are enough differences in RPC implementations that a conscious effort must be made to achieve such interoperability, and, even then, only the lowest common denominator of RPC services can be obtained (i.e., the minimum core set of features between the two RPC implementations).

Relative to the Open Systems Interconnection (OSI) stack, the RPC mechanism is a session-layer protocol. Above the session layer is the presentation layer, which is concerned with different forms of data representation (e.g., byte ordering, ASCII versus EBCDIC, etc.). As we will see later, most environments offering RPC provide a mechanism to deal with translation between different forms of data representation used by different computing platforms.

RPC provides a high level of abstraction for programmers, shielding them from low-level socket and low-level network API programming, but the core RPC protocol is very simple. All messages are either a request or a reply. RPC software development is carried out using RPC compilers, and these compilers often define additional functions that make the RPC concept more viable, such as offering error reporting and recovery features. These compilers define an RPC programming language, known as *Interface Definition Language* (IDL).

Traditional RPC is implemented over Transmission Control Protocol (TCP) or User Datagram Protocol (UDP); however, it most certainly can, and has been, implemented over other transports. Transport-independent RPC (TIRPC) libraries isolate the application from the transport selected, thereby allowing the same application to run over a wider range of transports.

Most network application frameworks, be they from a standards organization or from a particular product vendor, include an RPC implementation. Some examples include

- DCE RPC
- Sun ONC RPC
- Microsoft RPC (partially DCE RPC compliant)

Sun's ONC RPC is one of the most widely implemented RPC mechanisms. The Sun NFS and NIS system utilities are based on ONC RPC.

2.3.1 Application Development Concerns

Even though RPC shields the developer from many of the underlying network access issues, there are still network-related issues that must be addressed. Before developing an RPC application, or any other networked application for that matter, we should ask ourselves a few questions:

- What level of error reporting and recovery is required?
- What should the application do if the network connection breaks?
- Should there be different responses depending upon the type of network failure?
- Should an error be logged in a log file for later trouble isolation?
- What assumptions can be made about the reliability of the transport layer?
- What happens if the remote computer does not respond to an RPC even though there is no network error?
- What level of security is required?

All these design issues should be addressed in the application's design specification. RPC compilers offer features to aid the developer in understanding and responding to these issues. The application developer must make use of these features as well as those existing in the programming environment itself (e.g., C or C++) in order to guarantee that the needs of the organization are met by the particular RPC application.

2.3.2 Standard RPC Implementations

RPCs can be either nonblocking or blocking. *Nonblocking* RPCs use a one-way message approach—a client sends requests to the server and then moves on to whatever else it has to do. Since the client process is not waiting for a response from the server, it does not stop executing (block) while waiting for a server response.

Typically, RPC implementations are *blocking*—a request is sent and the calling process blocks until a reply is received. In multithreaded environments, the client can just block that thread but may continue to execute other threads so that the user can continue working while waiting for the RPC response.

Broadcast RPC is used to send a single client request to multiple servers. Broadcast RPC can be used for applications such as distributed data collection or parallel computing applications. In TCP/IP environments, UDP is used as transport for broadcast RPC. Batch-mode RPC is implemented through the transmission of a series of nonblocking RPC requests followed by a blocking request.

2.3.3 Data Representation

One of the important motivating factors for using RPC is its ability to link clients and servers based on different hardware platforms and different operating systems. The idea is that, if these two systems merely agree upon the same RPC implementation and, of course, a compatible transport layer, then RPC requests and replies can be passed between these two systems. Even if these two requirements are met, we still have another issue to deal with—data representation. For example, IBM mainframe systems often make use of the EBCDIC format to represent characters, while UNIX systems utilize ASCII. Another incompatibility might be byte order (big endian versus little endian). What happens if these two dissimilar systems try to exchange data? Unless there is a method to translate EBCDIC to ASCII and vice versa, the two systems cannot make use of the data received from each other. What is needed is a machine-independent method of data representation.

ONC RPC uses a single machine-independent format for data representation called *External Data Representation* (XDR). The XDR programming library provides filters for translating built-in C programming language types as well as other types such as strings and variable-length vectors to a common machine-independent format. XDR must be implemented on both ends of an RPC connection to be effective, and, therefore, if an RPC connection is established between two computers manufactured by different vendors, then both vendors must implement XDR consistently in order to achieve machine independence.

DCE RPC uses a similar mechanism called *Network Data Representation* (NDR). The process of converting from a machine-specific format to a machine-independent format is sometimes referred to as *marshaling*. The inverse of this process, the unpackaging of the data back into the machine-dependent format, is called *unmarshaling*.

2.3.4 Transactional RPC (TxRPC)

Suppose our program must support transaction processing. Then, *transactional RPC* (TxRPC), a transactional version of DCE RPC, can be considered. DCE borrowed the TxRPC standard from the X/Open Transaction Processing Reference Model.

TxRPC transactions are classified as transaction-*mandatory* or transaction-*optional.* This classification of the TxRPC transaction affects the amount of additional transaction-oriented processing performed on the RPC call to increase the probability of successful execution. TxRPC is based on a technology called *Remote Task Invocation* (RTI). RTI allows for the implementation of a two-phase commit for TxRPC transactions.

A two-phase commit algorithm is comprised of a series of individual commands and decision points grouped into two phases:

- *Phase I.*
  1. The coordinator of the transaction requests all participants in the transaction to prepare for a commit. Preparation consists of permanently storing all data required for a successful commit. If an error is encountered during this process, then the participant has not been able to prepare and cannot commit.
  2. The coordinator then waits for all confirmations to be received.
  3. After all confirmations are received, the coordinator determines whether or not to commit or roll back based on the ability of the participants to successfully prepare for the commit. If the coordinator decides to attempt to commit, it permanently stores all participant transactional data.

- *Phase II.*
  4. The coordinator requests all participants to commit or roll back. If the request is for a commit, all participants close files, remove locks on data, and update databases. If the decision is to roll back, all participants abandon the transaction, even if they have individually successfully prepared for the commit.
  5. After all participants have completed their work and returned acknowledgments, the coordinator can notify the calling application of the final result of the transaction.

2.3.5 Security

Different RPC implementations support differing options for security. Let's look at the DCE RPC security features as an example of one such implementation.

DCE RPC, for example, supports four methods of authentication. DCE RPC requires that the client and the server be registered in the DCE security database. The four types of authenticated DCE RPC service are as follows:

1. `rpc_authn_none` requires no authentication be performed.
2. `rpc_c_authn_default` defines a default authentication method in absence of a specific one signaled in the RPC request. This default is based on `rpc_c_authn_dce_secret`.
3. `rpc_c_authn_dce_secret` provides the DCE-shared secret key authentication service, based on Kerberos and DES.
4. `rpc_c_authn_dce_public` provides DCE RSA public key authentication.

2.3.6 API Programming

An RPC compiler and function library is required to compile and link RPC programs. Both the client and the server software requires use of this compiler and function library. The RPC request/reply communications model is implemented through function libraries known as *stubs*. Stubs are the communications interface between client and server, implementing the RPC protocol.

In order to find the server through the network, the client executes a process known as *binding*. Binding information is network communication and location information for a particular server. *Static* binding relies on hard-coded information, such as a configuration file that might provide information on the address of a remote server. *Dynamic* binding makes use of the directory service to locate the RPC server.

2.4 Common Object Request Broker Architecture (CORBA): Awakening of the Object Web

2.4.1 Introduction to CORBA

The ability of a Web browser itself to support objects, and for these objects to be capable of communicating with Web servers that also support objects, and for these objects to reference one another at will in a Weblike fashion—this is an exciting prospect. This vision has sparked the imagination of the many people working on this technology as they envision the potential of a livelier and more dynamic Web user experience. This experience would be one in which objects from across the world combine their strengths and specialties to respond on a moment's notice to the needs of individuals and the enterprise at large. It is this vision that has inspired many to adopt the *Common Object Request Broker Architecture* (CORBA) and embark on an industry campaign to further its broad acceptance. CORBA's impact is now reaching far and wide, beyond pure Web applications, moving deeply within the core of enterprise business processing.

While CORBA's popularity has recently catapulted, it is important to note that CORBA is not a new standard. The Object Management Group (OMG) was founded in 1989 and published its first *Object Management Architecture Guide* in 1990 and version 1.1 of CORBA in December of 1991. The group has over 700 members. CORBA version 2.1 was published in August of 1997.

CORBA is specified in great detail, offering a complete open standards-based framework for distributed object technology that allows objects and object platforms from multiple vendors to interoperate. CORBA is *multiplatform*, meaning it is not reliant on a particular operating system. CORBA scales quite well, from desktop to mainframe systems. It is also *language-independent*, meaning you can write CORBA applications in the language of your choice, be it C, C++, Java, COBOL, Ada, or whatever.

In this chapter, we will study CORBA. Later, in Chapter 7, we will look at Microsoft's component approach, which is known by a few names, including ActiveX, COM, and DCOM, and will briefly compare CORBA, the Microsoft component model, and the Java component model.

2.4.2 Interfaces: Standardizing Information Passing Between Objects

The CORBA *Interface Definition Language* (IDL) provides a formal standardized syntax for objects to communicate their capabilities and needs to one another. Programmers provide crucial information describing the object they are writing via the IDL. Objects use the CORBA *Object Request Broker* (ORB), discussed in more detail in a moment, to share IDL information with one another. When IDL instructions are written for an object, they are collectively referred to as the object's *interface specification*. The specifications for all objects known by an ORB are stored in the *interface repository*. Figure 2.9 illustrate these concepts.

The IDL shields one object from details about the internals of another. To communicate and leverage the capabilities of an object, you only need to

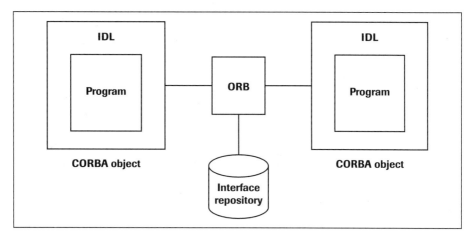

Figure 2.9 CORBA IDL and ORB

know how to communicate with it, based on its IDL, not how it actually does whatever it does. For example, if you want to use an object capable of checking the spelling of a document written in Italian, then you only need to know how to request spell-checking for a word in a document and in what format the results will be returned. In this context, *how* is defined entirely by the interface specification. That is, you do not have to know details about internal search algorithms used by the spell-checker's dictionary, about internal algorithms it uses to offer alternative spellings when you do a word-by-word spell-check, and so forth. Therefore, the CORBA IDL is said to *encapsulate* the object so that only the interface is relevant, not its implementation.

IDL is code added by programmers to "CORBA-ize" their objects. Tools such as Caffeine from Inprise generate IDL automatically from Java, simplifying the process of making a Java applet into a CORBA object.

As long as your programming language supports the CORBA IDL, you can use it. Remember, CORBA is language-independent, so you can use C, C++, Java, or COBOL. You could, for example, CORBA-ize a legacy CORBA application and bring it right into the world of objects.

2.4.3 Hop on the Object Bus: The Object Request Broker (ORB)

The ORB is often referred to as an *object bus*. This metaphor, as depicted in Figure 2.10, provides the imagery of the existence of a physical communications mechanism, such as the bus you plug cards into in the back of your PC,

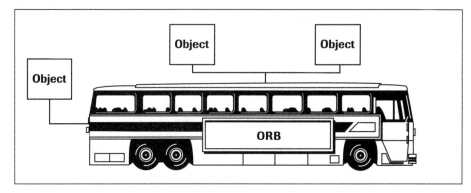

Figure 2.10 ORB, an object bus

for communication among objects. This imagery is appropriate since this is logically something the ORB does.

ORBs provide access to objects written by enterprise application developers and also to standard CORBA services. CORBA services, discussed later, are also accessed via the object bus.

2.4.4 Static Versus Dynamic Object Discovery

Fundamentally, for two objects to communicate with each other, we can assume one of two scenarios: static or dynamic.

First, suppose that one object is more or less predefined to take advantage of the functions (methods) of another specific object. In this case, the objects are statically configured (*statically* meaning in a predefined fashion) with information about the other object. This approach is called *Static Method Invocation* (SMI) because the functions (methods) of the object are called (invoked) by predefined instructions included within the object's IDL.

Now, suppose that one object—call it Alice for this example—knows nothing about the other object up front. Alice just knows she wishes to find an object somewhere, by querying its ORB, that is capable of achieving some function, such as Italian spell-checking, or meeting some other criteria. Alice makes use of the CORBA Trader Service, which provides a telephone directorylike service of available objects and functions, to query her ORB for an object capable of Italian spell-checking. The ORB returns information about Bob. Alice then uses this information to invoke Bob. The information returned by the ORB is essentially the same information that Alice would have used had she known about Bob up front (via preconfigured static information) and had she statically invoked Bob. This approach is called *Dynamic Method Invocation* (DMI).

    Let's discuss some of the pros and cons of DMI. First, what about reliability? Referencing our previous example, if Bob isn't available for some reason, then Alice might be able to use some other object also capable of Italian spell-checking if she uses DMI, but this is not necessarily so for SMI. It wasn't Bob himself and his unique personality that attracted Alice; it was Bob's Italian spell-checking capability. Alice can go elsewhere for this spell-checking capability if it is available. Figure 2.11 illustrates the principles of SMI and DMI.

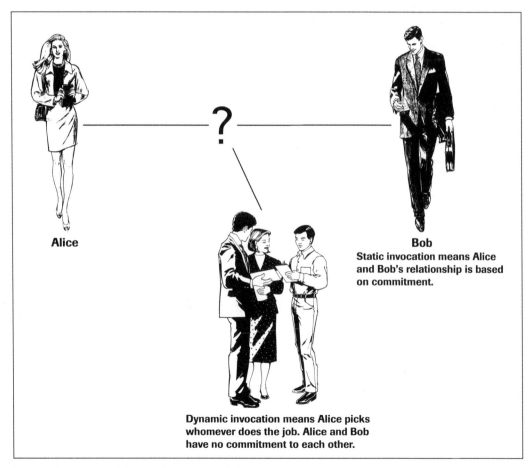

Alice

Bob
Static invocation means Alice and Bob's relationship is based on commitment.

Dynamic invocation means Alice picks whomever does the job. Alice and Bob have no commitment to each other.

Figure 2.11 SMI, DMI, and Alice's decision

Next, what about flexibility and adaptability? Suppose a better spell-checker than Bob comes along—one with an improved dictionary, for example. No problem. If Alice uses DMI, then she can just use that improved spell-checker without being reprogrammed or reconfigured.

Now, consider performance. DMI can slow things down simply because the queries and transactions required to locate and learn about the object to be invoked require time. The amount of time can, of course, vary wildly, depending upon whether the object to be invoked is remote or not, whether the machine doing the invoking is busy processing CORBA services for a large number of other objects, efficiency of interprocess communication within the operating system(s), utilization levels of the statically invoked object versus one that would be dynamically invoked, and so forth. So many variables, so little time. If your application is time-critical, you should run some tests simulating real loads and real networks (if present), and you can then compare results.

Finally, consider complexity in programming and error checking. DMI is more complex because there are more steps involved. Instead of knowing everything up front, the object is forced to find it out in real time. This yields more steps and more opportunities for the unexpected to occur. For example, SMI allows the IDL compiler to verify up front that all data types are compatible between the statically bound objects. This verification occurs during software development. DMI is much different in that it does this checking on the fly, at the time the object is executed by, for example, accountants in your company using their CORBA-enabled ledger system. Doing things on the fly can introduce risks since accountants typically have difficulty reacting to CORBA runtime errors.

2.4.5 Distributed Object Communication: Inter-ORB Standards and IIOP

In order for objects serviced by different ORBs to communicate, the ORBs themselves must communicate. So, it goes without saying that we do not have much of a distributed object framework here unless we have inter-ORB protocol standards.

The General Inter-ORB Protocol (GIOP) defines standardized data and message formats that allow one ORB to communicate with another. The Internet Inter-ORB Protocol (IIOP) provides a standardized method of communication between ORBs, be they located on the same computer or on remote ones, by defining an implementation of GIOP over TCP/IP. Through the

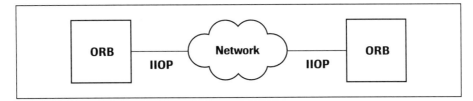

Figure 2.12 IIOP

functionality offered by the ORB and IIOP, an object need not care whether or not another object it wishes to communicate with is on the same computer or located on the other end of the world. IIOP is illustrated in Figure 2.12.

CORBA also supports Environment-Specific Inter-ORB Protocols (ESIOPs). ESIOPs allow ORBs to leverage other network and communication methods. For example, the DCE ESIOP—the DCE Common Inter-ORB Protocol (DCE-CIOP)—leverages DCE RPC for communication between ORBs. This is a step in the direction of leveraging the benefits of DCE and CORBA together.

One important issue with IIOP is that, in Internet/Intranet/Extranet applications where a firewall is involved, there has to be some way to accommodate IIOP traffic through the firewall. Firewalls are configured to deal with the HTTP protocol,which appears on TCP ports 80 and 443 (SSL-enabled HTTP); however, IIOP runs on its own port, which may vary depending upon how your administrator has configured your system. In order to deal with this issue, vendors are building gateways that encapsulate IIOP within HTTP up to the firewall, at which point an ORB may become involved that proxies object invocations back and forth between objects on either side of the firewall.

The topic of CORBA and firewalls is a complicated one. There is still no complete solution, and various standards efforts are under way to try to deal with the challenge. Ultimately, the solution will likely be rooted in the establishment of an intelligent gateway containment ORB at the firewall capable of authenticating and authorizing an incoming object and its requests and then proxying all communications and privileges granted to that object on its behalf behind the firewall.

2.4.6 CORBA Value-Added Services

CORBA value-added services are key to understanding issues associated with integrating CORBA into the enterprise network application framework.

2.4.6.1 Naming and Trader Services

The *CORBA Naming Service* allows an object to be located based on its name. CORBA objects can be named according to the standard CORBA naming format, or naming can be made more flexible through various CORBA naming extensibility mechanisms. For example, Visigenic, a supplier of CORBA products, allows objects to be identified via URLs. As previously mentioned, the *CORBA Trader Service* allows objects to be located and dynamically invoked based on their functions, not their name. In order for naming and trader services to reach their potential within the enterprise, ORB vendors need to provide manageable solutions to integrate them with the standard directory service infrastructure used by the network, be it LDAP, X.500, or Novell's NDS. Vendors are taking steps in this direction but aren't quite there yet in many cases. Novell, with their NDS product, discussed in Chapter 10, has taken steps to begin this integration process.

2.4.6.2 Event and Time Services

The *CORBA Event Service* allows objects to be triggered based on various conditions being met. For example, if inventory on a particular item in a warehouse falls below a certain level, an object could be invoked to place orders to replenish the inventory. The *CORBA Time Service* allows objects to be synchronized to a common clock, which is fundamental for event operations, since events can be triggered based on time as well.

2.4.6.3 Transaction Services

Transaction services provide ORB IDL extensions that allow transactions involving multiple ORBs to be carried out reliably. Transaction services are coupled with concurrency control services that manage contention for resources by blocking/unblocking access to them as needed. In Chapter 7, we'll discuss transactions in more detail along with their NT-specific COM-based product offering, the Microsoft Transaction Server (MTS), which can be viewed as competing with CORBA transaction services.

2.4.6.4 Security Services

The CORBA specification defines a broad range of security functionality. Why, then, do we hear so much about CORBA security challenges? First, because no matter how complete the specification, distributed objects are

not easy things to secure. By their very nature, they are dynamic and talkative, and they expect to make meaningful and impactful requests of one
another. You typically cannot put your CORBA objects into an overly protective sandbox and then ask them to perform mission-critical functions. Second, there are already so many competing security frameworks, as we have
seen in this chapter, that have or will require significant investment on the
part of the enterprise to deploy. Is it practical that we deploy yet another
security infrastructure for CORBA objects?

We typically think of security in terms of the user and the server that
controls access to resources accessible to the user and that, in the case of
SSL/TLS, authenticates itself to the user. But what of objects? One object
may call another that may then call another in order to get something done.
Who is the user? Who is the server? Objects therefore require *delegation,*
whereby an object can essentially inherit permissions from another object.
Figure 2.13 illustrates a common scenario: Bob, in trying to fulfill a request
made by Alice to update her bank records, has to invoke another object, Tom
the Bank Teller. Tom won't allow Bob to do anything to Alice's records without proper authority. If Bob were to impersonate Alice or otherwise prove he
is authorized to access Alice's records (of course, Alice doesn't give out blan-
ket authorization too easily, only authorization for specific transactions), then
Tom the Bank Teller would update the records.

Figure 2.13 Impersonation

Security services are implemented within the ORB. Therefore, the ORB takes on the responsibilities of managing the security fundamentals: authentication, authorization, privacy, integrity, and nonrepudiation.

CORBA defines the operations that allow these fundamentals to be implemented but does not specify how they are performed. While this is not a particularly intuitive thought, what it means, for example, is that the authentication operation defined by CORBA can be achieved through different means, including username/password, public key cryptography, Kerberos, or any other scheme. The authentication *interface* is defined, not the *implementation.* This allows CORBA to more easily leverage existing security technologies deployed within the enterprise. However, there are no existing technologies in broad deployment today that allow for all the CORBA security services to be implemented.

The user is authenticated by the Principal Authenticator object. Upon successful authentication, the user is issued a Credentials object. The Credentials object contains attributes that describe who the user is and what the user is authorized to do (his or her privileges).

CORBA supports delegation functions such as those required by Bob to update Alice's banking records. However, the underlying security mechanism must also be capable of supporting delegation in order to leverage the CORBA delegation functions. For example, if public key cryptography is used, the private key, the tool used to authenticate one's self, is not something you can just lend out to anyone else. If you do, you potentially break the whole set of assumptions upon which security in the system is based. This is not to say that you cannot delegate and leverage public key cryptography. It just means that a complicated arrangement of temporary certificates and private keys or some other adjunct mechanism must be employed.

Access control list (ACL) functionality is offered via policies configured within the ORB and via privileges within the object's credentials. The ORB will look at attributes within the credential, such as the role defined for the object (i.e., system administrator implies one set of permissions; salesperson, another) or the group it is a member of (for an employee in Information Systems versus Marketing, for example), and will also look at ACL policies defined within the ORB. For example, the ORB might have an ACL defined that states that members of the Information Systems group get full access rights to specific objects and methods whereas members of the Marketing group do not. CORBA also introduces the concept of domains, through which objects can be grouped into domains and subdomains, and security policies can be applied against those domains. CORBA security services provide a means of nonrepudiation by relying on message receipts, their storage, and concepts of evidence.

The issue here is that the ORB must have access to underlying secu. implementations to make all this work. It would need to provide enterprise wide scalable management solutions that compare with those offered by ones discussed in this book, including NT 4 Directory Services, NT 5 Active Directory, and Novell NDS.

Netscape took the simple and practical approach of offering IIOP over SSL. In this scenario, two objects on different ORBs can authenticate each other using SSL, plus get the rest of SSL's benefits. While simple, over time this approach needs to be augmented in order to support the full CORBA security services model. Also, delegation is not directly supported with this approach.

2.4.7 CORBA Versus RPC

Many CORBA ORBs, and even Microsoft's DCOM, are built on top of RPC. Right away that should tell you something about one versus the other—that object component object models actually *add* to the RPC concept.

RPC is based on a simple concept: two programs, each conforming to an agreed-upon interface, that call each other. In calling each other, if there is data to be presented, each program presents the data to the other outwardly.

CORBA and other component models are more sophisticated than that: You don't "call" a program; you invoke one of its methods, of which there may be many. Plus, you get all the other benefits relative to object technology, including classes, polymorphism, and so forth. But also, let's not forget the very important fact that component models include a wide range of well-defined services, such as the CORBA Trader Service and others we spoke of, all of which take advantage of object-oriented concepts.

2.5 X.500 and Lightweight Directory Access Protocol Version 3 (LDAPv3)

The *Lightweight Directory Access Protocol* (LDAPv3) brings open multiplatform standards-based directory services to mainstream corporate applications. While *X.500,* upon which LDAPv3 is based, is also an open standard, its success has been hampered by its complexity and the fact that its specifications were not originally adapted to the TCP/IP protocol.

LDAP defines a protocol for exchanging directory service commands between a client and a server as well as an API for adding LDAP functionality to applications. LDAP software development kits (SDKs) implementing this API are widely available.

As we will see, X.500 offers, in addition to a client/server protocol similar to LDAPv3, other protocols not defined by LDAP. For example, X.500 defines protocols specifically tailored for supporting the replication of the directory service database, whereas LDAPv3 does not define such a protocol. One could argue that, of course, LDAP does not define this since that was never what LDAP was intended for, and many argue that LDAP is merely a client access protocol and no more, their point being that LDAP does not define a directory service, but only a client access protocol. This statement, however, flies in the face of existing LDAP directory server products, such as those from Netscape, that are LDAP-based and that employ LDAP in various creative ways to provide a master/slave replication method, for example, without X.500 replication protocols.

The LDAPv3 protocol is flexible enough to be used as the basis for a directory service. However, it is hard for this simple and easily implementable protocol to compete with the large body of X.500 standards. And, for many, that is exactly the point—X.500 is too large and too complicated for them, and they want simplicity. They want LDAP.

LDAPv3's roots are in X.500. LDAPv3 is a lightweight version of an X.500 protocol, the Directory Access Protocol (DAP). LDAPv3 offers many benefits over DAP, including the most fundamental—support for TCP/IP.

Perhaps another reason for LDAPv3's popularity is that it exists in a more popular fast-moving standards body, the *Internet Engineering Task Force* (IETF). The *Committee for International Telegraphy and Telephone/International Standards Organization* (CCITT/ISO), the standards body responsible for X.500, is highly respected and has produced a wealth of standards implemented throughout the world today. However, it is not necessarily viewed by many as fast-moving or streamlined. Of course, the concept of being fast-moving is relative to whatever situation you are in at the moment—there are many who level similar criticism on the IETF.

The Joint CCITT/ISO Directories Working Group was formed in 1986 through a merging of various e-mail and directory service standards efforts going on at the time. The first complete X.500 standard was published in 1988.

2.5.1 X.500

When we look at X.500, we look at a specification for the entire directory service, one that defines the core elements of an enterprise directory service. Following is a list of the main functions of X.500 (an asterisk is placed by functions that are also specifically addressed by LDAPv3):

- ■ *Naming of directory entries
- ■ *Structure of directory information
- ■ *Client access to directory information
- ■ Partitioning of the directory service database tree
- ■ Replication/shadowing of the directory service database tree
- ■ *Security

2.5.1.1 X.500 Naming: It's All Relative

X.500 defines a standard for naming entries in the directory tree. This standard has been broadly adopted by a number of products, including Active Directory and Novell NDS, and by the LDAPv3 standard. It is considered to be counterintuitive by some, and alternatives are therefore offered by many vendors. We'll look at these alternatives when discussing other directory service offerings.

Components of an X.500 name are called *Relative Distinguished Names* (RDNs) because they are relative to one another. Each element of the name is relative to the element before it. The full name, the concatenation of all RDNs, is called the *Distinguished Name* (DN). Here's an analogy. If I were to tell you where I live, I might have said at one time in my life

Newport Beach, California, U.S.A.

Or, I could write this in the following manner to illustrate the hierarchical nature of this little spot on the West Coast of the United States:

U.S.A.
California
Newport Beach

Here, Newport Beach is relative to California, and California is relative to the U.S.A. If there is another Newport Beach in the world, there should be no confusion; the Newport Beach I'm talking about is in California, not anywhere else. Likewise, if there is a California somewhere else in the world, there should be no confusion; the California I'm talking about is in the U.S.A. Finally, at the root of this name is the country, U.S.A. It is assumed that everyone realizes there is only one of those; U.S.A. is relative to itself only. So, to make the analogy, Newport Beach is an RDN, California is an RDN, and U.S.A. is an RDN. The DN = RDN + RDN + RDN = Newport Beach, California, U.S.A. While the syntax in this example is not what is used specifically by typical X.500 installations (Country, State, City), the concept is essentially the same.

Within the X.500 directory service, this relative hierarchical naming scheme is formalized by defining identifiers at different points in the hierarchy (in the preceding example analogy, these were City, State, Country) and by providing rules for what can be stored within those identifiers, such as requiring that states be coded by two-letter symbols (in this case, the code would be CA).

X.500 is flexible in that it lets you define a multitude of naming structures. A good approach to naming objects and their containers while following the X.500 naming standard is provided by Novell NDS. In Chapter 10, we'll see how objects managed by the directory service (such as users, printers, and so forth) can be organized under a hierarchy of containers (RDNs): the root, country, organization, and organizational unit.

2.5.1.2 X.500 Components: Databases, Trees, and Agents

Each X.500 directory server maintains a database containing directory service entries. This database is referred to as the *Directory Information Base* (DIB). Relationships between entries in this database are expressed hierarchically in the form of a directory tree, such as the one we discussed in Chapter 1. The tree's data relationships are contained within the X.500 *Directory Information Tree* (DIT). The DIB/DIT can be partitioned (shared) among multiple directory servers.

A directory server employs a *Directory System Agent* (DSA) as the functional component that communicates with clients and with other directory servers. Clients access the DSA with the *Directory User Agent* (DUA) functional component. The relationship between these components and the DIB/DIT is illustrated in Figure 2.14.

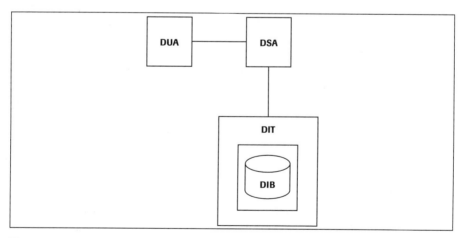

Figure 2.14 Relationship between DUA and DSA and the DIB/DIT

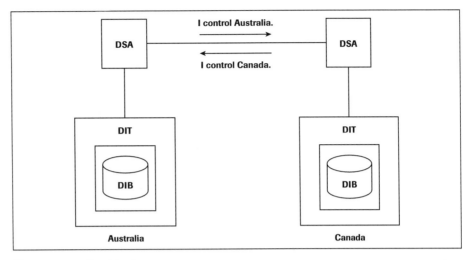

Figure 2.15 Partitioning

When the DIB/DIT is distributed among multiple directory servers, the DSAs within each server work together to share information so that, from the perspective of the user (DUA), there is one big database instead of many smaller ones spread across multiple servers. In order for one DSA to know what part of the directory tree other DSAs control, *knowledge references,* which essentially are pointers indicating what tree entries a directory server controls, are shared among DSAs. Figure 2.15 illustrates two DSAs sharing their knowledge references, one controlling the Australian network partition and the other controlling the Canadian partition.

The DIB/DIT can also be replicated for reliability and performance purposes. We'll discuss the protocols used to achieve this in the next section.

2.5.1.3 X.500 Protocols: Client Access, Agent to Agent, and Replication

DUAs use the *Directory Access Protocol* (DAP) to communicate directory service queries and commands with DSAs. To share knowledge references and to work together to satisfy DUA queries, DSAs use a protocol called the *Directory System Protocol* (DSP). The roles of DAP and DSP are illustrated in Figure 2.16. LDAP plays the same role as DAP.

It was mentioned earlier that X.500 supports replication. The *Directory Information Shadowing Protocol* (DISP) is used to implement this capability. DISP is used between DSAs to exchange information required to replicate

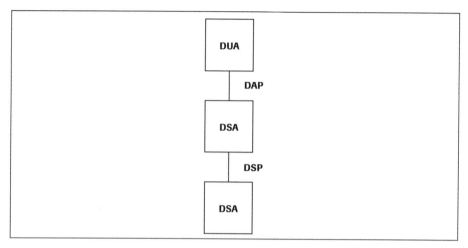

Figure 2.16 The roles of DAP and DSP

DIB/DIT partitions or, if so desired, the entire DIB/DIT. The *Directory Operational Binding Management Protocol* (DOP) allows two DSAs to dynamically communicate to each other exactly what data will be replicated and how frequently. DOP is an optional protocol, and the same parameters could be manually configured by the directory server administrators instead of dynamically configured via DOP. Figure 2.17 illustrates the roles of DISP and DOP in the replication of a directory database containing all enterprise entries for Australia.

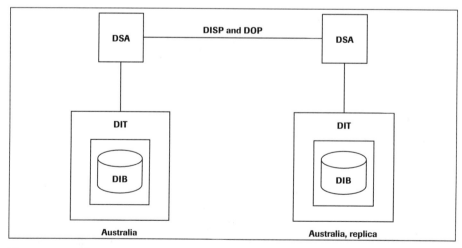

Figure 2.17 The roles of DISP and DOP in replication

X.500 supports a master/slave approach to replication, meaning that updates are ultimately controlled by the master (owner) of the DIB/DIT entries being replicated and that the master copy is always updated first, with shadow copies after that. Recall from the discussion in Chapter 1 that there are two fundamental approaches to doing this: master/slave and peer-to-peer.

Even though X.500 employs a master/slave model, the master itself does not have to update all of the shadows; it just must be updated first, with the shadows at some time and in some way afterward. X.500 supports a performance-enhancing feature called *secondary shadowing*. This feature allows shadows themselves to update other shadows and for those shadows to also possibly update others, in a treelike, trickle-down fashion. This removes the burden of updating all the shadows from the master. Instead, it need only update a select group of shadows, and those shadows can then update a select group of other shadows, which can then update other shadows, until all the shadows are updated.

2.5.1.4 Security

The X.500 authentication framework for client authentication to an X.500 server offers three fundamental services:

1. Simple authentication
2. Strong authentication
3. Digital signatures

Simple authentication is based on a username/password approach. There are two simple authentication choices:

1. With the Password in the Clear option, a username/password combination is sent in the clear over the network, which is a very unsecure and ill-advised approach.
2. The Hashed Password option is the same as option 1 except that the password is hidden via a hash algorithm, which offers slightly more security. These hash algorithms by themselves can be compromised by the determined hacker far more easily than they can crack the type of overall authentication and encryption scheme implemented by, for example, SSL. However, a hash algorithm still increases the effort required to crack the password; therefore, it is better than sending a password in the clear.

Strong authentication is based on X.509 certificates and public key cryptography. This approach offers additional security; however, it offers the disadvantage of requiring that a public key infrastructure be managed within the enterprise and that the issue of private key portability be addressed. Novell NDS, discussed in Chapter 10, takes an interesting hybrid proprietary approach, combining the username/password approach with public key cryptography, storing the private key on a server and distributing it to users dynamically.

Some X.500 installations replace the X.500 security offerings with other more familiar systems—for example, Kerberos. The manner in which this is achieved is dependent upon the security extensibilty features offered by your particular X.500 product.

2.5.2 LDAPv3

LDAPv3 is relatively simple. Even its name, with the word *Lightweight* in it, implies simplicity. There is an IETF RFC you can download off the Internet that defines it. Software development toolkits are freely available that allow you to integrate LDAPv3 access functionality into your application via the API defined for LDAP. And, it seems everyone is integrating an LDAPv3 gateway into their product. Even though it is simple, LDAPv3 is capable of issuing powerful directory service queries as well as allowing the client to issue commands that add, delete, or modify directory service entries. As we study LDAP, we'll focus on the following fundamentals:

- How LDAP directory servers are reached by your client (LDAP URLs)
- Allowing the use of multiple LDAP directory services (effective partitioning) and replication in your network
- Security and single-user logon with LDAP

2.5.2.1 LDAP URLs

Uniform resource locators (URLs) are the method used extensively within the Internet and Intranet—you use them all the time to visit Web sites. For example, the URL for Addison Wesley Longman's Web site is http://www.awl.com.

Your LDAP servers can be made reachable by URLs, as your Web servers can. For example, if you named your LDAP server directory.mycompany.com, an LDAP URL would be

```
ldap://directory.mycompany.com/<LDAP Command>
```

where `<LDAP Command>` would be filled-in by the LDAP client (such as your Web browser) and would represent the LDAP protocol command the client is issuing to the LDAP server.

2.5.2.2 Referral Mode and Effective Partitioning

LDAP lacks an X.500 DSP protocol equivalent that provides a means for two directory servers to share a partitioned database. Instead, LDAP supports another approach to achieve, from the client's perspective, a similar goal. LDAP defines a *referral mode* of operation as a method to satisfy a client query spanning multiple directory servers.

If an LDAP server does not hold information needed to satisfy a query it has received, it checks to see whether it has been administratively configured with information indicating what other server might contain that information (equivalent to a knowledge reference in X.500). If it knows of one, it sends an LDAP referral message back to the client, which causes the client to send a new LDAP request to the server being referred to.

With referrals, the burden is entirely on the client to attach to and resolve its query. If the first directory server the client attaches to cannot satisfy the query, then that server will refer the client to another directory server by providing that server's URL, and then to another, and so forth, until the query is resolved. LDAP provides mechanisms that prevent a client from looping in this state indefinitely in the event that there are circular knowledge references between LDAP servers.

2.5.2.3 Replication

Whereas X.500 defines a replication architecture and protocols, LDAPv3 does not, as we have already discussed. Therefore, when you purchase an LDAP directory server product, you might ask (1) if the product supports replication and (2) if it does, exactly how it is achieved.

For example, Netscape Directory Server 3.0 supports master/slave replication. Netscape states that this is achieved without the use of a proprietary protocol and that, instead, LDAP itself is used between the master and its slaves. Still, there obviously are timers and information exchanges that must occur between the master and the slaves, and Netscape has defined some parameters surrounding those variables and any error recovery conditions that must be handled during the replication process. So, if you had other LDAP-compliant directory service and you wished the Netscape tory server to replicate to that service, you would be wise to perform tests to determine whether it would work between the two implementations. In contrast to this, X.500 defines DOP, which would allow the disparate directory services to configure each other, and DISP, a peer-to-peer replication protocol, which would permit information exchange. Of course, even in this case, the ability to get two X.500 DOP/DISP servers to replicate to each other would also likely not be without its challenges.

2.5.2.4 Security and Single-User Logon

There are three commonly implemented methods for an LDAP client to authenticate to an LDAP server:

1. Simple authentication based on a username/password, with the password sent in the clear. This method is called out directly in the LDAPv3 specification.
2. Support for a replaceable authentication mechanism via the Simple Authentication and Security Layer (SASL). SASL is an IETF RFC standard, and the LDAPv3 specification refers to it.
3. Use of LDAP over SSL/TLS. This third approach is implemented by Netscape and others.

Let's take a closer look at methods 2 and 3.

2.5.2.4.1 SASL   SASL is a very simple specification that specifies a mechanism for an LDAP client and server to negotiate an authentication protocol. SASL itself does not define a particular authentication protocol. Also, SASL is not specific to LDAP—it can be used with any connection-oriented protocol.

   SASL defines two basic types of authentication mechanisms: registered and external. *Registered* mechanisms include Kerberos version 4 and S-Key (S-Key is an encrypted password authentication mechanism). In order for an authentication scheme to be registered, someone has to describe the protocol exchange and negotiation following a format defined within the SASL specification and then has to submit that description to the Internet Assigned Numbers Authority (IANA). IANA is the same group that registers standardized TCP and UDP port numbers (discussed in Chapter 3). *External* mechanisms are used for authentication mechanisms that are not as easily decoupled from their overall security implementation (which may include encryption, integrity, etc.). A good example of this is SSL/TLS. In this case, the LDAP server and client will utilize their own authentication mechanism, external to SASL, to perform authentication.

2.5.2.4.2 *LDAP over SSL/TLS*   LDAP over SSL/TLS requires that both the client and the server implement a version of LDAP that includes SSL/TLS support. As we discussed earlier, SSL/TLS allows the client and the server to authenticate each other via X.509 certificates and also provides a range of other benefits.

Exactly how would LDAP and SSL/TLS be combined to offer single-user logon within your enterprise? After all, the elements are here to achieve this—a directory server, Web servers with information requiring access control, and a secure protocol with a means of providing client/server authentication. Here is a very high level summary of one method that might be applied with Netscape's Web servers:

1. The client goes to the HR Web server and requests access to sensitive employee records.

2. SSL/TLS authentication is initiated between the client and the server.

3. As part of this process, the client presents its certificate and proves it holds the private key, as required by the SSL/TLS protocol.

4. The HR Web server then attaches to the LDAP directory server. This connection should also be made over SSL/TLS. Since the LDAP server holds security attributes, it is very important that it be highly secure. The HR Web server, because it identified itself to the LDAP server as a trusted Web server by having a properly signed certificate and proving ownership of the private key, is given access to the user's security attributes.

5. The HR Web server uses the DN contained in the user's certificate to look up its security attributes. The HR Web server discovers that this user is a member of the HR group.

There's the Server Connecting to the Directory Service and Other Observations

SSL integrated with LDAP, in the manner described here, provides an excellent example of one way a server may be required to access directory service information.

Let's take special note of the network design implication here. For this example, both the client and the server need to have access to the directory server in order for the client to achieve its goal (access to HR information). This means that both the client and the server need to have fast and reliable connections to a directory in order for this operation to succeed.

Also, as illustrated in this example, the directory server is holding very sensitive information. If it is successfully attacked, the entire authentication scheme could be compromised, and Bad Guy could gain access to anyone's HR records.

Finally, note that since the directory server is executing SSL, this will introduce additional server CPU load. If this directory server was not previously running SSL, it is a reasonable bet that, after SSL is enabled and running and transactions increase, CPU utilization will drive up faster than before and more computing capacity may be required.

6. The HR Web server then looks up the ACLs defined for the sensitive employee record files to which the user has requested access. These ACLs specify that members of the HR group are granted access to these files containing sensitive employee records. The client is then granted access to these files.

2.6 Conclusions

The technologies discussed in this chapter offer tremendous benefits to the enterprise network application framework. The rest of the book will help guide you to your own conclusions relative to the topics discussed here. Throughout the book, we'll discuss competing and complementary object technologies, including Microsoft's COM, and highly functional proprietary directory services, such as NDS from Novell, that, at the same time, support a number of the technologies we just studied.

FOR FURTHER STUDY

1. R. Atkinson. "RFC 1827 IP Encapsulating Security Payload." August 1995.
2. J. Myers. "RFC 2222 Simple Authentication and Security Layer." October 1997.
3. J. Bloomer. *Power Programming with RPC.* Sebastopol, Calif.: O'Reilly, 1992.
4. S. Garfinkel. *PGP: Pretty Good Privacy.* Sebastopol, Calif.: O'Reilly, 1995.
5. S. Garfinkel and G. Spafford. *Practical UNIX and Internet Security,* 2d ed. Bonn; Cambridge, Mass.: O'Reilly, 1996.
6. S. Garfinkel and G. Spafford. *Web Security and Commerce.* Sebastopol, Calif.: O'Reilly, 1997.
7. D. Gunter. *Client/Server Programming with RPC and DCE.* Indianapolis, Ind.: Que, 1995.
8. C. Kaufman, R. Perlman, and M. Speciner. *Network Security: Private Communication in a Public World.* Englewood Cliffs, N.J.: Prentice-Hall, 1995.
9. R. Oppliger. *Authentication Systems for Secure Networks.* Boston· Artech House, 1996.
10. R. Orfali and D. Harkey. *Client/Server Programming with Java and CORBA.* New York: Wiley, 1997.
11. R. Orfali, D. Harkey, and J. Edwards. *Essential Client/Server Survival Guide.* New York: Van Nostrand Reinhold, 1994.
12. R. Orfali, D. Harkey, and J. Edwards. *The Essential Distributed Objects Survival Guide.* New York: Wiley, 1996.
13 A. Vogel, K. Duddy, and Object Management Group. *Java Programming with CORBA,* 2d ed. New York: Wiley, 1998.

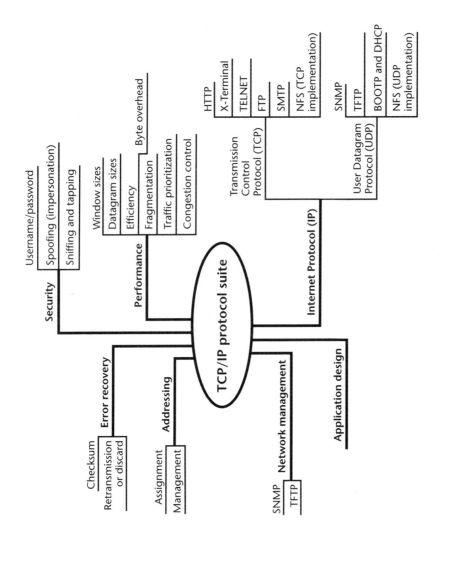

CHAPTER 3

The TCP/IP Protocol Suite

Topic	Benefits	Experience
IP, UDP, and TCP	We'll study the behavior of the TCP/IP protocol suite as it relates to the design parameters of functionality, performance, efficiency, and security.	Flow control, error recovery, windowing, maximum datagram sizes, and the like will significantly impact your corporate and Internet traffic. This chapter is intended to aid you in anticipating and understanding these issues.
Application design	The TCP/IP protocol suite is implicitly associated with a wide range of applications. We'll learn key application functions and design implications.	Suppose you have a legacy terminal-based (say, VT-100-based) application you need to bring onto your IP network. Should you use TELNET? X-Terminal? HTTP/1.0 or 1.1? TFTP or FTP? This chapter is intended to assist you with these and other similar questions.

CHAPTER HIGHLIGHTS

Topic	Benefits	Experience
Performance and efficiency	It is wise not to assume that all TCP/IP applications are efficient and perform well simply because they are standardized and broadly implemented. We'll learn why.	I have been in meetings with IS managers from some of the largest corporations in the world and have watched them turn pale as they learned about the *real* efficiency of their applications.
Security	With the ubiquitous connectivity of our day, we are assured of two things: (1) The hacker's thirst for intrusion is well fueled, and (2) corporations and individuals are becoming increasingly vulnerable. This chapter will help make you more aware of security vulnerabilities of the TCP/IP protocol suite and associated applications.	You may be surprised to find out that things are not as safe as you might have thought they were.
Addressing	How do you conserve IP addresses? What is VLSM?	For making important architectural decisions such as which routing protocol to use or for what to do when you can't get any more IP addresses (no matter how much the company's CIO demands otherwise), a grounding in addressing fundamentals is required.

3.1 Introduction

The collection of protocols commonly referred to as the *TCP/IP protocol suite* forms the basis of the Internet and is the protocol de jure for Intranets. To say you "know TCP/IP" is not saying much these days. It seems that everyone, technical or not, has heard of it. Even the least technical of folks know it has something to do with the Internet, and they may come to learn, usually through painful configuration bouts with their home computers, that they require it to get on the Web.

To really know TCP/IP is to know much more than this. For deploying applications that leverage this protocol suite, a full knowledge of its performance, efficiency, security, routing, addressing, congestion control, network management, and error recovery characteristics is well advised. This protocol suite is highly complex, and the right use of it can bring a smile and satisfaction to your workday. Use it the wrong way by not planning for or understanding its overhead processing, by not understanding its security capabilities and risks, or by otherwise relying on it for capabilities it cannot perform well or at all, and you could be in for one frustrating experience.

In this chapter, we will dissect the TCP/IP protocol suite and study its behavior. At times, it may seem that we are muddling down in the relatively unimportant bits and bytes layer. Try to stick with it, though, because these bits and bytes will eventually add up to a complex operational model that you will likely be rewarded for understanding.

3.2 IP, TCP, and UDP

The *Internet Protocol* (IP) is the common datagram (packet) format used in IP networks. The *Transmission Control Protocol* (TCP) "rides on top" of IP, meaning that IP transports TCP through the network. Think of TCP as the passenger and IP as the train. The *User Datagram Protocol* (UDP), an alternative to TCP, is also carried by IP.

The complete IP datagram format is illustrated in Figure 3.1. TCP and UDP are carried within the Data field of the IP datagram. The format shown in Figure 3.1 is called *IP version 4* (IPv4). IPv4 is the IP datagram format implemented throughout the world today.

Chapter 5 is dedicated to the next-generation IP protocol, called *IP version 6* (IPv6). Note that IP version 5 has essentially been "skipped" since the IPv5 specification never received widespread adoption.

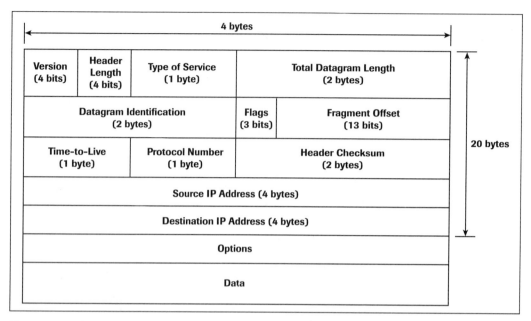

Figure 3.1 IPv4 format

3.2.1 IP in Detail

Let's explore each element (field) of an IP packet in detail and study its meaning and impact.

3.2.1.1 Version and Header Length

The 4-bit Version field defines the format of the IP datagram. Versions 1 through 3 are no longer used. Version 4 is illustrated in Figure 3.1.

The 4-bit Header Length field contains the length of the IP header only, excluding the Data field. The units for this field are in 4-byte increments. Thus, if the header is 20 bytes long—that is, there are no options in the header (see Figure 3.1)—then this field will contain 20/4, or 5 in it, signifying five 4-byte increments.

3.2.1.2 Type of Service

The 1-byte Type of Service (TOS) field indicates what level of service is best provided for the datagram. Various bit permutations can be set theoretically instructing the network to maximize throughput, minimize delay, maximize reliability, and minimize monetary cost. For example, your TELNET remote terminal emulation datagrams would, in an ideal world, incur minimum delay because they are part of an interactive session with a likely impatient user who is accustomed to near-instantaneous keyboard response time. You might, for example, want the TELNET interactive terminal packets to take precedence over packets from a file transfer. Products and protocols supporting TOS have not been widely deployed to date. Instead, router vendors have implemented various alternative priority queuing mechanisms to determine data priority, such as what protocol and application are carried within the Data field (determined by examining two fields we will talk about in this chapter, the IP Protocol Number and the TCP/UDP Port Number fields), the source address of the datagram, and so forth. The relative priority criteria are something that the network designer would implement in order to meet specific customer (user) response time requirements. These priority mechanisms are configured by the network designer in routers within the network. Figure 3.2 illustrates the dilemma of small packets queued behind those from, for example, a file transfer. Prioritization might help reduce the impact of the file transfer on the user computer's small packets.

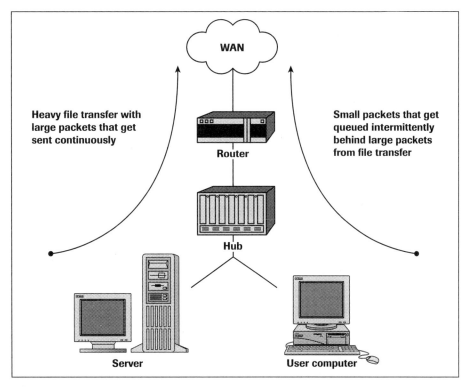

Figure 3.2 Poor little packets (no priority)

3.2.1.3 Total Datagram Length

The 2-byte Total Datagram Length field represents the total number of bytes in the datagram, including the IP header, any options, and the Data field. Two bytes allows us to represent a data field length of up to 65,535 bytes. However, due to the realities of buffer management and today's applications and their evolution, many devices operate with a *maximum transmission unit* (MTU) size of 576 bytes when sending data to devices on another network but use larger MTUs when communicating with devices on the same LAN (network).

3.2.1.4 Datagram Identification and Fragment Offset

The Datagram Identification field is a sequence number for each datagram sent. The need for this field is directly related to a capability in IP networks known as *fragmentation.* Fragmentation allows a router to break a large IP datagram into smaller ones. When it breaks these datagrams up, this identification field is used to group together all the individual fragments of the fragmented datagram, and the Fragment Offset field designates the sequence number of a given fragment so that the original IP datagram can be reassembled later.

A router or host that supports fragmentation can break a datagram into smaller ones (can *fragment* the datagram) if the next device along the path to the destination does not have buffers large enough to store the datagram and make a routing decision. In other words, the maximum allowable MTU of the sender is larger than that of the next recipient.

A detailed study of all the conditions and issues associated with fragmentation is rather complicated, so let's focus instead on how to avoid fragmentation. You should do so because it is bad in your network for many reasons—from the additional congestion caused by many small packets to the problems with those commercial implementations correct enough to support fragmentation and reassembly but flawed enough to crash often enough while attempting it. Two approaches for avoiding fragmentation are summarized here:

1. Make certain that all devices support an MTU of 576 bytes when transmitting to another network (as opposed to on the same LAN/network, in which case the devices may choose a larger MTU to get better performance). Many IP implementations will automatically reduce their MTU to 576 bytes when the destination is on another network, thus traveling through a router of some sort, and may use a larger one when communicating with devices on the same network (LAN).

2. Implement a feature called *MTU discovery* in your network. MTU discovery allows the source of an IP datagram to learn the maximum allowable MTU along a given network path to a given destination. The source of the datagram accomplishes this by sending a datagram of the size it wishes to send (say, for example, 1,024 bytes). Within the IP Flags field of this datagram, the source sets a "don't fragment" (DF) bit. The DF bit effectively instructs any device encountering the packet that can't route it without fragmentation to return an error message to the sender. This error message is an Internet Control Message Protocol (ICMP) "can't fragment" error packet. (We'll look at ICMP more in Chapter 4 on IP routing.) If no ICMP error packet is received, then the source assumes that a path exists to the destination supporting the MTU. The fact that paths through the network can dynamically change—and thus the maximum allowable MTU can change—does not exactly simplify things. Different TCP/IP implementations handle this differently. Some, for example, periodically rediscover the maximum MTU at fixed intervals. RFC 1191 suggests this interval be 10 minutes. Solaris 2.2, for example, uses a 30-second timer.

Some History

For the original designers of the IP protocol, fragmentation was a necessary feature to deal with the differing buffer capabilities of the new and old equipment that had to interoperate as the government networks grew.

3.2.1.5 Time-to-Live

Because IP datagrams are exchanged by routers executing complex routing protocols that respond dynamically to failures and sometimes create a few themselves, we need a way to prevent datagrams from *looping,* or taking an indefinite round-trip somewhere within your network due to a routing error or anomaly that has occurred within your routing protocol infrastructure. Such a thing is much more common than you would think, and, therefore, we are thankful for the Time-to-Live (TTL) field, which limits the time a datagram can survive before a router drops it in the bit bucket (discards the packet).

The source of an IP datagram sets the TTL field to a particular value—32 or 64, for example. Each router through which an IP datagram travels decrements the TTL field by 1, and, when the counter reaches 0, the datagram is discarded. The device discarding the datagram then sends an ICMP message to the source of the datagram indicating TTL has been exceeded.

Real-World Network Operations

Looping packets can become a real problem because they can artificially drive up utilization of network links and routers. Don't order more bandwidth or routers right away when you see high utilization (high network usage). Look closer. You could have a significant routing inefficiency in your network. Network usage statistics can be very helpful when troubleshooting routing problems within the network. Traffic statistics, for example, can be used in this way, detecting routing loops, inefficiencies, and other problems.

Looping within the network can have many causes. The causes and remedies are as broad as there are answers to why an automobile, for example, stops working. Common sources of looping are (1) buggy router software, (2) too many static routes configured within the network, and (3) improperly handled network upgrades.

For (1), you should fully test router software in a lab environment, simulating as much as you can and gaining familiarity with it before deploying it. Yes, this works. Yes, it is worthwhile. Yes, the cynics that say a lab can't simulate your network are right, but they are also wrong because whatever you do learn will typically be well worth your while. For (2), static configurations that override your routing protocols are hard to configuration-manage and often must be manually updated when the network changes (different static configurations being added and deleted in different routers). Avoid them. For (3), when upgrading router software, do it according to a careful plan and isolate parts of the network running old router software from new router software where possible. Interoperability problems between different router software versions, for example, can cause very bizarre buggy scenarios. Try to run as much of your network as possible on a common software revision.

3.2.1.6 Flags

The Flags field signals whether the datagram is a fragment of some larger IP datagram. One of the bits of this field is the "don't fragment" (DF) bit, which is used as part of the IP MTU discovery process.

3.2.1.7 Protocol Number

The Protocol Number field identifies the protocol contained in the Data field, which will usually be TCP or UDP. This field may also signal, for example, that the Data field contains routing protocol information. Table 3.1 provides some example protocol numbers.

Table 3.1 Example Protocol Numbers

Decimal	Keyword/Application
1	ICMP (IPv4)
6	TCP
17	UDP
88	EIGRP
89	OSPF

3.2.1.8 Header Checksum

The Header Checksum field is used to detect bit errors in the header only. The next layer up (TCP, UDP) has its own checksum. So, we have 2 bytes here for a checksum, and, as we will see later, we have another 2-byte checksum in the upper-layer TCP or UDP packet. That is a total of 4 bytes of overhead that gets sent along with every IP datagram carrying TCP.

3.2.1.9 Source and Destination IP Addresses

The Source IP Address and Destination IP Address fields uniquely identify the source of the IP datagram and its destination. Four bytes are allocated to each address. Due to the enormous and well-deserved popularity of the Internet, almost everyone, even the deli restaurant on the corner, has an Internet address. Addresses are assigned by a centralized Internet organization in the United States called *ARIN,* by an organization called *RIPE* in Europe, by *AP-NIC* in the Asia–Pacific region, and by other regional organizations. All of these organizations work to make sure that everyone connected to the Internet has a unique address and that addresses are conserved.

3.2.1.10 Options

The Options field is of variable length in order to signal any number of options, including security options, time stamping, and recording of the route traveled by the packet. These features can be useful for benchmarking and problem isolation but, in the scheme of things, can end up being the best friend of your worst enemy—the hacker trying to break into your network through the use of two features known as *loose source routing* and *strict source routing*. You may never need to use these source-routing options, and many routers allow you to disable them for good reason: While they can sometimes be useful for troubleshooting, the person finding them most beneficial is the hacker trying to break into your network in that they enable the hacker's computer to imper-sonate another computer on your network.

The hacker achieves this deception by specifying a source address in his or her datagrams that is trusted by the destination host. This type of attack is called *spoofing*. The trusted address might be that of a trusted management workstation. Because the source-routing option specifies the return path used by the host receiving the packet, the attacked host will respond to the hacker's datagrams with datagrams routed directly back to the hacker using the source-routing option, thereby defeating any of the honest (correct) routes to the true owner of that source IP address. One approach to prevent-ing this kind of attack is to disable source-routing support within the routers of your network.

3.2.1.11 Data

The Data field contains the next layer's packet, which will be TCP, UDP, or some other upper-layer protocol packet.

3.2.2 TCP in Detail

Figure 3.3 contains the TCP packet format. Right away, you should notice that, without options being set in the IP and TCP packets, there are already up to 40 bytes of overhead for every datagram (20 IP bytes + 20 TCP bytes). That is 40 bytes a datagram. You just can't ignore this number during your communications network design. This byte overhead, added to every packet, can have a dramatic impact on link utilization (percentage usage of your bandwidth) and performance.

Let's now move on to the next level, TCP, and explore it in more detail.

3.2.2.1 Source and Destination Port Numbers

The Source Port Number and Destination Port Number fields are used to identify a particular connection between the two computers communicating

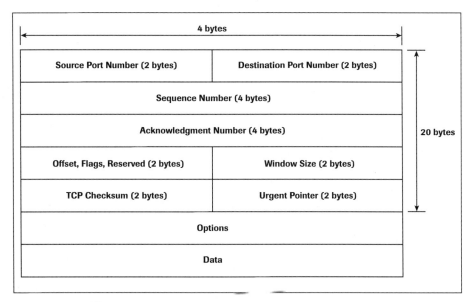

Figure 3.3 TCP format

over the network. Table 3.2 lists some well-known example port numbers. When a computer connects to another computer using TCP, it usually sets the destination port number to the well-known port number to indicate the particular application being accessed.

Table 3.2 Example TCP and UDP Port Numbers

Decimal	Keyword/Application	Description
7	ECHO	Echo
20	FTP-DATA	FTP file transfer data
21	FTP	FTP file transfer control
23	TELNET	TELNET
67	BOOTP/DHCP	BOOTP/DHCP server
68	BOOTP/DHCP	BOOTP/DHCP client
69	TFTP	TFTP
80	HTTP	HyperText Transfer Protocol
161	SNMP	SNMP
162	SNMPTRAP	SNMP trap event
177	XDMCP	X Display Manager Control Protocol
443	HTTPS	HyperText Transfer Protocol with SSL

3.2.2.1.1 *Other Applications*   These port numbers may also be used to prioritize traffic through network routers to, for example, prevent the file transfer traffic (FTP) from dominating the interactive terminal emulation traffic (TELNET) or other similar delay-sensitive applications. In this case, we use the port number to instruct the router as to which applications to give higher priority.

3.2.2.1.2 *Ephemeral Ports and Selecting Ports*   When a client application wishes to access an application on a host, such as a Web server, it uses a destination port number of 80 to indicate HTTP. But what about the *source* port number of this packet? What is it set to?

The client application selects what is commonly referred to as an *ephemeral port,* the word *ephemeral* meaning short-lived. Ephemeral ports are typically (but don't have to be) chosen from the range 1,024 to 5,000.

Ephemeral port numbers must be chosen carefully when establishing multiple connections between the same client and server for the same application. For example, suppose you wish to establish two different TELNET sessions to the same server. Then, your client will use destination port number 23 and choose some ephemeral source port number for the first TELNET connection. But, for the second TELNET session, your client must choose a second, different ephemeral source port number so that the client and server software can distinguish between the two different TELNET sessions.

3.2.2.2 Sequence Number

The TCP layer is concerned with error recovery (retransmission) and flow control. It utilizes sequence numbering to identify data that must be recovered or controlled. Flow control mechanisms allow for the source and destination computers to speed up and slow down transmission of datagrams, to retransmit datagrams with checksum errors, or to retransmit lost datagrams, all in a highly efficient manner by keeping track of the exact sequence of transmissions between the source and the destination. Note that the Sequence Number field used by TCP is represented in units of bytes, not datagrams. Each byte in a TCP session is numbered from 0 to the largest number you can identify in binary using 4 bytes, 4,294,967,296. That is a huge number. When a retransmission is needed, it is sent relative to the most recently and correctly received byte. Many people do not realize that TCP does not support selective retransmission of individual bytes. In the case of an error or lost data, the source must retransmit all bytes up to and including the first byte in error or lost byte, regardless of whether or not bytes received after that did not contain errors. This can be useful information when you are doing performance analysis and troubleshooting.

Why Was It Designed This Way?

Why did the TCP designers allocate 4 bytes for this problem instead of, say, only 1? With only 1 byte, there would be 256 sequence numbers, but with 4 bytes there are 4,294,967,296 sequence numbers. Why do we need so many? In order to reassemble datagrams at the destination and further assure that old data does not reappear and get confused with new data, this counter is made very large so that each datagram has as unique a number as possible before having to restart the counter (which would occur after about 4 billion bytes are sent).

3.2.2.3 Acknowledgment Number

The Acknowledgment Number field is the byte number of the most recently received byte that has been correctly received by the destination plus 1. One is added to indicate "the next byte expected," which is 1 more than the last correctly received byte.

3.2.2.4 Window Size

The Window Size field indicates the number of outstanding bytes that can be transmitted before the destination must provide an acknowledgment. The field is represented in units of bytes. It is *dynamic*, meaning that the two computers involved in the TCP session can change this value dynamically, depending upon changing network conditions, such as congestion, which would force the window size to decrease, thereby slowing the flow of traffic between the source and the destination.

Note that you can sometimes tune the computer operating system (e.g., UNIX) to encourage it to use larger window sizes wherever possible. For applications involving large amounts of data transfer over reasonably error-free links, this can improve throughput performance.

Comparisons

The dynamic window-size capability of TCP differentiates it from certain other protocols, such as X.25 and SDLC, which rely on fixed window sizes.

3.2.2.5 Offset

The Offset, or Header Length, field is used to identify where the header stops within the TCP packet. The header is defined as all the fields except the Data field. The Offset field is needed because of the Options field, which may cause the overall length of the header to vary.

3.2.2.6 TCP Checksum

The TCP Checksum field is a checksum for the *entire* TCP header including the Data field. You may recall that the IP header has its own checksum for the IP header only.

3.2.2.7 Urgent Pointer

The Urgent Pointer field signals an attempt at prioritizing data to accelerate, for example, the transmission of an important command. TELNET and Remote Login (RLOGIN) use urgent mode to signal that the user has pressed an interrupt key.

3.2.2.8 Options

The Options field is reserved for various uses, the most significant one being to signal the *maximum segment size* (MSS) during connection establishment. Each computer in the connection can set an MSS value. If one is not specified, then an MSS of 536 bytes is usually assumed, meaning that a 576-byte MTU value for the IP datagram is sufficient to carry TCP traffic having an MSS of 536 bytes (576 = 536 bytes of TCP data + 40 bytes of TCP and IP header overhead with no options). In many TCP implementations, the MSS will default to a higher value if the destination is on the same network (Ethernet, for example), and, if the destination is on a different network, it will default to 536 bytes.

3.2.2.9 Flags and Reserved Fields

The Flags field is used for various connection control functions, including connection setup and reset. The Reserved field is reserved for future use.

3.2.3 UDP in Detail

Figure 3.4 illustrates the much simpler UDP packet format. UDP only contains checksum, length, and source/destination port number fields. It has no retransmission scheme, so, by itself, it cannot support error recovery

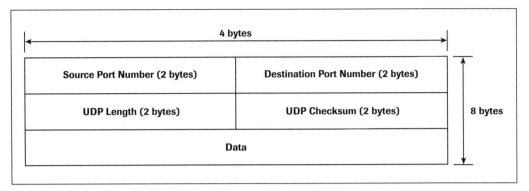

Figure 3.4 UDP format

or flow control other than by simply discarding the packet if an error occurs or congestion sets in. Therefore, applications using UDP either must not care about error recovery or flow control or must implement their own schemes at a layer above UDP. Table 3.3 provides a performance-characteristic comparison between TCP and UDP.

Table 3.3 TCP and UDP Performance-Characteristic Comparison

Characteristic	TCP	UDP
Flow control	Large, variable-length window. If buffers/resources are not available, the allowable number of outstanding bytes (the window size) will shrink. Retransmission will be requested for any data that must be discarded due to insufficient buffers/resources.	If buffers/resources are not available, packet is discarded. No flow control mechanism exists.
Error recovery	If checksum indicates error, re-transmission is accomplished via retransmission mechanism.	If checksum indicates error, packet is discarded. No retrans-mission mechanism exists.
Number of header bytes	40 bytes minimum.	28 bytes minimum.

3.3 Application Design

Applications such as TELNET, FTP, and SNMP use IP and either TCP or UDP. Figure 3.5 shows which of a common set of protocols use TCP and which use UDP.

Network File System (NFS)

NFS, shown in Figure 3.5 as either a TCP- or UDP-based application, is commonly employed by UNIX servers to allow remote access to their file systems. NFS implementors typically utilize RPC, which was discussed in Chapter 2. The RPC utilized by the NFS implementor can be either TCP- or UDP-based. Versions of NFS implementing advanced security often utilize TCP and are referred to as *secure NFS.*

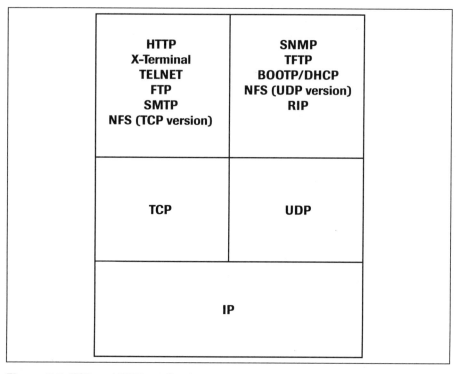

Figure 3.5 TCP and UDP applications

UDP applications, generally speaking, are simpler than TCP applications and do not require high levels of throughput, flow control, or error recovery. Applications based upon TCP, in contrast, benefit from the increased reliability and performance of TCP. Today, most application developers will choose TCP for the bulk of what they do since they need reliability and performance. In the days of more tightly constrained client/server protocol processing resources, experienced developers were more focused on the trade-off between UDP and TCP. This is not as much the case any longer, except in a few environments. Where might those be? Suppose you are a router vendor or some other kind of Internet network appliance manufacturer. In this case, you have limited CPU cycles and storage capabilities, and you may need to have some simple applications stored in, for example, the Read Only Memory (ROM) of your appliance. Consequently, you may be tempted by the simplicity of UDP-based applications such as TFTP or BOOTP/DHCP. UDP requires much less storage memory and fewer computer instructions than TCP. We'll take a closer look at TFTP and BOOTP/DHCP in a moment.

3.4 TCP and UDP Security and WAN Efficiency

Let's now explore security and WAN efficiency. The application summary in Table 3.4, while possibly a little overwhelming at first, provides an overview of security and performance considerations for common applications using TCP and UDP. Information in the table will be discussed in more detail in the next two sections.

Table 3.4 Application Summary

Application	Description	Performance	Security
TELNET	Remote nongraphic terminal emulation.	Very inefficient. Remote character echo is common implementation.	Login/password required. Login/password *tap* possible, meaning that login and password can be decoded if login sequence is intercepted within network.

Table 3.4 (continued)

Application	Description	Performance	Security
Remote Login (RLOGIN)	Remote nongraphic no-frills command-line terminal emulation.	Very inefficient; remote character echo.	Login/password required. Login/password tap possible.
HyperText Transfer Protocol version 1.0 (HTTP/1.0)	Command/response protocol used for transporting HTML-based Web pages and encoded attachments (graphics, Java programs, etc.).	Based on TCP, so adds byte overhead of TCP to network. Typical HTTP/1.0 request is small and represents a user clicking on HTML link and requesting information associated with that link. Typical response is very large. Therefore, relative to WAN, HTTP/1.0 produces an asymmetrical balance of traffic, which needs to be considered during design phase. HTTP/1.0, because it opens and closes TCP sessions repeatedly with each request, puts a reasonable CPU burden on servers responding to HTTP/1.0 requests.	HTTP/1.0 *Basic Authentication* is a weak username/password form of security and can be tapped. Username/password is sent in the clear unless coupled with SSL. Basic Authentication can be used by server admin-istrator to force user to enter username/password in order to receive desired response to HTTP/1.0 request. HTTP plus SSL (HTTPS) is discussed in Chapter 2.
HyperText Transfer Protocol version 1.1 (HTTP/1.1)	Improves upon HTTP/1.0, especially in area of performance, and is implemented by a number of vendors.	Allows connections to stay open, rather than constantly opened and closed as with HTTP/1.0, which significantly reduces CPU burden on Web server. HTTP requests can be *pipelined* (concatenated) together and processed in more of a parallel fashion, further enhancing efficiency.	Does not significantly improve upon HTTP/1.0 Basic Authentication mechanism.

Table 3.4 (continued)

Application	Description	Performance	Security
X-Terminal	Remote graphic terminal emulation.	Very inefficient; frequent and large screen updates. Newer low-bandwidth versions of X-Terminal attempt to remedy this.	Login/password required. Has various options that can be implemented, including host address authentication. Can be tapped. Can be easily *spoofed,* meaning that client may think it is talking to X-Terminal server, when, for example, entering username/password, when instead may be talking to Bad Guy.
TFTP	No-frills file transfer.	Very inefficient *stop and wait* protocol, meaning that, instead of allowing more than one data packet to be outstanding before requiring acknowledgment, TFTP insists on receiving acknowledgment for each packet before it will send the next. Maximum TFTP packet size is 512 byes. All of this combines to provide relatively slow file transfer performance.	No login/password!

Table 3.4 (continued)

Application	Description	Performance	Security
Boot Protocol (BOOTP) and Dynamic Host Configuration Protocol (DHCP)	Bootstrap protocol for providing devices with configuration information and IP addresses. DHCP is based on BOOTP.	Not intended for transfer of large amounts of data to individual device. BOOTP/DHCP uses broadcasts on local LAN. Its relay agents can be used to transfer BOOTP/DHCP requests received on LAN directly to remote BOOTP/DHCP server, eliminating broadcasts across WAN.	BOOTP/DHCP request and response broadcasts can be intercepted and spoofed by a hacker, potentially allowing for BOOTP/DHCP requests to be responded to with malicious configuration data and for BOOTP/DHCP responses to be intercepted and read by hacker, thereby providing potentially valuable configuration information to hacker.
Domain Name Services (DNS)	Directory service that maps IP addresses to more friendly *domain names* such as whitehouse.gov.	DNS servers should be distributed across network so that they are easily and efficiently reachable by clients and servers, who must query them at regular intervals in order to obtain mappings.	If DNS server is compromised or spoofed (replaced by hacker's DNS server), then clients and servers wishing to reach, for example, whitehouse.gov could be provided Bad Guy's IP address instead, thus connecting them to, for example, badguy.com.

Table 3.4 (continued)

Application	Description	Performance	Security
File Transfer Protocol (FTP)	More advanced file transfer.	Relatively efficient, offering much better performance than TFTP.	Login/password required. Two TCP control connections, one initiated by each end of FTP connection, make firewalls more difficult to implement because one connection must be allowed into firewall from outside network, and such a connection can be used maliciously by hacker to sneak into corporate network. However, today's quality firewalls typically handle this and are not usually confused or stressed by FTP. Anonymous FTP must be administered carefully.
Simple Mail Transfer Protocol (SMTP)	Used by mail clients to send mail messages to mail servers. Used by mail servers to route mail messages among one another.	Relatively efficient.	Hosts can be flooded by malicious transmission of SMTP packets sent by hacker attempting to stage denial-of-service attack on all users of mail server. SMTP mail messages are very easily impersonated. For example, e-mail message in your in-box saying it is from the president might not be. To deal with this, standards such as Secure MIME (S/MIME) add public key cryptography and X.509 certificate capability to e-mail.

Table 3.4 (continued)

Application	Description	Performance	Security
Simple Network Management Protocol (SNMP)	Used for network management, including service-level statistics gathering.	Protocol itself is relatively efficient, but network administrator's usage of SNMP can be quite inefficient if SNMP application is not designed and configured to control frequent polling and trap flooding. Protocol is also not particularly efficient for download of large configuration tables.	SNMP version 1 can be a security nightmare. *Sniffable* passwords are used to get/set data. SNMP version 2 was supposed to solve problem but never did. SNMP version 3 might solve problem, but wait to see vendor implementations before concluding anything.

Configuring HTTP Basic Authentication

While it is true that HTTP Basic Authentication offers a relatively weak form of security, it is also an excellent example of a security technology that is more easily managed and administered than others, such as public key cryptography. A security manageability versus security strength argument was made in Chapter 1. Basic authentication usernames and passwords can be easily stored on the local Web server in special files or managed via a directory service such as LDAP. For example, on Web servers installed in my home computer lab, I can configure password protection on a Web page in 5 minutes or less.

Again, the problem with technologies such as HTTP Basic Authentication is that its security is weak enough so that it simply won't stop a determined hacker who wants to put the CIO of the company under attack on the spot.

As part of the natural evolution of security technologies, there will come a time very soon when public key cryptographic-based security will also be this easy to configure. We are getting to this point quickly, and, when we do, what is meant by *manageable security* will be redefined.

3.5 Protocol Security: A Closer Look

In this section, we will explore security nuances of key TCP/IP protocol suite components.

3.5.1 Tapping and Sniffing

Table 3.4 contains the statement *"tap* possible," meaning that if someone can listen in on all the traffic on a given LAN or network connection, they can decode the login/password without too much effort, assuming that link encryption has not been implemented. This technique is commonly referred to as *sniffing.* It is usually launched by a hacker by (1) *remotely* breaking into a single weak system on the network/LAN and then (2) installing his or her own tap (sniffing) program on the system just compromised that reads information off the network/LAN and stores it for the hacker's snooping eyes. Once the hacker achieves this, he or she can obtain a wealth of username/password information plus all application data sent in the clear. All it takes is one weak link in this case—a single vulnerable host—to allow for the wreaking of significant havoc.

3.5.2 TFTP and Security

Looking at Table 3.4 again, you may be shocked to see that TFTP does not require a login/password. So, if it is enabled on your routers such that another device on the network can TFTP to them, then, for example, these routers can come under attack by a hacker writing over your configuration files and filling up the storage on your router.

3.5.3 BOOTP/DHCP and Security

DHCP and the protocol upon which it is based, BOOTP, provide a mechanism to dynamically deliver configuration information and IP addresses to installed routers, desktop computers, and diskless systems. Commonly called *plug-and-play,* this mechanism simplifies the administrator's job by eliminating the need to manually configure each and every desktop computer or other device requiring configuration information that could otherwise be dynamically delivered.

Because BOOTP/DHCP, by default, relies on a broadcast for everyone to hear that asks for configuration information it is vulnerable from a security perspective. Study any applications leveraging BOOTP/DHCP closely to determine how BOOTP/DHCP requests and/or responses could be spoofed by a hacker. Even if, for example, BOOTP/DHCP uses an optional random authentication scheme called *magic cookie,* the seed of the random authentication, the cookie, is itself sent unencrypted.

3.5.4 DNS and Security

DNS, briefly mentioned in Chapter 2, is a directory service that maps IP addresses to more friendly *domain names* such as whitehouse.gov or novell.com. DNS servers can be organized hierarchically and can work with one another to refer DNS directory service requests for IP-address-to-domain-name mappings among one another to the DNS server best able to service the request.

Since DNS servers translate IP addresses to these familar names, it is easy for them to become security holes. Suppose that Bad Guy breaks into your corporate DNS server, and, when the user types the URL for your accounting Web server (say, www.xyzaccounting.com), they attach to a server that looks like accounting.com but steals usernames and passwords instead. SSL and X.509 certificates protect against such impersonation by supporting a robust authentication mechanism. But, if you don't implement such a mechanism for all your applications, you especially need to protect your DNS server.

Note that, historically, DNS servers have been manually configured with IP-address-to-domain-name mappings. More recently, a dynamic DNS standard (RFC 2136) was developed, defining a means for DNS to be dynamically updated to reflect dynamically assigned IP addresses. Dynamic DNS brings along with it its own new security risk—the ability to dynamically update your DNS server can make it easier for Bad Guy to hijack it. There are also standards being developed to add security features to DNS.

3.5.5 SNMP and Security

SNMP is the core protocol used in your network to receive statistics and configuration information, and it also may be used, depending upon your implementation, to configure devices in your network, such as routers and modems. Allowing such configurations with SNMP version 1 introduces significant security risks because SNMP version 1 offers "security" through the use of unencrypted passwords sent every time an SNMP command is issued. As if that is not enough, many network administrators do not bother setting these passwords since getting everything up and running is enough to keep them busy and they need to sleep, too. The result is that some networks deployed today are using the default password in all systems, which is typically defined as PUBLIC (quite a self-explanatory choice of words). If you use SNMP version 1 for configuration, be sure to define unique SNMP passwords, change them often, and work to assure that they are difficult to sniff.

You will likely maintain the valuable SNMP Get capability (statistics-gathering capability), with the knowledge that a hacker can get SNMP information from your device if he or she knows your SNMP password. A way to help to make it harder for a hacker to gather statistics from your network device would be to configure it to look at the source IP address of any device requesting statistics. If it is not the IP address of your management station, many SNMP devices can be configured not to respond to the request. This technique is sometimes called *address filtering*. However, a determined hacker can still spoof the source IP address, thus defeating this approach.

SNMP version 2 was supposed to solve this security problem, but the needed security capabilities never made it into the final specification. SNMP version 3 is evolving right now, and it remains to be seen whether the standards process coupled with networking vendors pull together to provide products that enhance network management security. One hope is to see network equipment vendors implement IPSEC in conjunction with SNMP.

3.6 Efficiency: A Closer Look

3.6.1 TELNET and Efficiency

Applications such as TELNET and X-Terminal, which are often used to port old-style legacy terminal-based programs onto the LAN, can wreak havoc on the typical corporate private network if they are not planned for. TELNET, for example, uses *remote character echo*. This means that, for every character typed by the user, 40 bytes of overhead is added to it (for TCP and IP), then the packet containing the character is sent to the host, and then the character is echoed back to the client, as is illustrated in Figure 3.6. It is hard to imagine a more inefficient protocol.

Frequent use of TELNET by corporate enterprise developers is a perfect example of why application developers need to understand networking. If they or someone overseeing the project understood the networking impact of using TELNET and felt accountable for that impact, then it would be used far less frequently. Porting legacy applications to TELNET is a relatively easy thing, which is why it is such perfect bait for the developer, since TELNET

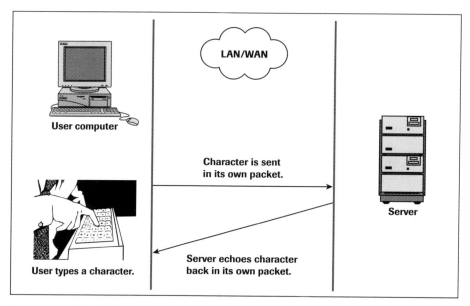

Figure 3.6 TELNET remote terminal emulation

supports *VT-100 emulation,* a terminal emulation standard that was very popular for many years and that many legacy applications leverage. Also, when the developer tests the application on his or her LAN, it works great because the problems don't surface until you add a WAN. I have witnessed TELNET-based applications that, when brought up at a remote site, literally choke off communication to parts of the network, flooding it with tiny packets. In one case, prior to getting the application modified, it was necessary to ask fewer terminal operators (customer service technicians in this case) to work at any given time since, combined, they typed too fast for the network.

The TELNET remote character echo problem is not just isolated to legacy applications. A number of newer popular accounting systems and databases rely heavily on VT-100-style interfaces that get translated to TELNET. Consider with great care any decision to deploy a new application based on TELNET in remote character mode. It may test well on your local LAN, but once you try to allow remote users access to the application, you may be in trouble.

3.6.2 X-Terminal and Efficiency

X-Terminal often is not practical, depending upon your application, for sub-T1 speeds. It depends upon what you are doing, and you should pilot-test it, along with all other traffic you expect to share on the WAN, before deploying it. X-Terminal is better designed for local LAN activity, from an efficiency perspective. Some work has been done on a low-bandwidth version of X-Terminal, but, in the end, if you can afford to redesign your applications according to an ultimately more effective client/server WAN-aware model, you are generally in for an easier time.

What About Header Compression?

Many network devices support header compression using the *Van Jacobson* (VJ) compression algorithm. VJ header compression can theoretically reduce the 40-byte TCP/IP header on average to as few as 3 to 5 bytes. However, there is a catch. The most popular usage of VJ compression is for lower-speed dial-up modem links leveraging the PPP or SLIP protocols. VJ header compression is not typically configured in network devices beyond the dial-up connection. For example, often it is not configured along high-speed network backbone links. Network routers are not typically configured for VJ compression since the CPU burden introduced by it is significant. So, its benefit is often limited to dial-up links.

3.6.3 TFTP and Efficiency

In spite of TFTP's efficiency, security, and reliability drawbacks, many network devices rely on it to obtain configuration files and operating system software. For example, your router configuration files may be downloaded via TFTP. The benefit of the compactness of TFTP (UDP) and the ability to put it into ROM are quickly forgotten once we realize that this unsophisticated and relatively unreliable protocol has become the central method by which we release new software updates into network devices, load configuration files, troubleshoot, and so forth—that this protocol has become the lifeline of our network. The manner in which we transfer new files for system upgrade is fundamental, and it is a shame that many device vendors felt that TFTP was a good approach for this.

3.6.4 SNMP and Efficiency

With regard to efficiency, SNMP is a polling and trapping (so-called event-driven) protocol that can be either quite efficient or inefficient depending upon how you use it. *Polling* means your central network management station requests information at fixed time intervals. *Trapping* means your SNMP device, such as your router, is configured to send SNMP-formatted information to the central management station when a certain set of conditions are satisfied, such as when, for example, a certain failure occurs or a performance threshold is reached.

The problem with polling is that its traffic impact on the network must be carefully watched, as well as the impact on the central management workstation's CPU resources and the SNMP device being managed. Such an impact is often underestimated, yielding sluggish and unstable management.

SNMP traps can also be quite dangerous. Failure and threshold trap conditions that we generally envision wanting to know about often occur repetitively and can be generated by many different devices in the network at once. When this happens, your network can become flooded with SNMP trap events, which either exacerbates the current problem or, commonly, creates an entirely new and much more severe one. Worse yet, when a flood of these things occurs, the network operator's first instinct is to go to the management workstation and try to do something. Here, they are often out of luck, as the management workstation has become essentially unusable as it tries to process the huge flood of SNMP traps it has just received, each requiring a database lookup, comparison to the network's hierarchical object-oriented layout, and then a write to a few other databases for storage, not to mention ringing the audible alarm bell a few times, changing and propagating color status changes on the workstation screen(s), and so forth. One approach at reducing such risks is to make sure your SNMP device has the ability to turn off SNMP trap generation for a certain threshold either until it receives a command to allow it to occur again or a preconfigured slowdown/stabilization time period has elapsed. This would limit the trap occurrence to as many times as you choose. This approach may require the network operator to reset the SNMP device for this particular trap threshold after a trap event is logged and resolved.

3.7 The World of Internet Addressing

Welcome to the world of Internet addressing. If you don't care for mathematical and binary aerobics, you might skip this section. Otherwise, read on, especially if you are responsible in any way for maintaining your company's scarce and valuable address space.

IP addresses are 4 bytes in length and are intended to be unique among all users in the world. There is an Internet group in your region of the world that we will refer to as an *Address Authority*, and also sometimes as an

Address Registry, that is responsible for assigning these addresses to org zations from the globally administered Internet address space. In the Unit States, the Address Authority is the *American Registry for Internet Numbers* (ARIN), and there are other groups, as mentioned earlier, around the globe that are responsible for different regions of the world. Due to the popularity of IP and the Internet, these groups are running out of addresses—hence, the new IPv6 specification.

There are five classes of IP addresses: A, B, C, D, and E. The difference between each of these, from your perspective, is the number of bits you will have to play with in your network as you subdivide it into subnetworks. Many textbooks imply that you, the small or large company developing an IP network, will receive, perhaps, some number of Class B or C addresses from the Address Authority for your use. This is often not at all the case. If you get just one Class B or C address, for example, how will you assign addresses throughout your network? The answer is through *subnetting.* Before we go any further, let's define what these addresses look like.

Internet addresses are represented in the form of four decimal digits, with each digit representing one of the 4 bytes of the IP address. This is called *dotted decimal notation.* An example of an address expressed in this notation is 192.1.2.45. The first byte of the address determines its class (A, B, C, D, or E). Table 3.5 provides the range of values of the first byte, in decimal, for each class of address.

Table 3.5 Range of First-Byte Values for IP Address Classes

First-Byte Range (in Decimal)	Address Class
0 through 127	A
128 through 191	B
192 through 223	C
224 through 239	D
240 through 247	E

Each class of address offers a different number of bits for you to subnet for your network. The more bits you have, the more addresses you have available. A Class B address offers you more address space than a Class C address. Class A offers the most bits, and Class E offers the least. The first byte of a Class A address is defined by the Address Authority, and the rest is available for subnetting. The first two bytes of a Class B address are defined by the Address Authority, and the rest is available for subnetting. The first three

signed for Class C. Classes A, D, and E are not important to most
~~e~~ they will not deal with them for their standard applications.
~~mmary~~ of available subnetting fields for Classes A, B, and C (an
~~it~~ you will be able to divide up (subnet) this address space as you

- Class A: <0–127>.X.X.X
- Class B: <128–191>.<0–255>.X.X
- Class C: <192–223>.<0–255>.<0–255>.X

3.7.1 Subnet Masks: Organizing Your Network Address Space

If we are assigned a Class B address, for example, then we would subdivide
the last two bytes in order to provide addresses for our own subnetworks and
hosts. We indicate this subdivision through a *subnet mask.* This is a binary
mask used to indicate which bits in the byte are significant for the subnetwork and which indicate the host. For example, suppose we have the Class B
address 181.142.X.X. Then suppose we had no more than, say, 180 subnetworks (LANs at remote sites, for example) to connect and no more than 200
hosts at each site. We could then define a subnet mask indicating that the
first three bytes of the address are for subnetwork addresses and the remaining byte is for host addresses on each subnetwork. This is indicated by the
mask 255.255.255.0. The number 255 represents eight binary 1s in the byte
(11111111), which means *all* of the byte is significant. The mask is Boolean
"ANDed" with the address to obtain the full subnetwork address. For example, if we have the address 181.142.1.12 and we have a subnet mask of
255.255.255.0, then we are merely saying that the first three bytes represent
subnetwork addresses and the remaining byte is for host addresses on each
subnetwork.

Suppose we needed more host/computer addresses and fewer subnetwork addresses. In this case, we could have chosen a different mask, such as
255.255.240.0, where 240 is equivalent to binary 11110000, which indicates
that half the byte is significant for the subnetwork address and the other half
is not. Therefore, we allow ourselves 2^4, or 16 subnetworks, and 2^{12}, or 4,096
host addresses.

Suppose we had a Class C address. Our only choice is to subdivide the
final byte. In this case, we might choose a mask such as 255.255.255.240 if

that met our needs, allowing us 16 subnetworks with 16 host addresses on each subnetwork.

3.7.2 Variable-Length Subnet Masks (VLSM): Conserving Your Address Space

It used to be that network designers could keep things simple when defining subnetwork masks, often keeping one mask for all Class B addresses in the network and one mask for all Class C addresses in the network. However, with the era of scarce address space, conservation-minded engineers, and evolving networks, subnet masks can be quite complicated, with a technique known as *variable-length subnet masking* (VLSM). VLSM allows more than one subnet mask to be used for the same address.

Here's the problem VLSM is intended to solve. Suppose we have a network that requires 100 hosts at a site in New York, 50 hosts at another in Paris, and 50 more in Washington, D.C. Suppose we have only one Class C address to work with, 209.152.138.0. How can we achieve this? If we choose a subnet mask of 255.255.255.128, then we have 128 host addresses but only *two* subnets, and we need at least three subnet addresses, one for each of the three sites. If we choose 255.255.255.192, then that gives us 64 host addresses and four subnets, which is not good either since we need 100 host addresses for New York. The solution to this problem is VLSM.

We use VLSM to assign two different subnet masks for use with the single Class C address, 209.152.138.0. Here's how we might solve our problem:

- New York: subnet mask of 255.255.255.128
- Paris: subnet mask of 255.255.255.192
- Washington, D.C.: subnet mask of 255.255.255.192

Depending upon the routing protocols used in your network, VLSM may not be an option. We'll discuss this situation in Chapter 4.

VLSM in your network can be dangerous if you do not carefully manage how addresses are assigned and can also lead to confusion during network troubleshooting for those engineers less inclined to think in binary. For network designs employing frame relay, an ever more popular and appropriate choice for many, as well as other virtual-circuit-based WANs, VLSMs can be useful in conjunction with bandwidth-efficient routing protocols such as OSPF. Because of the high level of meshing/connectivity available through frame relay networks, for example, quite a few addresses can be required, though the router vendors are now offering features that reduce this requirement. Nonetheless, these features are not always available or applicable, and, therefore, the designer is forced to divide up the address space as efficiently as possible, which may drive him or her to a VLSM implementation.

3.8 Conclusions

As we have seen, the TCP/IP protocol suite is highly involved, offering considerable flexibility and complexity at the same time. Clearly, the protocol is a winner, given its widespread adoption. Enterprise networks leveraging the TCP/IP protocol suite should consider its performance characteristics, transmission overhead burden, and application-level security implications.

FOR FURTHER STUDY

1. D. D. Clark. "RFC 813 Window and Acknowledgment Strategy in TCP." July 1982.

2. J. Postel. "RFC 879 TCP Maximum Segment Size and Related Topics." November 1983.

3. J. Nagle. "RFC 896 Congestion Control in IP/TCP Internetworks." January 1984.

4. P. V. Mockapetris. "RFC 1034 Domain Names—Concepts and Facilities." November 1987.

5. P. V. Mockapetris. "RFC 1035 Domain Names—Implementation and Specification." November 1987.

6. Sun Microsystems. "RFC 1094 NFS: Network File System Protocol Specification." March 1989.

7. T. J. Socolofsky and C. J. Kale. "RFC 1180 TCP/IP Tutorial." January 1991.

8. R. Droms. "RFC 1534 Interoperation Between DHCP and BOOTP." October 1993.

9. B. Callaghan, B. Pawlowski, and P. Staubach. "RFC 1813 NFS Version 3 Protocol Specification." June 1995.

10. S. Alexander and R. Droms. "RFC 2132 DHCP Options and BOOTP Vendor Extensions." March 1997.

11. P. Vixie, ed., S. Thomson, Y. Rekhter, and J. Bound. "RFC 2136 Dynamic Updates in the Domain Name System." April 1997.

12. P. Albitz and C. Liu. *DNS and BIND.* Sebastopol, Calif.: O'Reilly, 1997.

13. C. Kaufman, R. Perlman, and M. Speciner. *Network Security: Private Communication in a Public World.* Englewood Cliffs, N.J.: Prentice-Hall, 1995.

14. M. Miller. *Troubleshooting TCP/IP.* New York: M&T Books, 1996.

15. W. R. Stevens and G. R. Wright. *TCP/IP Illustrated.* Reading, Mass.: Addison-Wesley, 1994.

16. A. S. Tanenbaum. *Computer Networks*, 3d ed. Upper Saddle River, N.J.: Prentice-Hall, 1996.

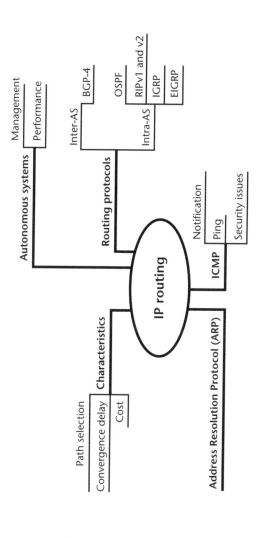

CHAPTER 4

IP Routing

CHAPTER HIGHLIGHTS		
Topic	**Benefits**	**Experience**
Address resolution and routing	We'll look at answers to these questions and others: How do you design complex IP networks? Where are the single points of failure in a given network design? How does routing on the Internet work? How does routing impact overall network and application performance? Which routing protocol should you choose and why?	A poorly designed routing infrastructure can effectively paralyze a corporation's applications. Network design requires knowledge of protocol behavior and dynamics, both of which we'll study in this chapter.
Autonomous systems (AS)	ASs can enhance network stability, security, and performance and play a fundamental role in the operation of the Internet.	Understanding the AS concept allows you to understand how to interface with the public Internet and provides an additional tool for you to consider using to deal with challenges associated with complex network designs.

CHAPTER HIGHLIGHTS		
Topic	**Benefits**	**Experience**
Address Resolution Protocol (ARP)	ARP is the fundamental method by which devices on the same subnetwork, such as a LAN, share information needed to establish physical connectivity.	Understanding basics such as ARP can be helpful in troubleshooting problems and in building an appreciation for the role of routing protocols.
Routing Information Protocol versions 1 and 2 (RIPv1 and 2)	RIP is still a popular protocol for use on very simple, small networks. At the same time, it introduces significant challenges as networks grow in size. It is a good protocol to study when developing an understanding of basic IP routing concepts.	You will likely bump into RIP in one form or another frequently, so it is necessary to have a fundamental understanding of its capabilities and limitations.
Open Shortest Path First (OSPF) protocol	OSPF addresses the shortcomings of RIP and provides a rich and open standards-based protocol for simple and complex networks.	OSPF is a very popular routing protocol for good reason: It provides the efficiency and flexibility demanded by today's IP networks. At the same time, it is a very complex routing protocol to understand. This chapter removes some of its mystery and reveals key underlying OSPF design concepts.
Interior Gateway Routing Protocol (IGRP) and Enhanced Gateway Routing Protocol (EIGRP)	EIGRP and its predecessor IGRP offer a Cisco proprietary routing-protocol alternative to OSPF.	EIGRP has important features, capabilities, and ease-of-use demanded by today's complex networks. However, it offers the disadvantage of encouraging reliance on a single vendor because it is proprietary.

CHAPTER HIGHLIGHTS		
Topic	**Benefits**	**Experience**
Border Gateway Protocol 4 (BGP-4)	BGP-4 is an advanced protocol used for interconnecting autonomous systems.	BGP-4 is heavily used on the Internet and within corporations either to connect to the Internet or to interconnect separate ASs. BGP-4 is becoming increasingly important for corporations that must manage multiple connections to the public Internet and therefore require an inter-AS protocol such as BGP-4 to route across the multiple links.

4.1 Introduction

In this chapter, we will study important technologies and design strategies for IP networks ranging in size from just a few sites to the largest of them all, the worldwide public Internet. Building medium-to-large-scale networks to route IP is a very complex task. You need to become knowledgeable in everything from binary calculations to the dynamics of the most advanced path selection protocol. The benefits to learning this are obvious—a well-run system and the pride of having become another member of the underground society that has transformed the way the world communicates.

The downside of not understanding IP routing becomes painfully evident when poorly designed networks and applications behave in such seemingly irrational way that you spend every waking hour chasing down their symptoms of poor health, routinely solving one problem while creating others. And, if you ever get the opportunity to build a dynamically routed connection to the public Internet at large, running a protocol such as BGP-4, which we'll study in this chapter, you will need to take great care to avoid disrupting regional or worldwide Internet traffic flow. In building such a connection, if you dare to make an error and violate what has become the collective consciousness that holds the Internet together, look out. You not only run the risk of disrupting the network but also will quickly learn the wrath of e-mail flaming and public chastising at its finest and on the scale and impact of cyberspace.

4.2 The Autonomous System (AS): Keeping Things Separate

The first concept we'll consider is one of isolation—the ability to shield one part of the network from other parts. Why would we want to do this? After all, the network is all about getting everything connected, right? Not always. The first and perhaps most obvious reason to create such shielding relates to security: You may want to limit the amount of information you share about your network to other networks. Routing information is quite valuable to the hacker trying to break into your system. You want to share only as much as you need to and no more. Routing provides the superhighway to your hard disk, from the hacker's perspective.

The other reasons are a bit more subtle. They relate to performance and reliability and the ability to shield one part of the network from potentially disruptive activity occurring in another. The processing of routing information can be CPU- and memory-intensive. The total number of routes distributed within the core of the public Internet today exceeds 45,000, which is enough to crash anything but the biggest and most powerful routers used within its backbone. And, when a change occurs in any route, which, on a worldwide scale, you might imagine occurs very frequently, routers in the network must recompute their routing algorithms to determine the revised best path to a given destination. Even if you don't intend to take on the number of routes on the scale of the Internet, a network with just 20 sites can quickly become unstable if the routing infrastructure is designed improperly or is suffering from software malfunction (routing software bugs, for example), simulating a network hundreds of times its size in performance overhead. By subdividing a network into *autonomous systems* (ASs), routers in one AS can be shielded from instability occurring within neighboring ASs. A network constructed of two ASs is illustrated in Figure 4.1.

In formal terms, networks in different ASs are said to be managed by *separate administrative entities.* Historically, this might have meant two universities, each one having its own group of network engineers, not knowing much about each other and not necessarily wanting to, other than to allow connectivity between their two networks. Sometimes, this is the case—that it is two separate organizations (groups of people) between two connecting ASs. Sometimes, it is merely the case that you, the network designer, have chosen to keep one part of your network separate, more or less, from another for some of the reasons we just discussed.

ASs are assigned unique numbers. Internet Service Providers (ISPs), discussed in the later BGP-4 section, must obtain unique AS numbers from

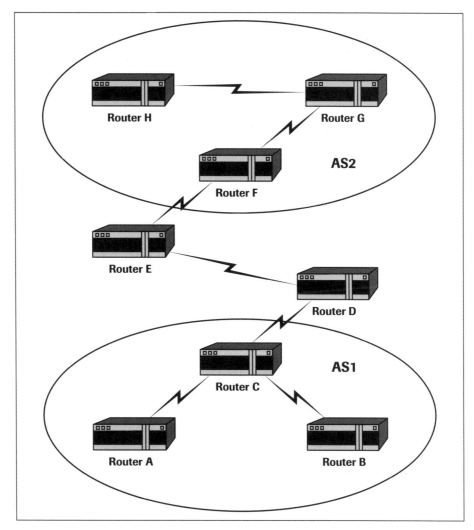

Figure 4.1 A network with two autonomous systems

a centralized registry, which, in the United States, is *ARIN*. AS numbers are 2 bytes long (16 bits) and are typically expressed in decimal format in the range from 0 to 65,535.

In the remainder of this chapter, we'll consider two classes of routing protocols: those used within a single autonomous system, called *intra-AS* routing protocols, and those used between autonomous systems, called *inter-AS* routing protocols. Inter-AS protocols are used to link separate ISP networks that today form the fabric of the public Internet. They are also often used in large corporate networks to maintain security, stability,

efficiency, and acceptable performance by localizing certain routing information to only the parts of the network where it is needed. In this chapter, we'll
study BGP-4, the most broadly implemented inter-AS protocol today, as well
as the following intra-AS protocols: RIPv1 and v2, OSPF, IGRP and EIGRP.

4.3 Fundamental Routing Characteristics

In order to select an optimal routing protocol and associated implementation
for a given networking requirement, the IP network designer must focus on
three fundamental routing-protocol characteristics: (1) The method used by
the routing protocol to select paths (*path selection*); (2) The time required for
the protocol to react to changes in the network such as router or link failures
(*convergence delay*); (3) The cost associated with using the routing protocol
in terms of bandwidth, CPU utilization, memory, and maintainability.

We begin this study with an overview of the most basic form of IP path
determination, *address resolution.* Address resolution is used when both the
source and the destination are on the *same* IP subnetwork.

4.4 Address Resolution Protocol (ARP)

IP devices communicating over the same local area network (LAN) utilize
the *Address Resolution Protocol* (ARP) to associate a destination IP address
with the physical LAN address of the destination device. Physical addresses
are needed by the source and the destination because connection mechanisms such as Ethernet LANs do not know anything about IP—they rely on
their own physical addressing mechanism. For the case of the Ethernet,
this is a 48- or 64-bit address commonly referred to as *media access control*
(MAC) address. In order to instruct the Ethernet to deliver an IP datagram
to its destination, the source of the datagram must give the Ethernet the
physical Ethernet address of the destination.

4.4.1 ARP Example

Suppose there are two workstations, Alice and Bob. Alice would like to
exchange data with Bob. Alice and Bob are interconnected via an Ethernet
LAN. For this example, to avoid getting concepts confused with numbers, we'll
use symbols for addresses instead of numbers. Therefore, we'll write Alice's IP

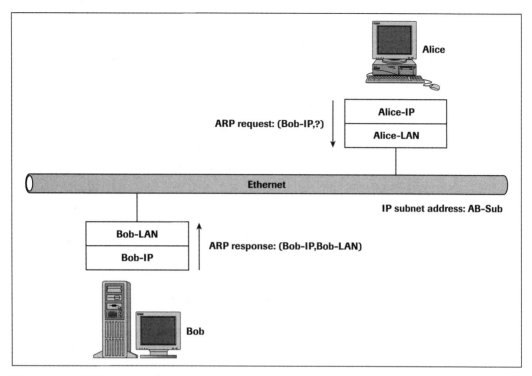

Figure 4.2 ARP example

address as *Alice-IP* and Bob's IP address as *Bob-IP*. Alice and Bob are assigned to the same IP subnetwork, which we'll designate as *AB-Sub*. We'll write Alice's physical Ethernet LAN address as *Alice-LAN* and Bob's physical Ethernet address as *Bob-LAN*. All of this notation is illustrated in Figure 4.2.

Assume that Alice has just been powered up and that she has an IP datagram she would like to send to Bob. Alice will follow these steps:

1. Alice first checks to see whether Bob is on the same IP subnetwork as she is (AB-Sub). Alice determines this by applying her own subnet mask (Alice knew this already, having been preconfigured with it) to Bob-IP and observing that the result equals AB-Sub. Alice concludes she can use ARP to obtain a path to Bob. Note that, had Alice and Bob not been on the same subnetwork, Alice either would have needed to be preconfigured with a default gateway router to which she could send all her packets not destined for her own subnet (AB-Sub) or would have had to execute a routing protocol such as one of the protocols we will study in this chapter.

2. Since Bob is on the same subnetwork as Alice, Alice broadcasts an ARP request onto the Ethernet (see Figure 4.2), requesting that the device having IP address Bob-IP respond with its physical Ethernet address. This message is an Ethernet broadcast message, so it is received by all workstations on the LAN.

3. All the workstations on the LAN hear Alice's ARP request, but only Bob responds since he recognizes his IP address, Bob-IP, in the request packet. Bob responds to Alice's ARP request with a message containing both his IP address and his physical Ethernet address, Bob-LAN (again, see Figure 4.2). Note that Bob will also record the address association (Alice-IP,Alice-LAN) since he can easily learn that mapping by simply looking at Alice's ARP request packet and since he will need it in order to send datagrams to Alice.

Alice and Bob may now exchange IP datagrams over the Ethernet. Both Alice and Bob will maintain an *ARP cache*. From Alice's perspective, this means that the mapping (Bob-IP,Bob-LAN) is stored in a temporary table (cache) for an administratively preconfigured period of time, after which the mapping entry will be purged. The entry is purged, rather than maintained permanently, for two reasons: (1) Bob-IP can potentially be reassigned to a different workstation with a different physical Ethernet address, and (2) Bob may simply be removed from the subnetwork (AB-Sub) altogether.

4.5 Internet Control Message Protocol (ICMP) for IPv4

Let's now explore an important protocol providing a common vehicle for the exchange of routing status and control information among all IP devices—the *Internet Control Message Protocol* (ICMP). ICMP provides various services to routers, workstations, and servers, including

- Router alert and network informational messages
- Network congestion notification
- Time stamp capabilities (used by ping, which we'll talk about in a moment)
- Dynamic delivery of subnet mask information, allowing for auto-configuration of IP subnet masks
- Important statistics-gathering capability by supporting the ping application

ICMP allows an IP router to alert a source of IP datagrams, such as a workstation or server, that it (the router) is having difficulty forwarding its traffic due to congestion, bit errors, or some other failure condition. This alert does *not* indicate that ICMP is retransmitting the traffic the router may have dropped. Retransmission must be handled by the upper layer operating between the two endpoints, such as TCP. Instead, ICMP informs the sender that some of its packets may have encountered a problem, implying that specific actions by the sender might be appropriate. When a device such as a workstation or a server receives this message, the workstation user may, for example, be notified by its application that there is a temporary disruption in communication to the destination.

ICMP offers the ability to directly influence routing such as with the ICMP *Redirect* function. This feature is intended for situations where a LAN has more than one connected router, and an IP device such as a workstation is configured to always direct datagrams destined for another IP subnetwork to a single default router on its connected LAN. If this default router recognizes that it does not have the lowest-cost route to the destination, it will inform the workstation via an ICMP redirect packet to send its datagrams to the other IP router on the same IP subnetwork having the lower-cost route. The workstation will extract the IP address of the lower-cost IP router from the ICMP redirect packet, send and ARP request on the LAN to determine the physical address of the lower-cost IP router, and then forward the appropriate datagrams to it.

A Security Risk

Despite its good intentions, the ICMP Redirect feature can present a security risk. If you don't need it, it should be disabled in your routers. It can allow a hacker to send phony Redirect messages to your routers and workstations, forcing them to route traffic through the hacker's computer, where they can be secretly recorded, or perhaps even modified, and then sent back through the network to their final destination.

ICMP also provides the basis for an important statistics-gathering and troubleshooting application called *ping*. Ping allows the network engineer to verify the reachability of any IP destination. In addition, it provides round-trip total delay associated with the transmission of a test packet to and from any destination. The ability to consistently reach IP destinations with an acceptable level of delay is the primary mission of an IP network. Ping can be used to measure this reachability and delay on a regular basis and, therefore, provides one vehicle for assessing network quality.

It is important to note that routers and computers (clients and servers) will typically treat ping packets as low priority, meaning that heavily congested routers may either discard ping packets or put them in the back of the transmission queue, sending higher-priority user datagrams first and making ping packets wait longer. Therefore, in such scenarios, it is possible for ping to return higher delay values than those actually experienced by user datagrams. This observation should not deter you from using ping because, when you study network statistics indicating larger ping delays due to router congestion, you learn something. When you see larger ping delays, you can use that in conjunction with router congestion statistics you might be gathering (such as link utilization) and, combined, get a very useful view as to what is going on in the network.

4.6   IP Routing Protocols

ARP, as discussed, allows IP devices on the *same* subnetwork to obtain reachability information about other devices on the *same* subnetwork. But what about communication between devices attached to *different* subnetworks? *IP routers* are connected to one another and to *different* IP subnetworks and dynamically share information concerning the reachability of IP subnetworks among one another. Each IP router builds and maintains a detailed routing table that summarizes available paths to different subnetworks. The router utilizes a path selection algorithm for choosing among those paths when routing IP datagrams to their destination. Routing tables and path selection are determined by the routing protocol being used. In this section, we will study several important routing protocols.

4.6.1   Routing Information Protocol Version 1 (RIPv1)

The *Routing Information Protocol version 1* (RIPv1) is a very simple IP routing protocol relative to others and is now implemented more as a LAN-access routing protocol, as opposed to one running in the backbone of a large network. UNIX workstations are frequently configured with RIP, allowing them to communicate with IP routers on their local LAN so that the optimal one can be chosen to reach a given IP destination. In such cases, an IP router will implement RIP on its LAN interface and usually some other more advanced protocol over its connections to other IP routers.

RIPv1 was originally documented in RFC 1058. Version 2 (RIPv2) is described in RFC 1388.

4.6.1.1 Operation

Figure 4.3 shows an example RIP network with five routers interconnected by various links, as illustrated by straight lines. All routers and servers in this example are running RIP. The Ethernet segment at the top of the figure is assigned subnetwork address A. The *distance vector* to A, as perceived by each router, is shown to the side of each router.

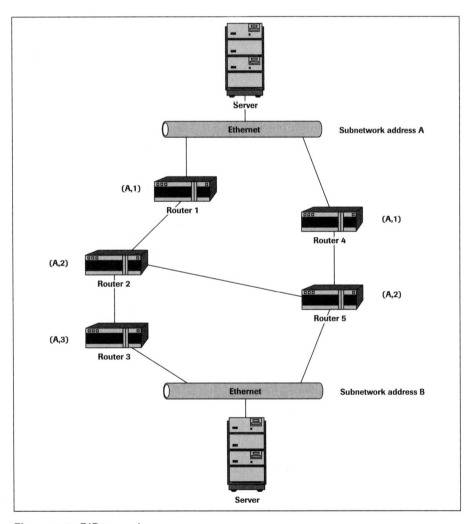

Figure 4.3 RIP example

Let's look at router distance-vector values for reaching subnetwork A based on the current state of the network:

- Router 1 can reach A in one hop, so it offers a "distance" of 1 to A.
- Router 2 can reach A in two hops by going through router 1 (longer if going through routers 5 and 4, but this is not an optimal route because it has more hops to it).
- Router 3 can reach A in three hops by going through routers 2 and 1 (longer if going through router 2 and then through routers 5 and 4).
- Router 4 can reach A in one hop.
- Router 5 can reach A in two hops by going through router 4 (longer if going through 2 and then router 1).

Based on this routing, the server on Ethernet subnetwork B will choose router 5 for all packets destined for subnetwork A, under the current conditions, because router 5 offers the least number of hops (the shortest distance) to the destination.

RIP routers share their individual subnetwork distance vectors with other directly connected RIP routers. This allows each router to form its own routing table containing its cumulative distance to each subnetwork destination. Because RIP builds its routing table in this fashion, it is said to be a member of the *distance-vector class* of routing protocols.

What's a Hop Again?

In the RIP example, *one hop* is defined as the transit through one router. Each router in this particular example always adds 1 to account for itself. Router 1 shows itself as being one hop away because it includes itself. If router 1 didn't include itself, it would be zero hops away since it is directly connected to subnetwork A.

In this example, each router added 1 to the distance value of the next router capable of reaching subnetwork A, and we referred to these distances by using the physical metaphor of a *hop*. Many router vendors allow this distance value to be configurable so that you can make one router path appear farther way (more costly) than another. For example, router 1 could have added 5 instead of 1, thus offering a "distance" of 5 to A, in which case the distance no longer fits the physical metaphor of hops but is instead, more generically, simply an assigned cost metric. You might assign different costs within your network in order to make one route appear more favorable than another.

What are some of the reasons for doing this? Maybe one path through the network is slower (say it uses a satellite link) or more expensive than another. You have to be careful with the metric values you assign, though, because one of the important limitations of RIP is that the sum total of all metric values for a given network path (the total distance-vector value) cannot exceed 16.

Now, returning to the example, what would happen if the connection between router 5 and Ethernet subnetwork B fails? This situation is illustrated in Figure 4.4. Here, router 3's distance to A is longer than the distance previously available from router 5. However, the server on subnetwork B has

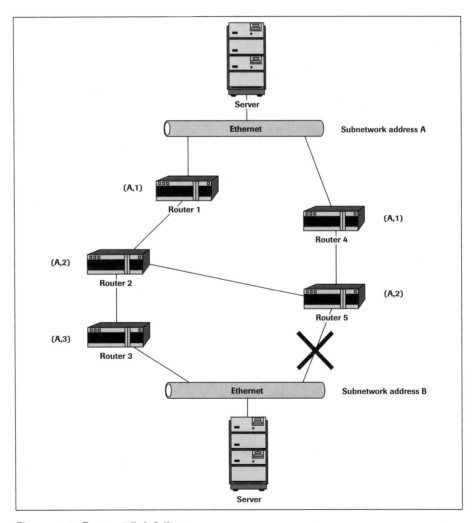

Figure 4.4 Router 5 link failure

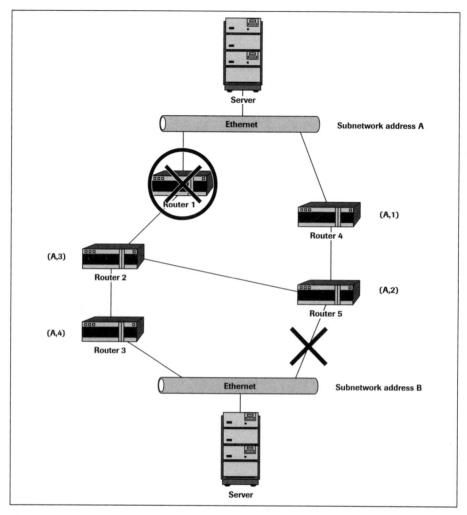

Figure 4.5 Multiple failures

no choice but to choose router 3 to send datagrams to subnetwork A since router 3 provides the only available path.

Next let's imagine that, in addition to this failure, router 1 completely crashes and can no longer route IP datagrams. This situation is illustrated in Figure 4.5. Note that the figure shows updated distance values to reflect the current failures within the network. Here, the only path to subnetwork A for datagrams originated by the server on the subnetwork B is

subnetwork B → router 3 → router 2 → router 5 → router 4 → subnetwork A

What is the total distance for this new path? Router 2 has an updated cost to subnetwork A of 3 because it must pass through router 5 and router 4 to reach A. Router 3 learns of this incremental distance and increases its distance to 4. Router 3 therefore advertises a cost of 4 to A.

Finally, suppose that the Ethernet connection from router 5 to subnetwork B becomes operational again. In this case, the server on subnetwork B will begin routing packets to router 5 because it now offers a lower cost of 2 for reaching subnetwork A.

4.6.1.2 Packet Formats

RIPv1 and v2 packet formats are illustrated in Figure 4.6. Both RIP versions use UDP to exchange routing updates. A RIP packet contains the IP address

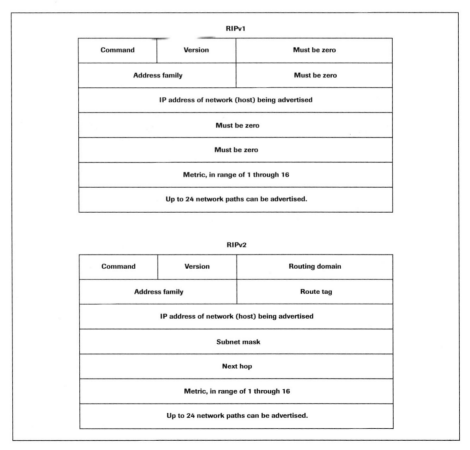

Figure 4.6 RIPv1 and RIPv2 datagram formats

of each reachable subnetwork along with the distance (metric) to reach it. By advertising metrics to one another, RIP routers can choose optimal paths (the lowest-cost ones) for IP datagrams, as we saw in the previous example.

RIPv2 makes use of the zero fields that existed in RIPv1 to add new functions, thereby theoretically making the software development impact of implementing and decoding RIPv2 less painful. However, it *is* different from RIPv1, which means that RIPv1 devices won't know what to do with RIPv2 packets. RIPv1 is, by far, the more commonly implemented of the two protocol versions.

4.6.1.3 Unreliable UDP and Rebroadcasting

RIP sends UDP routing update packets on their way with no required acknowledgment. Also, RIP rebroadcasts its routing table every 30 seconds, in contrast to other protocols that use a reliable transport mechanism to share routing information, such as OSPF, which is discussed in a later section. With RIP, the *entire* routing table is rebroadcast every 30 seconds, not just changes to it. This persistent rebroadcast of the full routing table makes RIP less bandwidth efficient.

A Common Misconception

It is important not to confuse the concept of a distance vector with the approach of rebroadcasting a routing table every 30 seconds. RIP rebroadcasts its routing table every 30 seconds, but that is not why RIP is a distance-vector protocol. Many incorrectly believe that a distance vector protocol, by definition, rebroadcasts its table at fixed intervals, whereas other protocols, such as shortest path first protocols, do not. The issue of distance vector or shortest path first has nothing to do with the rebroadcast of the table. If RIP had been designed to run over TCP or some other reliable data link protocol and implemented a keep-alive mechanism such as the Hello protocol, there would be no need for rebroadcast. Later, we will study EIGRP, which is an example of a distance-vector routing protocol that does not routinely rebroadcast its routing table.

4.6.1.4 Routing Loops and Convergence Time Reduction

Various techniques are employed by RIP for preventing routing loops and reducing the time required to converge when the network topology changes. The three most commonly used are split horizon, poison reverse, and triggered updates.

4.6.1.4.1 Split Horizon   Suppose we have two directly connected routers imaginatively named X and Y. *Split horizon* is a configuration option that instructs router X not to transmit RIP information received from router Y back to router Y over the same communications link. The problems that can arise when split horizon is not enabled can be illustrated through a simple example.

Suppose that, in Figure 4.3, routers 1, 2, and 3 are removed, leaving only routers 4 and 5. In this scenario, router 4 can reach A on one hop, and router 5 can reach A in two hops. Now suppose that router 4 were also to listen to advertisements from router 5 about reaching subnetwork A instead of ignoring them, on the basis that they are merely a reiteration of its own route. Next, imagine the connection between router 4 and subnetwork A fails. If router 4 were to listen to router 5, it would be looping because router 5's path to A is through router 4.

Virtual Circuits and Split Horizon

The original split horizon specification was focused on the problems associated with routing information distributed at the *interface* level. Split horizon uses the interface address (IP address) to determine whether routing information should be broadcast to a given address. In a private line environment using a protocol such as HDLC or PPP, this is not a problem. However, in X.25, ATM, and frame relay networks using multiple virtual circuits on a single interface, "native" split horizon can cause the routing tables to be improperly updated. Proper updating of tables may be prevented because routes learned from one virtual circuit of the physical interface will not be shared with any other virtual circuits on the same interface.

Many router vendors have resolved the problem of split horizon over virtual-circuit-based networks by allowing each individual virtual circuit to be treated as its own separate IP interface, thereby allowing split horizon to be individually enabled or disabled for each virtual circuit.

4.6.1.4.2 Poison Reverse   *Poison reverse* is a configuration option that instructs a router to advertise a network route as down for an extended period of time after it has been determined to be down in order to make sure all routers clear the route from their tables. This is done by advertising the network with a cost of 16, meaning that any other router, when adding its hop cost to this path, will overflow its distance field and therefore treat this path as down. This is why the cost of 16 is often referred to as an *infinite cost*.

4.6.1.4.3 Triggered Updates   If the *triggered update* option is enabled in a router, it will immediately issue a RIP update in the event a metric changes for any network in its routing table. If the triggered update option were not configured, the router would wait for the expiration of the 30-second broadcast timer before issuing the update. Thus, triggered updates can speed up convergence by communicating network changes sooner.

This approach provides for faster convergence; however, a price is paid. Rapid changes in network reachability can cause a rapid increase in triggered RIP routing traffic overhead through the network. A rapid increase in RIP routing traffic can increase bandwidth consumption and router CPU utilization. Rapid network changes are not uncommon in large networks. Physical links and routers often cycle through rapid up/down phases when experiencing various failure conditions—a single router can potentially flood the network with a stream of updates caused by some rapidly oscillating malfunction. This phenomena is sometimes referred to as *route flapping*.

The alternative to triggered updates, waiting for the 30-second broadcast timer to expire and sending the update with all others, has a dampening effect on routing update traffic by shielding the network from these rapid changes and allowing them to take effect only once every 30 seconds. The downside of this is slower convergence.

4.6.2 Routing Information Protocol Version 2 (RIPv2)

The three most significant improvements offered by the *Routing Information Protocol version 2* (RIPv2) over the original RIP are

1. The addition of variable-length subnet masking support

2. The addition of a security authentication mechanism

3. The addition of a route tagging feature

4.6.2.1 VLSM

The original RIP does not support variable-length subnetting because the RIP packet format does not include the subnet mask along with the advertised network number. Returning to the example in Figure 4.3, if subnetwork A had a mask of 255.255.255.128 and subnetwork B had a mask of 255.255.255.192, then we could potentially have a problem with RIP because the router connected to subnetwork A would assume its subnetwork mask (255.255.255.128) for networks advertised to it by other routers, but that assumption, in this case, would be incorrect. RIPv2 solves this problem by adding the transmission of the subnet mask along with every network address advertised.

4.6.2.2 Authentication

The RIPv2 authentication feature is intended to prevent a router from accepting routes from another router that is not trusted (known). The original RIP does not have any type of authentication, meaning that if a hacker somehow gains access to your LAN by appearing as a local device, and on that LAN you have routers listening to RIP advertisements, the hacker can send a barrage of phony paths through your network, causing, for example, your traffic to route straight into the hacker's computer for analysis, decode, or what have you. However, the RIPv2 authentication scheme itself is relatively weak, and, therefore, it does not offer much more security than RIPv1.

4.6.2.3 Tagging

Tagging solves a few potential problems with a fundamental activity in many networks today called *route redistribution*. Route redistribution occurs when a route learned from one routing protocol such as RIP is redistributed (shared) with another routing protocol such as OSPF. In some cases, tags can be used to prevent loops when doing this redistribution by preventing the receiver of the redistributed route from advertising the route right back to the originator, which would create a loop.

Tagging is also a way to provide *policy-based routing*, meaning that a learned route can be handled differently depending upon its tag. The routing decision made based upon the contents of the tag can be guided by the routing policies configured by the network administrator.

4.6.3 Open Shortest Path First (OSPF) Protocol

4.6.3.1 Why OSPF

The *Open Shortest Path First* (OSPF) protocol offers significantly more functionality and flexibility than RIP and, in doing so, better meets the needs of more advanced network designs. Sophisticated network designers choose OSPF over RIP because it solves many of the problems RIP introduces in large networks, including

- Excessive traffic overhead caused by rebroadcast of the RIP routing table every 30 seconds.

- Limitations brought on by the maximum RIP distance metric of 16. This maximum is often insufficient for larger networks. OSPF's metric is 24 bits long, yielding a maximum value of 16,777,216.

- The slower convergence delay of RIP in large-diameter networks.

In addition to improving upon RIP in these areas, OSPF offers the ability to conserve valuable IP address space through support for variable-length subnet masks, offers the ability to hierarchically organize routing information within an autonomous system, and allows for load sharing. Finally, in comparison to the two proprietary routing protocols we'll explore later in this chapter, IGRP and EIGRP, OSPF comes from an open standards body (the IETF), and implementations of it are thus available from many different vendors. This increased capability does, however, come with a price—more complexity and therefore a much steeper learning curve.

4.6.3.2 Hierarchical Architecture

OSPF employs a hierarchical routing approach whereby routers can be organized into *areas*, and areas communicate with one another through a single *backbone area,* as illustrated in Figure 4.7. The term *area* is an OSPF technical term used within the specification. The area concept allows routers that would commonly exchange data among one another to be grouped and interconnected optimally. If, for example, a company has three divisions and each division mainly communicates with itself and rarely communicates with the other divisions, then each division can be placed into its own area, allowing for optimal interconnection between users in the same division. Within each area, the routing table is limited to paths within the area, to information about the best router to use to reach destinations in other bordering areas, and also to external autonomous system (AS) routes, which we will discuss later. By limiting the routing table size in this way, resources are conserved (router CPU, memory, bandwidth).

Any paths to destinations outside of the area but within the same AS must pass through an *area border router,* as shown in Figure 4.7. The area border router provides connectivity to networks reachable in other areas within the same AS. As shown in Figure 4.7, area border routers are interconnected via the backbone area.

Area border routers are concerned with the routing of traffic between areas. They are not concerned with the routing of traffic within areas they do not border. This offers a significant cost benefit by limiting the size of the routing tables within area border routers to only those routes needed to achieve area interconnection.

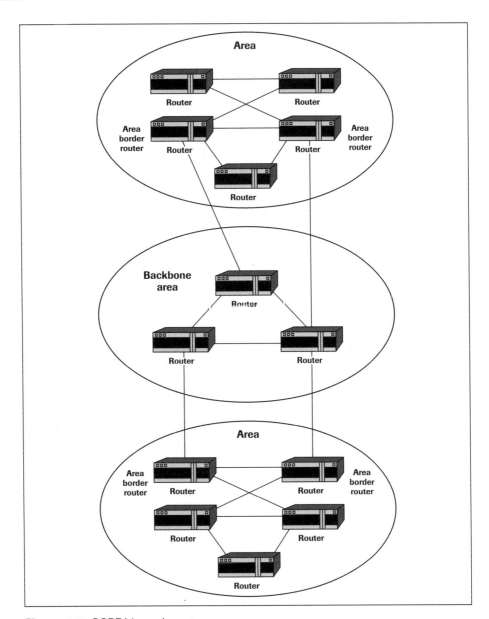

Figure 4.7 OSPF hierarchy

Figure 4.7 illustrates that an area can have multiple area border routers, which can be important for reliability because, if an area loses connection to the backbone, it cannot communicate with other areas. OSPF has the concept of virtual backbone links that allow area border routers to establish paths through other areas in order to reach the backbone area. This feature is often used to enhance reliability further by allowing for alternate paths to the backbone through other areas.

4.6.3.3 Path Selection Algorithm

The path an IP datagram takes from source to destination within an area is determined by the path selection algorithm utilized by OSPF. IP routers running OSPF employ a shortest path first approach known as *Dijkstra's algorithm* within each area. Each router within the area assembles a tree diagram of the entire topology within its area and places a cost, assigned by the network administrator, onto each link. The router then runs the Dijkstra shortest path first (SPF) routing algorithm against this topology. The algorithm takes into account each link's cost as well as all available physical paths between source and destination. The router then uses the result of this computation to determine which of its outgoing links to use in order to forward an IP datagram to its destination.

OSPF Versus RIP

The fundamental difference between the OSPF approach and the RIP distance-vector approach is that routers using a distance-vector approach only share information about what they consider to be the lowest-cost link available to reach a destination, whereas OSPF routers construct a topological view of an entire portion (area) of the network. There are pros and cons to either approach.

The Dijkstra SPF algorithm has a computational complexity of $n \times \log(n)$, whereby overall router CPU load within an area increases as the number of subnetworks (n) within an area increases. The usefulness of this type of approximation is simply to reinforce that the CPU utilization of the routers within an area may increase at an unexpectedly high rate as router subnetworks are added to it. Network managers accustomed to seeing somewhat smooth increases in CPU utilization as they grow their networks can easily be caught by surprise with routers running protocols such as OSPF. They need to carefully monitor the CPU utilization of all routers in an OSPF area, paying special attention whenever subnetworks are added.

Let's make one final observation relative to OSPF path selection. One of OSPF's most valuable path selection features is its support for load sharing.

Load sharing is supported across equal-cost links and is part of the OSPF specification. This is an important advantage over the RIP specification, which does not itself specify load sharing, although there are proprietary implementations of load-sharing mechanisms based on RIP.

4.6.3.4 Different Types of OSPF Networks

IP routers within an area allow for the interconnection of some number of OSPF networks. OSPF has its own definition of *network,* and it is important for the reader to pay close attention to the definition of the word *network* within the context of the OSPF specification. This section will define each of the OSPF network types, providing examples and design trade-off considerations.

OSPF defines a dedicated leased line connection between two routers as a *point-to-point* (PTP) network. The two other types of OSPF networks are the *broadcast multiaccess* (BMA) network and the *nonbroadcast multiaccess* (NBMA) network.

LANs are BMA networks. This name is derived from the following LAN characteristics:

- A LAN is a *broadcast* medium. When one device sends a message, all other devices on the LAN have the ability to receive it.

- A LAN can be accessed by more than two devices. Therefore, a LAN is a *multiaccess* medium.

When we talk about connections between IP routers utilizing virtual-circuit-based protocols such as X.25, ATM, or frame relay, the issue gets a little more complicated. OSPF allows virtual circuits on the same physical port to be treated as individual PTP networks (one for each virtual circuit), or, instead, all virtual circuits can be grouped together and treated as a single network type, which, in OSPF terminology, is a nonbroadcast multiaccess (NBMA) network. The characteristics of virtual-circuit-based protocols making them capable of NBMA operation are summarized next:

- A single frame relay port, for example, can support multiple access to many virtual circuits. Therefore, the port is *multiaccess.*

- There is no mechanism to physically transmit a packet just once across a frame relay interface and then have it received by all virtual-circuit destinations. While it is true this can be simulated by retransmitting the packet *N* times, once for each of *N* virtual circuits, this is not a true broadcast mechanism. It is not like a LAN, where the packet is sent just once and then heard by all. Therefore, the frame relay port is *nonbroadcast.*

Finally, it is important to understand that the OSPF specification uses the terms *BMA* and *NBMA* to refer to *both* the transmission facility characteristics and the fact that all devices within a specific BMA or NBMA network are part of the *same* logical IP subnet.

4.6.3.5 Building Routing Tables

Different OSPF network types were developed in order to leverage the capability of the underlying transmission technology. Each OSPF network type is based upon a different method of routing information exchange.

The exchange of routing information in a PTP network is achieved in the following manner:

- The two routers in a PTP network exchange full knowledge of the area's topology with each other. The two routers form an *adjacency* in order to exchange this information. This routing information is shared over a reliable IP-based connection offering error detection and recovery, unlike RIP, which uses UDP only.

- Hello status messages are sent regularly between the two routers so that each one is aware of the other's health.

- PTP routers share information about topological changes in the area such as router failures or link failures only when changes occur. The exchange of this topological change information is called a *link-state update.* For this reason, OSPF is often referred to as a *link-state protocol.*

OSPF Versus RIP

Note that OSPF differs significantly from RIP in that it transmits routing status information only when it is needed as opposed to rebroadcasting it at fixed intervals.

Each OSPF adjacency places an additional CPU load on the router and an incremental bandwidth load on the network because each adjacency requires the exchange of significant area topological information and must be maintained with link-state updates.

In BMA and NBMA networks, all routers form two adjacencies, one with the network's *designated router* (DR) and the other with the network's *backup designated router* (BDR). The DR and BDR are central repositories for routing information within the BMA/NBMA network. The BDR is a hot standby version of the DR. Because each router in the network need only establish an adjacency with the DR and BDR, and not with each other, the number of adjacencies in BMA and NBMA networks is kept to a minimum.

A BMA network is illustrated in Figure 4.8. The BMA network's DR and BDR perform the same functions as the NBMA DR and BDR, with the LAN providing full connectivity among all LAN devices and the DR and BDR.

Because all routers in the OSPF NBMA network are part of the same IP subnetwork, additional virtual circuits may be required beyond those established to the DR and BDR. Because all devices within the NBMA network share the same IP subnetwork, the DR and BDR have no way of routing traffic received from one router within the NBMA network to another router within the same NBMA network. Because all members of the OSPF NBMA network are members of the same IP subnet, they are assumed to be directly reachable, just as all devices within an IP subnet on a LAN are directly reachable. Therefore, to allow for full reachability between devices within the same NBMA network, a virtual circuit must be established

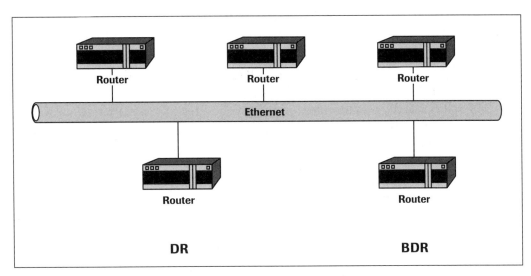

Figure 4.8 BMA example

between all of them So, if there are N sites, for example, then $N*(N-1)/2$ virtual circuits would be required. This kind of connectivity is called a **full mesh**. Therefore, to achieve full IP connectivity between all devices within an OSPF NBMA network using only the OSPF NBMA mechanism itself, a fully meshed frame relay implementation is required. If you don't have a direct virtual circuit between any two sites within the NBMA and you wish to route packets between them, you must either employ some other routing protocol or configure static routes (hard-coded routes) so that routers between the two sites know how to utilize some sequence of virtual circuits to reach the destination.

In the preceding discussion, it is important to differentiate between the mere existence of a virtual circuit and its impact on router CPU and memory utilization versus the impact of requiring an adjacency across that same virtual circuit. The OSPF specification calls for adjacencies with the DR and BDR only—adjacencies are not formed over other virtual-circuit connections between devices within the same NBMA network. Adjacencies represent a significant CPU and memory load; however, mere virtual circuits typically do not.

4.6.3.6 PTP Versus NBMA

As mentioned earlier, routers interconnected by virtual-circuit-based protocols can utilize either the PTP method across each of its virtual circuits or can utilize the NBMA method. The decision to use PTP or NBMA in this case is important to the overall network design,

Suppose we are designing a network for a large corporation, and this corporation's main computing center is maintained at a single site, headquarters. The corporation also has four offices that must be connected to headquarters (total of five sites). The network designers have chosen to use frame relay and fully mesh the sites together (every site connected to every other) as illustrated in Figure 4.9. In this configuration, there are four virtual circuits from each site to every other. If we choose to define each virtual circuit as its own PTP network, then every router in the network will have four adjacencies. However, if NBMA is used, each router will have only two adjacencies. As the number of routers meshed via frame relay increases, the decreased number of required adjacencies with the NBMA approach becomes more dramatic. For example, if we have 100 routers in the network, then each router would have 99 adjacencies with the PTP approach, one for each of the other 99 routers; however, only two would be required with the NBMA approach.

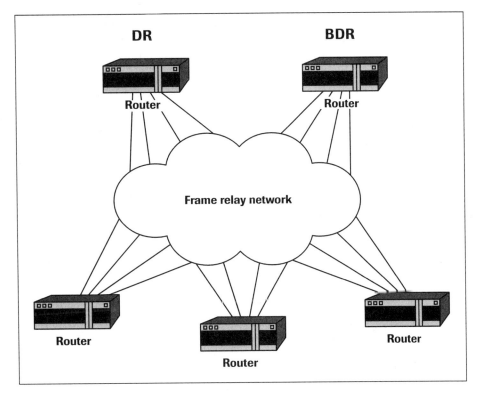

Figure 4.9 NBMA example

4.6.3.7 Route Redistribution and External AS Routes

Earlier in this chapter, *external AS routes* were mentioned. External AS routes can become quite a problem in large OSPF networks. You might think that, because a collection of routers are configured for a single autonomous system, there would be no external AS routes—after all, where is the "external AS"?

The concept is relatively simple. Many devices on LANs today are still running protocols other than OSPF, such as RIP. When a router running OSPF receives routing information from a router running a routing protocol other than OSPF, the OSPF router will, if so configured, redistribute the information into OSPF and then share it with all other OSPF routers in the AS. This activity is called *route redistribution*. OSPF assumes that these redistributed routes are from another AS and are therefore considered external AS routes.

External AS routes are shared among every router in the entire OSPF autonomous system, except for OSPF *stub areas,* which will be discussed in a moment. Therefore, they undo the routing table size efficiency benefits produced by dividing the network into areas. With stub areas as the exception, this means that every external AS route can take up routing table space in every router in the AS configured for OSPF. It does not take long, in networks comprised of as many as 100 to 200 routers, for the number of external AS routes to reach well into the hundreds because each site may redistribute multiple routes from RIP into OSPF. These routes consume precious bandwidth, memory, and CPU capacity. External AS routes can become a very serious problem in large OSPF networks.

Any OSPF router that offers connectivity to another autonomous system or series of autonomous systems such as the Internet or any OSPF router that redistributes routes is called an *AS boundary router.* An AS boundary router is responsible for advertising its external AS routes to all OSPF routers except those routers contained in special OSPF areas defined as stub areas. Therefore, any router redistributing routes from another routing protocol, such as RIP, is considered an AS boundary router.

One approach to dealing with this problem in large OPSF installations is to divide routers into separate autonomous systems and to establish an addressing methodology and inter-AS protocol implementation that would shield one AS's external AS routes from the other. Another approach is the use of stub areas.

The purpose of the stub area is to save bandwidth, router CPU, and memory usage within the stub area for OSPF autonomous systems having large numbers of external AS routes. Stub areas will not accept external AS routes; thus, their routing tables are not flooded with a large number of external AS entries. Instead, to reach external AS destinations, routers within a stub area are instructed (via an OSPF default routing message) to use one of the stub area's area border routers as the default device through which external AS traffic is routed. This area border router itself will have knowledge of external AS routes.

There is a subtle problem with all of this, however. Suppose there is a router within the stub area that is connected to an Ethernet LAN on which there is a RIP router advertising some important routes. The router within the stub area would like to advertise these RIP-originated routes to other routers within the overall OSPF AS. However, as previously discussed, these RIP-generated routes are considered external AS routes. Given the current

OSPF specification definition of a stub area, there is no way for the router within the stub area to share these external AS routes. Routers within a stub area can default routes for external AS destinations; however, they themselves are not allowed to share external AS routes. Therein lies the problem. It is not uncommon for corporate networks to have RIP or other routing devices on their local LANs and for these routes to represent valuable routing information that must be known by OSPF-based routers. So, while external AS routes become a heavy burden, the protection mechanism we have to deal with them (the stub area mechanism) takes away another needed feature—the ability to share external AS routes with other OSPF routers.

An RFC describing a newer OSPF option designed to deal with this problem is defined in RFC 1587. The RFC specifies a new type of area called a *not so stubby area* (NSSA).

4.6.3.8 OSPF Case Study

The goal is to design an IP network for a large corporation according to the following basic requirements:

- Minimize monetary cost.
- Provide full connectivity between all sites, meaning that any site can share IP datagrams with any other site.
- Optimize performance for the most probable everyday traffic patterns.

This company is actually a collection of business units. Each business unit has its own set of products. For example, one is in the light bulb business, while another is in the jelly bean business. Although the light bulb folks don't communicate too much with the jelly bean folks, there has been increased pressure for business units to work together to reduce costs. Synergies do exist in certain areas of these businesses (believe it or not), and, therefore, there is some light traffic (no pun intended) among the business units, such as common need for data warehousing. There are a few large corporate data centers with which all business units must communicate. This communication is considered mission-critical and includes employee records, accounting records, and so forth. Each business unit site is not necessarily a small office of three or four people and a router—some of these sites are large campuses with hundreds of employees. These sites have, for

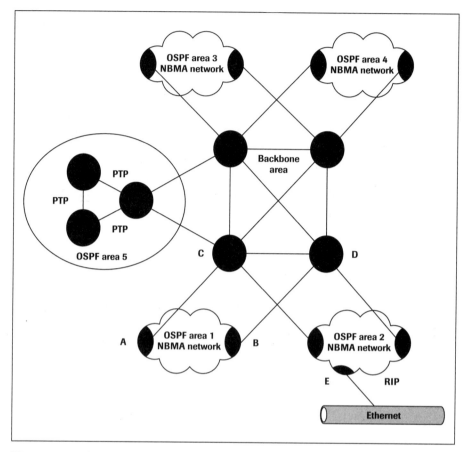

Figure 4.10 OSPF case study (light bulbs and jelly beans)

years, operated by themselves (i.e., without a corporate backbone) and have a wide range of legacy systems. IP-based systems on the campuses generally run RIP.

After careful review of the requirements, the network designers propose the design shown in Figure 4.10. Each business unit is organized into its own OSPF area. OSPF areas 1, 2, 3, and 4 are configured as NBMA frame relay networks, while OSPF area 5 uses dedicated leased lines. OSPF area 5 has three point-to-point (PTP) OSPF networks.

Areas 1, 2, 3, and 4 have two area border routers, while area 5 maintains a single area border router with two connections to the backbone. These area border routers connect to the high-speed corporate backbone consisting of four main routers. Backbone routers are fully meshed using dedicated leased lines.

Because each business unit has its own area, communication is optimized for traffic within each unit. A frame relay full-mesh NBMA implementation means that there is a direct frame relay connection between each router within the area (business unit). Therefore, all sites within the NBMA can communicate with one another directly.

Different business units communicate with one another through the corporate backbone. The corporate backbone performs all routing between areas (business units). Corporate systems connect directly to the backbone. Therefore, corporate-level traffic originated by a business unit leaves the area, hits the backbone, and then is routed directly to the corporate computing systems.

Hardware must be carefully selected to accommodate this design. The area border routers—for example, A and B for area 1—must be powerful because they are both members of their own area and members of the backbone area. They must service a large number of adjacencies, especially as more business units are added to the corporate backbone. They must have sufficient memory to carry all routes, and their particular CPU utilization should be carefully monitored on a regular basis. The network designers have chosen more powerful router models with significantly expanded memory to support this requirement.

Routers within the business unit areas are typical lower-end models. However, their memory has been expanded to handle the large number of external AS routes that are propagated throughout the corporate network. The Ethernet LAN connected to OSPF area 2, router E, is just one of many such LANs that have one or more RIP systems on it, thereby generating external AS routes.

This network design is highly reliable. The backbone routers are maintained as fully redundant high-end units because failure of a backbone router affects many companies. Each OSPF area has two connections to the backbone for reliability purposes. This protects the area from backbone isolation from a single backbone node failure or a single area border router failure, excluding area 5, which has both links to the backbone coming from one area border router and represents a single point of failure.

4.6.4 Interior Gateway Routing Protocol (IGRP) and Enhanced Gateway Routing Protocol (EIGRP)

The *Interior Gateway Routing Protocol* (IGRP) and the *Enhanced Gateway Routing Protocol* (EIGRP) are proprietary distance-vector routing protocols developed by Cisco Systems Incorporated—*proprietary* meaning that the specification is not controlled by an open standards body in the way OSPF is, limiting the ability to obtain implementations of IGRP and EIGRP from multiple vendors. For some, this reason alone makes IGRP and EIGRP unattractive.

IGRP was released by Cisco in 1986. By significantly improving upon RIP, IGRP quickly won popularity. Cisco followed up with EIGRP in 1993. EIGRP enhances the distance-vector approach by incorporating an as-needed-only path update mechanism and a new path selection algorithm. Both IGRP and EIGRP support a similar set of routing metrics.

IGRP and EIGRP can be less complex to deploy, from the network design and implementation perspective, than OSPF. In contrast to OSPF, IGRP and EIGRP do not demand that the network engineer learn as many new terms. Nonetheless, the flexibility, openness, and structure offered by OSPF can often make it the more desirable approach.

4.6.4.1 IGRP

Three critical shortcomings of the RIPv1 protocol are addressed by IGRP:

1. Instead of a simple metric limited to a maximum value of 16, a more involved and much larger collection of metrics is used to characterize paths, thereby allowing the network designer to have more influence over the path selection mechanism.
2. Instead of always choosing the single path with the smallest metric for destination IP datagrams, traffic can be split among several paths with metrics in a specified range, thereby allowing for load sharing.
3. Several features are introduced to improve stability in situations where the topology is changing.

Like RIP, IGRP broadcasts its routing table at fixed time intervals, but, in contrast to the 30-second default if RIP, IGRP's default update period is 90 seconds and can be increased or decreased by the network administrator. By shortening the update period, overhead traffic is increased due to the increased number of routing updates being transmitted. Extending the period increases the time it takes to communicate changes in the network, thereby increasing the amount of time it takes for IGRP to converge on a new route. IGRP declares a route inaccessible if it does not receive an update from the first router in the route within three update periods. After seven update periods, the router removes the route from the routing table. IGRP supports split horizon, triggered update, and poison reverse options, just as RIP does, to speed up the convergence of the routing algorithm.

4.6.4.2 EIGRP and DUAL

EIGRP maintains a distance-vector approach for communicating and computing routes. However, it does not broadcast its table at regular update intervals like IGRP or RIP for three reasons:

1. It implements a reliable transport protocol for guaranteed ordered delivery of EIGRP routing update packets among all routers, as does OSPF.

2. It utilizes a keep-alive Hello protocol implementation to monitor the health of its neighbors, so it does not rely on getting a new copy of the routing table every 30 seconds to know the neighbor is still alive, as does RIP.

3. It employs an algorithm for determining when it is necessary to request updated routing information and when and how it is necessary to distribute it. This algorithm is based upon the *distributed update algorithm* (DUAL).

It is important to understand that DUAL is not a routing algorithm. Instead, it is an algorithm for determining when and how to update information that is fed to the routing algorithm. DUAL can be applied to either shortest path first or distance-vector route determination methods. The original DUAL researchers concluded, through an argument based upon simulation results, that DUAL offered better performance when combined with a distance-vector approach.

DUAL offers, for many network designs, the fast convergence and bandwidth efficiency that OSPF offers, and, therefore, EIGRP is often considered as a proprietary alternative to OSPF. Cisco has implemented a multi-protocol version of EIGRP supporting Novell and AppleTalk routing in addition to IP routing.

4.6.4.3 DUAL: A Closer Look

In this section, we will take a high-level look at the distributed update algorithm. Note that the algorithm behavior described here does not necessarily match the exact operation of any specific release of Cisco software implementing DUAL. Particular software implementations may vary, and Cisco developers may choose to optimize or modify various behaviors.

DUAL makes use of three messages:

1. *Update* informs a neighboring router of a distance change.

2. *Query* issues a router's query for reachability to a specific destination when the router has lost its current lowest-cost route and has exhausted its table of *feasible successors*. If, at the moment a router is informed of a distance change, it can locate a route through one of its neighbors that is equal or lower in cost compared to the route it just lost, then that router is considered to have a feasible successor to the destination. If, however, an equal or better route does not exist, then the router must issue a query. The word *successor* is used because a router offering an equal- or lower-cost alternate route to the destination is the next hop (successor) for packets forwarded to the destination.

3. *Reply* is a reply in response to a router's query for routes to a specific destination.

EIGRP uses a reliable link-layer error detection and retransmission protocol to exchange these DUAL messages and uses the Hello protocol to monitor the health of its connected neighbors.

DUAL is loop-free algorithm. Whenever routes must be recomputed, packets are guaranteed not to loop through the network for the duration of the recomputation. DUAL achieves this by locking the routing tables being used to forward packets while performing route recomputation in the background. By locking the tables, packets affected by the recomputation will be dropped rather than looped through the network.

Routers running DUAL are always in one of two states: active or passive. A node will always stay *passive* if a feasible successor exists. The passive mode is the standard mode for a router in a stable (nonchanging) EIGRP network. If the router loses its current lowest-cost route to a network destination, it will remain in the passive state and issue a query to its neighbors to determine whether any feasible successors exist. If they do, it will remain in the passive state and adopt one of the feasible successors for packet forwarding to the destination. If, however, no feasible successors exist, the router will enter into the *active* state and begin recomputing its distance-vector table in order to determine the next-best available route to the destination.

EIGRP does not have the concept of OSPF areas but instead offers the ability to establish multiple EIGRP processes on the same router, whereby routes will not be redistributed between the two processes unless the router is so configured. This allows the administrator to determine the best method of this redistribution, which may include the implementation of a routing hierarchy.

Both IGRP and EIGRP use a similar set of metrics to derive an overall value for routing distance to each destination in the network. They do not use the simple hop metric employed by RIP. The following elements are combined to form the routing metric: bandwidth, delay, reliability, load (average link utilization), and hop count (for detecting loops). Each of these elements is weighted according to a relatively bizarre-looking equation (by their very nature, optimization-based equations typically look that way) that, in the end, yields a routing metric. Cisco commands are available that theoretically allow you to alter the variables used in the metric computation. Some of the elements are computed dynamically, while others are or can be static. For details on the manner in which the version of EIGRP you are using exactly computes the metrics, you should consult with Cisco directly since different releases may perform computations differently.

4.6.5   Border Gateway Protocol 4 (BGP-4)

The *Border Gateway Protocol 4* (BGP-4) is designed for routing between autonomous systems, in contrast to the previously discussed protocols, which are designed for routing within a single autonomous system. The public Internet is a collection of interconnected IP autonomous systems, with different ASs operated by *Internet Service Providers* (ISPs). ISPs use BGP-4 within their network and also at *exchange points,* which are locations where groups of ISPs interconnect their BGP-4 networks and exchange routes with one another, thereby enabling global connectivity. ISPs that exchange routes to reach destinations within one another's own ASs are said to be *peering.* If these ISPs also carry traffic for one another to destinations other than within their own ASs, they are said to be in a *transit routing* relationship.

The commercialization of the Internet has required government and commercial Internet network providers to form more complex policy-based peering and transit routing relationships. BGP-4 allows for the enforcement of these policies. Also, BGP-4 provides features allowing for reduction in the size of the Internet routing table, which is currently difficult to process and maintain due to its larger size. BGP-4 is used in private (corporate) networks that have become so large as to either require separate autonomous systems or, for security or other policy-based reasons, require separation into multiple ASs. It is also often used by corporations with multiple connections to their ISP. With just one connection to an ISP, only a default route is required, but with multiple connections BGP-4 can be used to choose the optimal ISP connection for a given diagram.

4.6.5.1 Path Selection

BGP-4 is a *path-vector protocol*. BGP-4 routers exchange lists of AS numbers that must be traversed to reach each network advertised. By sending AS numbers with the route advertisement, the receiving router can detect a routing loop (i.e., it knows whether the path contains an AS of which it is a member). Also, the transmission of AS numbers allows the receiving router to make various path attribute *policy decisions,* such as, for example, a decision to favor a route through one AS over another.

Internet engineers can configure their routers to favor certain routes simply because they represent the shortest AS path. However, it is very common for them to have preferences for certain ASs over others, even if going through these preferred ASs represents a longer AS path than some other to the destination network. These BGP-4 preferences are hand-configured, or *statically configured,* into the router.

One of the biggest challenges of BGP-4 routing administration in the Internet is the dependence most Internet designers have on statically configured preferences. This is a fallout of the underlying principle of the Internet that each autonomous system can be run in a manner different from any other; therefore, one autonomous system is less likely to trust anything but the AS path provided by another. Because of this, preferences are more commonly manually configured by Internet engineers in the routers connecting to other autonomous systems instead of dynamically learned.

4.6.5.2 Routing Table Distribution

BGP-4 sends its table once and then issues incremental updates, which is possible because BGP-4 uses TCP, a reliable transport protocol, to exchange routing information. When multiple BGP-4 routers are connected to the same AS, a consistent view of the interior routes of the AS can be maintained by establishing a direct TCP connection between each and every BGP-4 router (a so-called full mesh). Also, policies can be applied between the routers so that a consistent agreement can be arrived at for determining which routers provide exit and entry to or from the AS for particular destinations.

The requirement that all BGP-4 routers connected to the same AS be fully meshed via TCP creates a problem for ASs containing many routers. The TCP connections required between each router place a significant load on even the most powerful routers in today's largest ISP networks. One solution to this is through the use of **route servers**. A route server allows routers within the AS to be assigned to individual route servers.

These route servers are interconnected to one another and together simulate the required full-mesh TCP connectivity.

4.6.5.3 CIDR

Perhaps the most significant feature of BGP-4 is support for **classless interdomain routing** (CIDR). CIDR is a simple concept that allows for a single routing update to signal reachability to a whole range of network addresses rather than to just a single one. In this way, the addresses are aggregated, or *supernetted.* The term *supernet* implies that a single supernet address represents a range of individual network addresses. Because the Address Registries around the world (ARIN in the United States, RIPE for Europe, AP-NIC for the Asia–Pacific region) are distributing a great many Class C addresses, which make the Internet routing tables much larger without some form of aggregation, CIDR is now effectively required in order to keep routing in the Internet under control.

Today, ISPs are typically provided large blocks of Class C addresses. ISPs are then responsible for distributing addresses from these blocks to their customers. The issue of who actually owns these addresses is a subject of significant debate. The requirements of route aggregation, however, demand that CIDR blocks not be broken up, which means that if one ISP hands out part of its block to a large customer and this customer moves to another ISP, the block would be broken, causing an increase in the overall Internet routing table. To prevent this, customers must usually renumber their entire network if they change ISPs. There are creative ways to try to deal with this problem; however, the current Internet address aggregation strategy fundamentally implies address ownership by the ISP.

Network Address Translation (NAT)

One creative way to deal with scarce IP addresses and to shield yourself from ISP changes is to utilize private IP addresses that are reserved by IANA, the overseer of all IP Address Registries. These private addresses are not guaranteed to be unique when used on the public Internet—they must never be included in datagrams leaving the safe haven of the private corporate network. To use these addresses, you just choose them from the reserved private address block—you don't even need to ask the Address Registry for permission. After choosing your addresses, you place a server acting as a *network address translation* (NAT) server (often just a proxy server) at the firewall between your private network and the public Internet.

Network Address Translation (NAT) (continued)

The NAT can be configured to translate any private IP address to a public Registry-assigned Internet address (one assigned by ARIN, for example). The NAT will act as a proxy device, translating addresses between the public and the private networks. From the perspective of the public Internet, it will always see public, globally unique Internet IP addresses. Within your private network, however, you are free to assign the private IP addresses you choose from the IANA-designated address blocks. If you ever change ISPs, you won't need to assign new IP addresses. Instead, you need only change the address within the NAT. The reserved private address blocks are summarized next:

- 10.0.0.0 through 10.255.255.255
- 172.16.0.0 through 172.31.255.255
- 192.168.0.0 through 192.168.255.255

There are two methods of representing a CIDR block of addresses. The first method, the "slash" (/) method, involves simply stating the number of significant bits in a given address. The second method involves the use of an address mask that contains binary 1s in all bit positions that are significant in the address. These two methods are used interchangeably in documentation, specifications, and even when configuring routers. Before getting into the details of these representations, let's review some of the addressing concepts discussed in Chapter 3 and practice some mathematical and binary aerobics.

IP addresses are expressed in dotted decimal notation, with each decimal representing an 8-bit quantity called an *octet*. With 4 octets, an IP address is thus comprised of 32 bits. An octet can take on decimal values in the range from 0 to 255. The value 255 indicates that 1s are contained in all bit positions:

- Bit position: 76543210
- Contents of octet containing a value of 255: 11111111

To convert binary to decimal, we take the value of the bit in each bit position (either a 0 or a 1) and multiply it by 2 to the power of the bit position, the values of which are listed next:

$$2^7 = 2 \times 2 \times 2 \times 2 \times 2 \times 2 \times 2 = 128$$
$$2^6 = 2 \times 2 \times 2 \times 2 \times 2 \times 2 = 64$$
$$2^5 = 2 \times 2 \times 2 \times 2 \times 2 = 32$$
$$2^4 = 2 \times 2 \times 2 \times 2 = 16$$
$$2^3 = 2 \times 2 \times 2 = 8$$

$$2^2 = 2 \times 2 = 4$$
$$2^1 = 2$$
$$2^0 = 1$$

So, binary 11111111 is equal to

$$(1 \times 128) + (1 \times 64) + (1 \times 32) + (1 \times 16) + (1 \times 8) + (1 \times 4) + (1 \times 2) + (1 \times 1) = 255$$

Suppose we have the quantity 11110000. In decimal, it is equal to

$$(1 \times 128) + (1 \times 64) + (1 \times 32) + (1 \times 16) = 240$$

The slash method of CIDR block representation uses an IP address in dotted decimal notation (for example, 192.77.172.0) coupled with a slash followed by a number representing the number of significant digits in the address (for example, /16). Suppose we are presented with a block of addresses represented as 192.77.0.0 /16. What range of addresses does this represent? The /16 indicates that the first two octets are significant and that the remaining bits can take on all possible values (i.e., the remaining two octets can each take on any values in the range from 0 to 255). Note, however, that all 1s and all 0s must be avoided because these addresses are sometimes used for broadcasting/multicasting. The value of 192 in the first octet means this block is comprised of Class C addresses, and the ability to vary the third octet over its full range (0 to 255) means that 192.77.0.0/16 represents a block of 256 Class C addresses, all beginning with 192.77 in the first two octets. This same CIDR block can be represented using the mask notation as 192.77.0.0 255.255.0.0, where 1s in the first two octet positions mean that the first two octets of the address are significant and that the remaining octets can take on any values.

These two examples are relatively simple. Let's consider a slightly more difficult one. Suppose we advertise the block 200.8.64.0/18. What does this mean and what is the mask representation for this block? The first two digits of the address (16 bits) are clearly significant because /18 is greater than /16. There are two remaining bits in the third octet that are considered significant. Let's represent the third octet of the address in binary so that we can see which bits are significant:

01000000

The first two bits are significant, and the remaining bits in the third and fourth octets may take on any values. The mask used to indicate the significant bits must have 1s in the first two bit positions of the third octet. That is

11000000, which is equal to 192. So, our mask for a /18 is 255.255.192.0. Therefore, this block can also be represented as 200.8.64.0 with mask 255.255.192.0. By allowing the varying of the remaining six bits in the third octet, we are indicating that this CIDR block represents $2^6 = 64$ different Class C addresses.

Table 4.1 summarizes different CIDR block options using the slash notation and assuming Class C address blocks. Note, however, that CIDR is in no way confined to advertising ranges of Class C addresses. It can be used for all classes of addresses and is, therefore, referred to as *classless*.

Table 4.1 CIDR Blocks

Number of Significant Digits	Mask	Number of Class C Networks
/24	255.255.255.0	1
/23	255.255.254.0	2
/22	255.255.252.0	4
/21	255.255.248.0	8
/20	255.255.240.0	16
/19	255.255.224.0	32
/18	255.255.192.0	64
/17	255.255.128.0	128
/16	255.255.0.0	256
/15	255.254.0.0	512
/14	255.252.0.0	1,024
/13	255.248.0.0	2,048

ISPs are sometimes assigned addresses in /16 blocks. They then divide them up over their own internal customer base. For example, an ISP can divide its /16 block into two /17 blocks, or four /18 blocks, and so forth. When peering and transit routing at exchange points, ISPs are beginning to establish policies in order to encourage maximum aggregation. Today, it is unlikely that anything less specific than a /24 CIDR block will be accepted by ISPs at exchange points. Some ISPs are even making this more stringent, demanding aggregation to the /19 level. This trend will likely continue.

4.6.5.4 Operation

BGP-4 routers are called *BGP speakers* in the specification. BGP speakers have either *internal links* or *external links* with other BGP speakers, as illustrated in Figure 4.11. Internal links are links between two BGP speakers

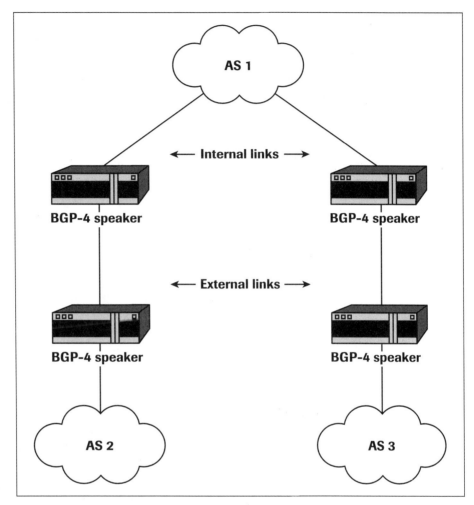

Figure 4.11 BGP internal and external links

having connections to the same AS. External links are between two BGP speakers having connections to different ASs.

BGP-4 routers connected by internal links are fully meshed using the TCP/IP protocol, as illustrated in Figure 4.12. Note that this is a TCP/IP *logical* full mesh. As shown in the figure, the BGP-4 routers connected by internal links are not necessarily physically connected, but they must all be logically connected via TCP/IP. The figure also has notations for *IBGP* and *EBGP*. It is common to refer to routers connected by internal links as participating in the Internal BGP-4 Protocol (IBGP) and those connected by external links to be using the External BGP-4 Protocol (EBGP).

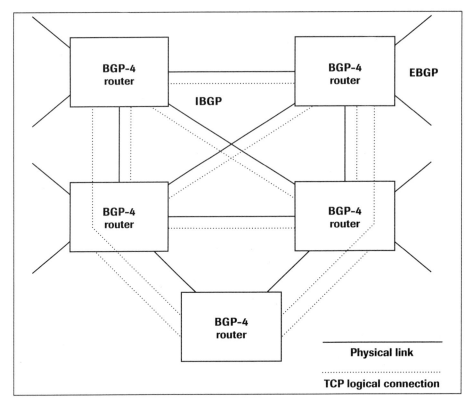

Figure 4.12 BGP-4 internal links fully meshed

A BGP speaker's routing information is stored in a *Routing Information Base* (RIB). There are three types of RIBs. Routes received from other BGP speakers are stored in *Adj-RIBs-In,* routes used by the local BGP speaker are stored in *Loc-RIB,* and routes advertised to other BGP speakers are stored in *Adj-RIBs-Out.* The routing decision process is based upon a configured *Policy Information Base* (PIB) within the BGP-4 router that articulates routing preferences based upon contents of the route's path attributes. These policies are applied against Adj-RIBs-In, and the result is placed in Loc-RIB and Adj-RIBs-Out, as shown in Figure 4.13.

There are four BGP-4 message types:

1. The Open message is used to establish the TCP connection between two BGP speakers.

2. Routing information is exchanged with Update messages, including the first transmission of the routing table once the connection is opened and, after this, the incremental addition and deletion of

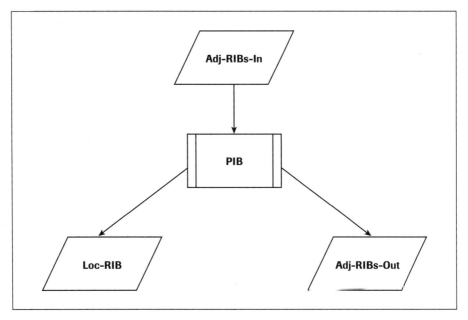

Figure 4.13 Routing information base

routes based upon changing network conditions. Path attributes are included in Update messages. Because update packets contain the full path of ASs traversed for the advertised route, the receiving BGP-4 router can detect loops and therefore discard looped routes instead of placing them in Loc-RIB or Adj-RIBs-Out.

3. The Notification message is used when an error condition is detected. In response to this message, the BGP-4 connection is immediately closed.

4. Keepalive is essentially a Hello protocol used to verify operation of a neighboring BGP speaker at regular intervals, the default being the transmission of a Keepalive message every 30 seconds.

The following path attributes contained in the Update message are defined:

1. The origin field contains the number of the AS originating the routing information in the Update message. All BGP speakers propagating the routing information maintain this attribute.

2. The AS_Path attribute is a record of all ASs through which the routing information has traveled. Update packets contain a single AS_Path and a list of networks that can be reached by traveling that

AS_Path. The AS_Path information allows BGP speakers to detect loops and, very importantly, to implement policies to determine the next best path. The BGP speaker could choose the shortest AS_Path or could implement a policy to favor one AS over another by examining the contents of the AS_Path field. It is not uncommon to pad this field in the BGP-4 packet in order to force routing in a direction other than through the shortest AS path. Padding is usually performed by replicating the same AS number more than once in the BGP-4 update packet. This is also referred to as AS *path prepending*.

3. The Next_Hop field contains the IP address of the border router used to reach the networks listed in the Update message.

4. Multi_Exit_Disc (MED) is used on BGP-4 external links to segregate between multiple exit and entry points to the same neighboring AS. The exit or entry point with the lower metric is preferred, when all other factors are equal. MED is used between ISPs to control routing across multiple links between their networks. MED can be set within one ISP's network for certain routes, and the connecting ISP can, if so configured, utilize these MEDs to control routing toward its connected ISP. An example of the use of MED is provided later.

5. The Local_Pref attribute represents the degree of preference the BGP speaker has for the advertised route. The *higher* the value of Local_Pref, the higher the preference for the route. This is the opposite of the way we may be accustomed to thinking. For example, in OSPF, the *lower* cost field is preferred, and, in the case of RIP, the *lower* hop value is preferred. The Local_Pref value is 32 bits long and can therefore take on values in the range from 0 to 4,294,967,296. Local_Pref is used by ISPs to favor different exit and entry points into and out of their AS to specific network destinations. The Local_Pref administrative weight is assigned by the router receiving the route via an external BGP-4 link. This weight is then redistributed into IBGP and used by other internal BGP speakers to determine their level of preference among multiple IBGP speakers advertising a path to the same network destination.

6. The Atomic_Aggregate field indicates that the BGP speaker has chosen a less specific route, as opposed to a more specific one, from a set of overlapping routes that have been received by it.

7. The Aggregator attribute is included when the Update message contains an aggregated route.

8. The Network Layer Reachability Information (NLRI) field of the
Update message contains the IP network address(es) for which
reachability is being transmitted. The term *IP prefixes* is used in the
specification to indicate that CIDR, or supernetting, could be signaled here. The AS_Path field contains the sequence of ASs associated with the route to the networks contained in the NLRI field. All
of the networks in the NLRI field must follow the same AS path and
the next-hop router. This is important because it means that the BGP
speaker must be reasonably intelligent, if it is to be optimal, in recognizing a set of routes taking the same AS path and then placing them
into the same message. If the router implementation does not do
this, then more update traffic will be sent than is otherwise necessary
and table sizes will be larger than necessary. Ask your router vendor
about its aggregation capabilities. Because the Internet is so large,
updates can occur frequently and table sizes can become extremely
large; such compression of multiple networks into one message can
therefore be of significant value.

4.6.5.5 BGP-4 Case Study

A national network has been proposed consisting of a main core backbone
and separate regional networks, as illustrated in Figure 4.14. For the initial
implementation of the network, a single ISP has been chosen for Internet
connectivity outside of the country.

The core backbone runs IBGP and is assigned the AS number of AS-1.
OSPF is configured to allow routing for the internal TCP sessions used by
IBGP. The backbone maintains two high-speed links into the ISP and runs
EBGP over these links. Routes learned through the ISP international gateway
are *not* redistributed into the core backbone's OSPF routing process. Redistribution of the current Internet table (approximately 45,000 routes) generally
destabilizes current routing technology— the task is simply too memory- and
CPU-intensive given the real-time requirements of a dynamic routing protocol. So, IBGP carries the full Internet table, and OSPF carries information for
routing IBGP management channel TCP connects between backbone routers
only. That is, the TCP/IP connections used to carry IBGP routing updates
need to, themselves, get routed—OSPF provides that function.

Each regional network is its own AS, and each region represents a significant portion of the country. Each regional network runs OSPF to route all
local customer traffic and makes use of dedicated leased lines for connections

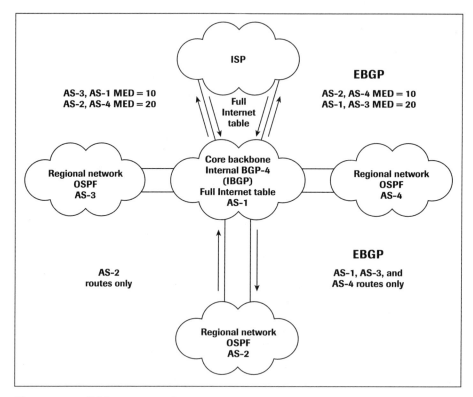

Figure 4.14 BGP-4 case study

between routers within the region. Let's examine the routing between the
region and the core, using AS-2 as one example that all regions follow.

As stated previously, within AS-2, OSPF is used. IBGP is not used
within the AS-2. AS-2 maintains two connections to the backbone (to two
separate physical nodes on the core for redundancy purposes, though not
shown). The area border routers in AS-2 execute EBGP with the core backbone. The area border routers redistribute all AS-2 routes into the core backbone. The core backbone takes these AS-2 routes and places them into its
IBGP routing table and advertises them to the ISP and to other regional networks. The core backbone advertises all countrywide ASs to AS-2—that
would be all regional ASs and the core backbone AS. Because the regional AS
routes are redistributed into OSPF, AS-2 can choose the shortest path to any
AS within the country by selecting one of the two links as the shortest path to

the destination—for example, the rightmost link might be the shortest path to AS-4.

For routes outside of the country network (to the ISP international gateway), the regional network uses OSPF equal-cost load sharing across each of its two links to the core. This is achieved by redistributing an equal-cost default route into the regional OSPF area. Load balancing, as opposed to shortest path routing, is used for destinations outside the country because shortest path routing would require the regions to have full knowledge of the Internet topology (the full routing table, complete with policies, etc.). The overall benefit of such a capability when only two links can be chosen from is questionable, and its cost would be very high. In order to support the full Internet table within a regional network, there would be a very significant increase in router hardware requirements (CPU, memory) and routing over-head bandwidth utilization within the region. So, instead, for packets routed to and from the ISP international gateway, load balancing is used.

Let's return to the ISP connections. It is desirable to distribute load across these links. We must consider both direction of transmission.

Each of two core backbone nodes has a connection to the ISP from the perspective of the core. The router with the left link is topologically nearest to AS-3 and AS-1. The right link is connected to a router that is topologically near-est the AS-2 and AS-4. We use the Multi-Exit-Discriminator (MED) with the ISP to signal to the ISP which link to prefer for AS traffic back into the country. The ISP has agreed to redistribute the MED we provide as a routing metric into its routing tables. The ISP will then route AS-3 and AS-1 traffic primarily over the left link (and thus to its topologically nearest point of entry into the country) and only route AS-2 and AS-4 over this link on a backup basis (i.e., if the rightmost link fails, AS-2 and AS-4 will be routed over the left link because it is preferable to having no route at all). Traffic preferences for the right link are simply the reverse of the left. For traffic in the opposite direction of trans-mission (leaving the country and entering the ISP), Local_Pref and other pol-icy approaches are used to distribute traffic across these links. Note that this design, depending upon how outbound traffic is policed, might allow asymmet-rical routing leaving the country. For this small set of links, this is not neces-sarily an issue. However, on an Internet-wide basis, it is the generally accepted practice to avoid asymmetrical routing, the idea being that it is easier to trou-bleshoot and predict performance in symmetrically routed networks. However, it is sometimes advantageous to distribute traffic in one direction differently from the other in order to maximize bandwidth utilization.

4.7 Conclusions

In this chapter, we reviewed routing methods and particular routing protocols. Table 4.2 summarizes the *intra-AS* routing protocols studied here. (Note that the abbreviation DV is used in this table to indicate distance vector.)

Table 4.2 Intra-AS Routing Protocol Summary

Protocol	Path	Update Mechanism	Convergence in Large Networks	VLSM	Standard	Load Balancing	Learning Curve
RIP	DV	Broadcast, UDP	Slow	No	IETF	No	Low
RIPv2	DV	Broadcast, UDP	Slow	Yes	IETF	No	Low
OSPF	SPF	Incremental, reliable link layer for updates	Fast	Yes	IETF	Yes	High
IGRP	DV	Broadcast, UDP	Slow	Yes	Cisco	Yes	Low
EIGRP	DV	Incremental-DUAL, reliable link layer for updates	Fast	Yes	Cisco	Yes	Low

BGP-4 is an *inter-AS* routing protocol. ISPs use this protocol to share Internet traffic at exchange points. Some private networks use this protocol to support complex routing policies between different portions of the network and to connect to multiple ISPs. BGP-4 is a path-vector protocol. Routing updates are sent using a reliable protocol, TCP. Updates are sent incrementally. BGP-4 policies can be set using approaches such as AS path prepending, Local_Pref weighting, and MED.

FOR FURTHER STUDY

1. M. Little. "RFC 1126 Goals and Functional Requirements for Inter-Autonomous System Routing." October 1989.
2. K. Varadhan. "RFC 1403 BGP OSPF Interaction." January 1993.

3. R. Coltun and V. Fuller. "RFC 1587 The OSPF NSSA Option." March 1994.

4. P. Traina. "RFC 1656 BGP-4 Protocol Document Roadmap and Implementation Experience." July 1994.

5. G. Malkin. "RFC 1721 RIP Version 2 Protocol Analysis." November 1994.

6. G. Malkin. "RFC 1722 RIP Version 2 Protocol Applicability Statement." November 1994.

7. Y. Rekhter and T. Li. "RFC 1771 A Border Gateway Protocol 4." March 1995.

8. Y. Rekhter and P. Gross. "RFC 1722 Application of the Border Gateway Protocol in the Internet." March 1995.

9. P. Traina. "RFC 1773 Experience with the BGP-4 Protocol." March 1995.

10. P. Traina, ed. "RFC 1774 BGP-4 Protocol Analysis." March 1995.

11. J. Hawkinson and T. Bates. "RFC 1930 Guidelines for Creation, Selection, and Registration of an Autonomous System." March 1996.

12. P. Traina. "RFC 1965 Autonomous System Confederations for BGP." June 1996.

13 K. Hubbard, M. Kosters, D. Conrad, D. Karrenberg, and J. Postel "RFC 2050 Internet Registry IP Allocation Guidelines." November 1996.

14. J. Moy. "RFC 2178 OSPF Version 2." July 1997.

15. T. Bates, R. Chandra, D. Katz and Y. Rekhter. "RFC 2283 Multiprotocol Extensions for BGP-4." February 1998.

16. D. Comer. *Internetworking with TCP/IP.* Englewood Cliffs, N. J.: Prentice-Hall, 1995.

17. M. Dickie. *Routing in Today's Internetworks: The Routing Protocols of IP, DECnet, NetWare, and AppleTalk.* New York: Van Nostrand Reinhold, 1994.

18. B. Halabi. *Internet Routing Architectures.* Indianapolis, Ind.: Cisco Press New Riders Publishing, 1997.

19. C. Lewis. *Cisco TCP/IP Routing Professional Reference.* New York: McGraw-Hill, 1997.

20. R. Perlman. *Interconnections: Bridges and Routers.* Reading, Mass: Addison-Wesley, 1992.

21. J. S. Quarterman. *The Matrix: Computer Networks and Conferencing Systems Worldwide.* Bedford, Mass: Digital Press, 1990.

22. J. S.. Quarterman and S. Carl-Mitchell. *The Internet Connection: System Connectivity and Configuration.* Reading, Mass: Addison-Wesley, 1994.

23. A. S. Tanenbaum. *Computer Networks.* Englewood Cliffs, N. J.: Prentice-Hall, 1996.

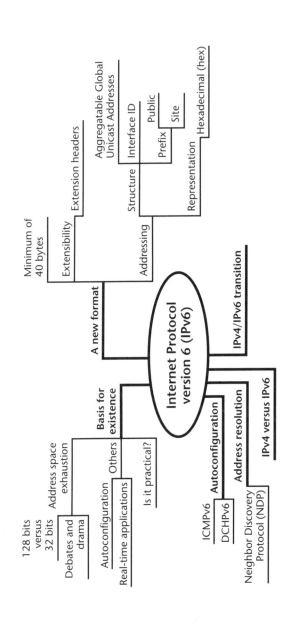

CHAPTER 5

Internet Protocol version 6 (IPv6)

A new format
- Extensibility
  - Minimum of 40 bytes
  - Extension headers
- Addressing
  - Structure
    - Aggregatable Global Unicast Addresses
    - Interface ID
    - Prefix
      - Public
      - Site
  - Representation
    - Hexadecimal (hex)

Basis for existence
- Address space exhaustion
  - 128 bits versus 32 bits
  - Debates and drama
- Others
  - Autoconfiguration
  - Real-time applications
  - Is it practical?

Autoconfiguration
- ICMPv6
- DCHPv6

Address resolution
- Neighbor Discovery Protocol (NDP)

IPv4 versus IPv6

IPv4/IPv6 transition

Internet Protocol Version 6 (IPv6)

CHAPTER HIGHLIGHTS		
Topic	**Benefits**	**Experience**
Internet Protocol version 6 (IPv6)	IPv6 deals with the address exhaustion problem in the Internet today and offers some compelling features.	The adoption of IPv6 will be difficult, given the broad impact a transition from IPv4 to IPv6 would have on our applications, routers, configurations, and so forth. At the same time, a large number of vendors are providing IPv6 support in one way or another, and IPv6 is receiving much attention. Unless we solve our Internet address exhaustion challenge in some other way, IPv6 could become a baseline requirement.
IPv6 header format, address structure, autoconfiguration, and address resolution	IPv6 offers significant changes in these areas. Understanding these changes is a prerequisite for planning IPv6 deployment.	IPv6's dramatic changes translate to equally dramatic costs and benefits. We'll explore these.

5.1 Introduction

The push behind specification and adoption of *Internet Protocol version 6* (IPv6) is, for many, rooted in the fear that we will exhaust the existing IPv4 address space. Current predictions have us running out of addresses sometime around the end of the first decade of the new millennium (year 2000), assuming we continue to assign addresses and use them in the manner we have to date. As a result, in the eyes of some, the Internet would effectively collapse without IPv6. For those looking at the world this way, the IPv6 standardization effort, earlier known as *IP Next Generation* (IPng), is an effort to save the Internet and to save their virtual world. No wonder there continues to be so much debate and so many proposals surrounding IPv6 and its broad pattern of impact across anything that touches IP—from routers, to desktops, to hosts, to applications.

Some downplay address space exhaustion as being the primary justification for IPv6, and they do have a point. IPv6 offers some very compelling features, especially those relating to autonconfiguration. In spite of the attractiveness of these features and others as well, we must be careful not to underestimate the impact of a worldwide migration from IPv4 to IPv6. The scale and impact of such a transition have never before been seen, and network managers won't be anxious to make wholesale changes. Just look at the large existing installed base of technologies dating back many years, many of which we discuss in this book, including Novell IPX and IBM SDLC.

We must accept that a transition to IPv6 impacts virtually everything. Routing protocols need to support it, as well as autoconfiguration mechanisms, filters and security, and applications that speak to sockets and make any assumptions about things they should or perhaps should not. This is not trivial. It is serious.

Also serious is the observation that the exhaustion of IPv4 addresses may be a reality at the rate we are going. What is debatable is whether we could make better use of the existing IPv4 address space, thereby eliminating this requirement that we transition and swap out the worldwide IPv4 infrastructure to an IPv6 one. Techniques to achieve this include use of VLSM for scarce public Internet addresses (as discussed in Chapter 3) as well as proxy server/network address translation servers coupled with reserved private Internet addresses (see BGP-4 discussion in Chapter 4). These approaches do introduce various complications and complexity, so it is not as easy as saying we should just follow them and forget about IPv6. Still, though, all options must be, and will continually be, considered.

A large number of vendors are supporting IPv6 in one way or another at this time. It is getting considerable attention, and, unless we solve our address exhaustion problem some other way, if may indeed be the savior of the Internet. In this chapter, we will review the design of IPv6 and its new addressing structures, will consider IPv6 impacts, and will compare IPv6 to IPv4.

5.2 Datagram Header Format and Options

An IPv6 packet must contain the minimum header information illustrated in Figure 5.1. This header is 40 bytes in length, which is 20 bytes more than the IPv4 header length, but IPv6 can be extended, so the header can contain even more bytes. Additional overhead could impact performance, so keep an eye out for extensions to headers if you proceed with IPv6.

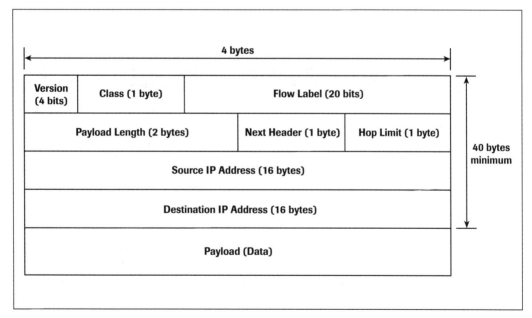

Figure 5.1 IPv6 format

5.2.1 The Minimum IPv6 Header

Let's look at each element of the header.

5.2.1.1 Version

The 4-bit Version field indicates the version of the IP protocol. For IPv6, this field contains the number 6.

5.2.1.2 Class (Priority) and Flow Label

The Class and Flow Label fields theoretically allow traffic to be prioritized and routed according to its specific performance needs. For example, quality voice applications require that the delay between datagrams carrying voice samples be minimized, and, as discussed earlier, interactive traffic such as TELNET has different response-time requirements than file transfer. The existing IPv6 RFC does not precisely define how the fields would be required to be used, so we will have to see how this evolves. (Note that RFC 1883 references a *Priority* field. Further work by the IPv6 standards groups resulted in this field being renamed *Class.*)

It's Never That Easy

Historically, we have not seen fields such as Flow Label and Class (Priority) clearly specified and broadly implemented for protocols perhaps because these concepts do not have clear answers to them—they are all about optimization. The problem of optimization, by its very nature, does not typically inspire cut-and-dried solutions. The best way to prioritize and favor some traffic over others is a complicated and highly debated topic. Also, from the router vendor perspective, implementing complex mechanisms in software and hardware is nontrivial. So, it is not uncommon for a great deal of effort to be put forth but for there to be little agreement and, ultimately, little real progress made. It would be nice if meaningful agreement is reached in the standards committees on flow labels and classes (priorities) and among all vendors since they could provide considerable quality-of-service benefits and possibly realistically open the Internet up to broader real-time delay-sensitive applications such as better voice and video. We'll just have to wait and see.

5.2.1.3 Payload Length

The Payload Length field indicates the length of the Payload (Data) field of the IPv6 packet. The Payload Length field is 16 bits long, so, by itself, it can signal a payload of up to 65,535 bytes. There is an option to signal longer lengths by placing a 0 in this field. A 0 indicates that the Jumbo Payload Hop-by-Hop option has been selected, and it leverages an *extension header,* which we'll discuss in a moment.

The Payload Length field is similar to IPv4's Total Datagram Length field, but it is not exactly the same. Whereas IPv4's Total Datagram Length includes the bytes of the IPv4 header in the total byte count, IPv6's Payload Length includes only Payload (Data) field bytes.

5.2.1.4 Next Header and Extension Headers

The Next Header field is analogous to the IPv4 Protocol Number field, but it offers the capability of extending IPv6 functionality be adding headers called *extension headers.* When not used with extension headers, this field contains the same protocol numbers as used with IPv4.

Let's examine how the header could be used to extend IPv6. Here, we'll look at the mechanism to do this; later, we'll take a closer look at different types of extension headers.

Suppose we use the minimum IPv6 header with no additional headers (extensions), and suppose the payload contains a TCP packet. The datagram would contain the following fields:

> (Version)(Class)(Flow Label)(Payload Length)
> (Next Header=TCP)(Hop Limit) (Source Address)
> (Destination Address)(Data)

Suppose we wish to add two extension headers. Then, the datagram would look like this:

> (Version)(Class)(Flow Label)(Payload Length)(Next Header=
> First Extension Header)(Next Header=Second Extension
> Header)(Next Header=TCP)(Hop Limit)(Source Address)
> (Destination Address)(Data)

So, we can stack the headers one after another. The last Next Header field will indicate the protocol carried by the IPv6 packet in the Data field. Table 5.1 contains important values defined for the Next Header field.

Table 5.1 Next Header Field Values

Decimal	Keyword/Application
0	Hop-by-Hop
1	ICMP (IPv4)
4	IP encapsulated in IP (e.g., IPv4 in IPv6)
6	TCP
17	UDP
43	Routing Header (IPv6)
44	Fragmentation Header (IPv6)
50	IPSEC Encapsulating Security Payload (ESP)
51	IPSEC Authentication Header (AH)
58	ICMP (IPv6)
59	No Next Header
60	Destination Options Header
88	EIGRP
89	OSPF

5.2.1.5 Hop Limit

The Hop Limit field serves the same function as IPv4's TTL. It is decremented by 1 for each device that forwards the datagram. The datagram is discarded if the hop limit reaches 0.

5.2.1.6 Source and Destination IP Addresses

An IPv6 address is 128 bits long (16 bytes), as opposed to the 32-bit (4-byte) length for IPv4. This represents a huge increase in the number of available addresses.

5.2.1.7 Additional Capabilities with Extension Headers

The IPv6 header can be extended, as we saw earlier, and thus features and options added, through the Next Header mechanism. This allows IPv6 to grow and evolve over time and to meet changing needs.

5.2.2 Extension Headers

There are various types of extension headers. Let's look at some important ones.

5.2.2.1 Hop-by-Hop and Destination Options Extension Headers

The Hop-by-Hop extension header must be examined by every router along the path from source to destination. In contrast, the Destination Options extension header is examined only by the source and destination, not by any routers or other devices embedded within the network. This distinction is made because it allows us to maximize router performance by not forcing it to read and interpret headers in every packet that have nothing to do with it (Destination Options).

The specific action required for the extension header is signaled in its Options field. For example, one Hop-by-Hop option is the Jumbo Payload option, which is used to signal that the payload is larger than 65,535 bytes. The actual length of the payload is signaled within the Options field of the Hop-by-Hop extension header. As previously noted, the Payload Length field must contain a 0 in order to activate the Jumbo Payload option.

5.2.2.2 Routing Extension Header

The Routing extension header is used to enable capabilities similar to the loose/strict source routing options we discussed with IPv4. Without the use of IPSEC, it offers similar security vulnerabilities.

5.2.2.3 Fragmentation Extension Header

IPv6 does not support fragmentation within the network, as does IPv4. In order to avoid the problem of sending a datagram greater than the path to the destination can sustain, IPv6 devices are required to use MTU discovery, which was optimal with IPv4. IPv6 does support fragmentation, however, between the two endpoints, the source and the destination—but just not by routers within the network. So, for example, if a source application has a 2,048-byte message to send but the maximum MTU to the destination is 1,024 bytes as learned through MTU discovery, then it can still fragment the datagram into two 1,024-byte datagrams. The destination IPv6 device will then reassemble the datagram into a 2,048-byte message and pass it onto the destination application. This feature can be useful to application developers since they can send larger messages than the MTU and neither worry about reassembly within the application at the destination nor worry about inefficiencies of fragmentation within the routing infrastructure. However, as a result, the application will be dependent on the robustness of the fragmentation and reassembly code in the IPv6 implementations (stacks) in the source and destination computers. Given the history of fragmentation implementations in general not being done very well (my personal experience), application developers are advised to test their application well on target platforms for fragmentation behavior if it is to be used, making sure they can respond to all error conditions returned by IPv6. They should especially test over congested networks wherein fragments may have larger delay variance between their delivery, forcing the destination IPv6 stack to handle higher interfragment delay cleanly as part of its effort to reassemble the full message for delivery to the destination application.

5.2.2.4 Authentication and Encapsulating Security Payload Extension Headers

In Chapter 2, IPSEC was introduce. IPv6 supports IPSEC natively, through the use of extension headers.

5.3 Addressing

In this section, we will explore IPv6 address structure and representation. A prerequisite to interpreting IPv6 addresses is knowledge of hexadecimal representation. So, let's take a moment and review that.

5.3.1 Hexadecimal Representation

We use decimal representation in our everyday lives. Each digit of a decimal number may take on values from 0 through 9:

   0, 1, 2, 3, 4, 5, 6, 7, 8, 9

Imagine a new numbering scheme whereby each digit can take on values from 0 through 15. To make things clear, we want a single symbol to identify each of these values. There is no problem with the numbers 0 through 9, but what happens to 10, 11, 12, 13, 14, and 15? We use letter symbols for those numbers. So, in our new numbering scheme, with a single digit, we count to 15 as follows:

0, 1, 2, 3, 4, 5, 6, 7, 8, 9, A, B, C, D, E, F

where A = 10, B = 11 , C = 12, D = 13, E = 14, and F = 15. This is called **base 16 (hexadecimal) representation.**

Recall that a byte is 8 bits. The 8 bits can be divided into two groups of 4 bits. Using binary arithmetic, 4 bits can be used to represent the numbers 0 through 15:

Binary	Decimal	Hexadecimal
0000	0	
0001	1	
0010	2	
0011	3	
0100	4	
0101	5	
0110	6	
0111	7	
1000	8	
1001	9	
1010	10	A
1011	11	B
1100	12	C
1101	13	D
1110	14	E
1111	15	F

Recall that an IPv6 address is 16 bytes (128 bits) long. If we view each individual byte of the IPv6 address as two groups of 4 bits, then we can represent each byte of the address by two hexadecimal digits.

IPv6 (RFC 1884) specifies that an address will be represented in the following form:

$x:x:x:x:x:x:x:x$

Each x represents 16 bits, which is equivalent to 2 bytes, which is equivalent to four hexadecimal digits. Using this notation, we can represent x as four hexadecimal digits. Here are two examples of IPv6 addresses:

FEDC:BA98:7654:3210:FEDC:BA98:7654:3210
1080:0:0:0:8:800:200C:417A

Notice that whenever x contained all 0s or leading 0s, they were not required. If they were, we would have written

1080:0000:0000:0000:0008:0800:200C:417A

We are allowed to make another simplification. Because we have so many addresses and because of the way we will assign them, there may often be many 0s inside an address. To make it easier to represent these addresses, a double colon(::) can be used to indicate multiple groups of 16 bits of 0s. Whenever you see ::, you can assume that all 0s are that portion of it. Returning to our example, we could rewrite the address as

1080::8:800:200C:417A

As another example, the address 0:0:0:0:0:0:0:1 could simply be represented as ::1.

5.3.2 Structure and Assignment

An address space of 128 bits is quite a lot of space. It yields 2 to the power of 128 different addresses. That is thousands of billions of addresses. It is clear the IPv6 designers were intent on putting the risk of further address space exhaustion to rest.

We should not become disillusioned with such a large number. It is not as simple as choosing a different address for every IPv6 device in the world. We need to organize our addresses into a hierarchy to allow for efficient routing, and thus 128 bits is used to organize the address space hierarchically and to allow for addresses that map to individual endpoints (so-called Unicast addresses) and to groups of endpoints (multicast and anycast addresses).

IPv6's address space can be organized in a manner similar to the way CIDR was employed for IPv4. The IPv6 addressing format that accomplishes this is the *Aggregatable Global Unicast Address* format. Addresses conforming to this format would be used to communicate across the worldwide public Internet. They would contain the necessary hierarchical routing information so that IPv6 routers could route traffic to and from the address efficiently. This format is illustrated in Figure 5.2.

The Prefix field is divided into a Public field and a Site field. The public portion would be used by Internet Service Providers (ISPs) to route among

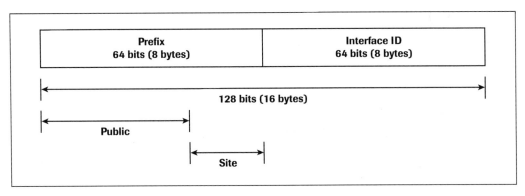

Figure 5.2 Aggregatable Global Unicast Address format

themselves at exchange points and within their own network. The site portion would be used, for example, inside a corporation.

What we are after with the Interface ID field is some number that uniquely identifies the IPv6 endpoint device (host or desktop computer, for example). The IPv6 designers observed that most endpoint devices already have unique addresses embedded in them. So, they asked, why not leverage them? In the case of hosts and desktops connected to Ethernet, this address is called the *MAC layer address.* It is typically 48 bits long and is burned into your LAN card. This address, allocated by a centralized organization (the IEEE), is guaranteed to be unique worldwide. Newer Ethernet standards introduced by the IEEE 802 standards committee extend this address to 64 bits. Note that the Interface ID field *can* contain the MAC address or other physical link-layer address (for ATM or what have you), but it is *not required* to. The only requirement is that it be unique within the site. IPv6 defines an address called a *link local address* that contains essentially nothing but the interface ID plus some other bits to indicate that this IPv6 address contains link (i.e., MAC) address in it but no prefix.

As we saw in Chapter 4, to route IP, we require more than a unique address—we need a routing hierarchy so that we can pass around routing information that is aggregated to the network level. Imagine if every router in the world had to have an entry for each individual endpoint IPv6 address. The tables would be unmanageable. This is a problem the prefix solves: It provides aggregation capability. However, we will see a use for link local addresses in the next section.

5.4 Autoconfiguration

Earlier in this book, DHCP and BOOTP were discussed. These two protocols are used for *autoconfiguration* of endpoint IPv4 devices with their IP
addresses and other configuration data. For IPv4, there was no concept of
link local addresses, so the device had no unique IP-level address it could
use to communicate with DHCP servers and the like upon bootup. Instead,
broadcasts and hacks within the operating systems (for example, modifying
the UNIX ARP table on the fly) were required. Availability of direct IP-level
addressing upon bootup is cleaner.

With IPv6 link local addresses, a DHCP server on the local LAN can
cleanly and directly communicate with the endpoint IP device using its link
local address. The DHCP server can then deliver directly to the endpoint
device its full IPv6 address as well as any other configuration information it
might need, such as available DNS servers and default routers. Note that the
DHCP server need not be on the same LAN. A DHCP *relay agent* can add
the local prefix to link local addresses and forward DHCP messages to their
destination.

In addition to DHCP, IPv6 allows the use of ICMP as a method to assign
addresses. ICMP was extended to support allocation of IPv6 addresses, and
the new version is known as *ICMPv6*. One advantage of using ICMPv6
instead of DHCP is that you are not required to configure a DHCP server.
All routers are required to implement ICMP so that any device might be
capable of delivering the prefix. It is likely, though, that administrators will
continue to favor DHCP because of its robust configuration capabilities
beyond delivering IPv6 addresses and other minimalist information. DHCP
has the benefit of being a centralized place where you can configure stateful
information.

Note that the IPv6 specification does not preclude DHCP from delivering a new interface ID to the device along with the prefix. It just seems so
convenient to leverage the Ethernet MAC address (following our example)
or similar address on the endpoint. When might we need to not use the Ethernet MAC address, for example, as the interface ID? One example would
be if a host requires more than one IP address. Since this host may have only
one Ethernet MAC address, there would need to be some mechanism to
produce additional interface IDs that are different from single available
MAC address.

5.5 Address Resolution

The *Neighbor Discovery Protocol* (NDP) effectively replaces ARP as a mechanism for resolving IPv6 addresses. NDP is based on ICMPv6. Also, NDP provides a mechanism for endpoint devices on the LAN (generally speaking, the link) to learn about any connected routers. Endpoints could also learn about available routers via *DHCPv6,* so administrators will have a choice. NDP functions similarly to ARP.

It is fair to ask the question, why not bypass NDP altogether and simply take the Ethernet MAC layer address directly from the Interface ID field of the IPv6 address? The answer is that, while the Interface ID field *may* contain the MAC layer address, it is *not required* to do so. We already saw one example of where this would not be the case—where one host has multiple IP addresses.

5.6 Impact on Applications

Depending upon how your application has been written, it may or may not be impacted by IPv6:

- If your application becomes involved at the address level (address data structures) in any way, then either it will need to be shielded from the new IPv6 address format through middleware or it will need to be modified.

- WinSock version 2, discussed in Chapter 7, supports IPv6. Changes to UNIX socket support are required to support IPv6. The extent to which these changes affect your application would need to be assessed.

- If applications developers wish to take advantage of certain advanced features of IPv6, such as flow labels, then applications may need to be modified.

5.7 IPv4/IPv6 Migration and Interoperability

Various proposals are being made at this time for ways to accomplish IPv4/IPv6 migration and interoperability. We will not go into detail on them here, so you might want to check a few of the references included at the end of this chapter. The proposals are changing, and what will really transpire will be driven by the availability of products, services, and administrative tools for making the transition easier.

Fundamentally, migration and interoperability involve shielding parts of the network from packet formats they don't know about (either IPv4 or IPv6 packets, depending upon their capabilities) while at the same time leveraging the transport capabilities (bandwidth) available in both parts of the network.

Presuming that IPv6 backbones begin to pop up—for example, your ISP decides the ISPs to convert to IPv6 within their own backbone—then the ISP might tunnel your IPv4 packets through their backbone to the destination. Likewise, the ISP could also convert between the two formats, depending upon the destination.

Within the corporations, both IPv4 and IPv6 computers would require autoconfiguration, support, and maintenance. Finally, applications may be affected and may require upgrade. Also, security mechanisms based on addresses, such as address filters configured in routers, firewalls, and hosts, would all need to be reconfigured.

5.8 Conclusions

While we should be careful to recognize the realities and challenges of deploying IPv6, we should not underestimate its significance and the energy and commitment of those pushing for its adoption. A large numbers of vendors already support IPv6 in one way or another. IPv6 offers benefits beyond dealing with address exhaustion.

FOR FURTHER STUDY

1. W. Stevens and M. Thomas. "RFC 2292 Advanced Sockets API for IPv6." February 1998.

2. C. Partridge. "RFC 1809 Using the Flow Label Field in IPv6." June 1995.

3. Y. Rekhter and T. Li, eds. "RFC 1887 An Architecture for IPv6 Unicast Address Allocation." December 1995.

4. J. Bound, B. Carpenter, D. Harrington, J. Houldsworth, and A. Lloyd. "RFC 1888 OSI NSAPs and IPv6." August 1996.

5. R. Hinden and J. Postel. "RFC 1897 IPv6 Testing Address Allocation." January 1996.

6. R. Elz. "RFC 1924 A Compact Representation of IPv6 Addresses." April 1996.

7. R. Gilligan and E. Nordmark. "RFC 1933 Transition Mechanisms for IPv6 Hosts and Routers." April 1996.

8. S. Thomas and T. Narten. "RFC 1971 IPv6 Stateless Address Autoconfiguration." August 1996.

9. M. Crawford. "RFC 1972 A Method for the Transmission of IPv6 Packets over Ethernet Networks." August 1996.

10. M. Crawford. "RFC 2019 Transmission of IPv6 Packets over FDDI." October 1996.

11. D. Mills. "RFC 2030 Simple Network Time Protocol Version 4 for IPv4, IPv6, and OSI." October 1996.

12. Y. Rekhter, P. Lothberg, R. Hinden, S. Deering, and J. Postel. "RFC 2073 An IPv6 Provider-Based Unicast Address Format." January 1997.

13. G. Malkin and R. Minnear. "RFC 2080 RIPng for IPv6." January 1997.

14. R. Gilligan, S. Thomson, J. Bound, and W. Stevens. "RFC 2133 Basic Socket Interface Extensions for IPv6." April 1997.

15. D. Borman. "RFC 2147 TCP and UDP over IPv6 Jumbograms." May 1997.

16. R. Callon and D. Haskin. "RFC 2185 Routing Aspects of IPv6 Transition." September 1997.

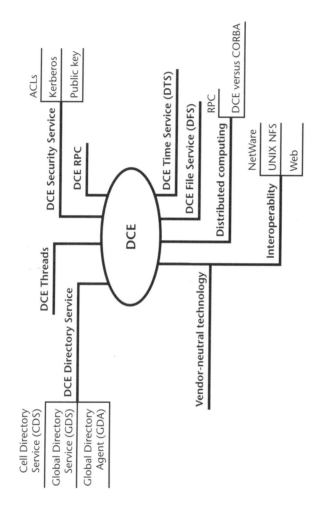

CHAPTER 6

The Open Group Distributed Computing Environment (DCE)

CHAPTER HIGHLIGHTS		
Topic	**Benefits**	**Experience**
Distributed Computing Environment (DCE)	DCE is well worth studying even if only to see what a fully architected set of distributed services looks like.	From RPC to X.500 to its file system to Kerberos, you will notice that DCE has more than a few things in common with popular network application frameworks.
Integrated platform-independent services	DCE is intended to fulfill the vision of hardware and software platform-independence. DCE provides platform-independent security directory, and file- and time services, as well as important application programming facilities, including threads.	While DCE as a whole has not received widespread adoption, the technologies that comprise it and its vision have significantly impacted the evolution of network application framework technology.

6.1 Introduction

The Open Software Foundation (OSF) was a nonprofit organization formed in 1988 to support the research, development, and implementation of vendor-neutral technology and industry standards. The OSF adopted the **Distributed Computing Environment** (DCE) from an earlier proposal, named DECORUM, submitted by Digital Equipment Corporation, IBM, Apollo, Transarc, and the Locus Computing Corporation. In 1996, the OSF merged with another standards group, X/Open, which was itself founded in 1984. This merged entity became known as the **Open Group**. DCE is one product of all this openness.

DCE was created to fulfill the vision that any computer could exchange information with any other, independent of who manufactured the computer's hardware or software. The resulting specifications produced from this vision have proven to be an important influence on the evolution of distributed computing, as pointed out a number of times in this book. However, the all-encompassing DCE environment never achieved its ambitious goal of broad ubiquitous deployment. Instead, elements of it were adopted, and concepts were borrowed from it by other competing and complementary standards and products.

This chapter does not purport to give you the ins and outs of deploying DCE inside your corporation, though you may gather information from it that helps you achieve that end. Instead, its purpose is to convey to you two things:

1. An understanding of what an all-encompassing distributed network application framework looks like. If there is one thing DCE is, it is all-encompassing.

2. Enough information for you to gain an appreciation for how DCE and its well thought-out approach has influenced the other network application frameworks discussed in this book.

DCE provides a comprehensive solution for file services, directory services, security, management, RPCs, machine-independent data representation, internationalization, and multitasking (threads). Even if you don't intend to use DCE, studying it is worth your time. It is an excellent example of how various fundamental components can be integrated in a very complete manner.

And for Nonbelievers . . .

DCE does receive some criticism. The skeptics argue that its consistency is taken to bizarre extremes, that it is proprietary because the Open Group requires membership ($) and its member companies have the voting rights, and that it duplicates well-known and widely implemented standards. While there may be some isolated support for such criticisms in a few instances, on the whole, they are probably neither entirely fair nor accurate.

In the remainder of this chapter, you will occasionally notice that the specific release of DCE is called out. The reason is that DCE has had, to date, the following releases:

- DCE 1.0
- DCE 1.1
- DCE 1.2 released in two phases, 1.2.1 and 1.2.2

Many existing textbooks discuss version 1.0. This chapter discusses features through version 1.2.2. The particular versions are pointed out here so that you can differentiate between the software releases. This differentiation is important since specific vendor products implement different releases and, therefore, if and when selecting these products, you will need to know which features are there and which ones are not. Also, by learning the new features added by release, you can get some idea of the evolution and direction of DCE.

6.2 DCE: Not Necessarily an Operating System

DCE itself is not necessarily an operating system. Instead, it can optionally ride on top of one, and, if it is implemented in this fashion, it places certain demands on the underlying operating system. Alternatively, native operating system implementations of DCE are available, such as OSF1.

When implemented on top of some other operating system, DCE assumes the availability of a layered transport service such as TCP/IP and requires that the underlying operating system provide a standard socket-style interface. The operating system must also offer the following services:

- Multitasking
- Timers
- Local interprocess communication
- Basic file system operations
- Memory management
- Local security mechanisms
- Threads or the ability to allow DCE Threads to be ported to the operating system
- Various commonly implemented system utility functions

UNIX meets these requirements, and, for that reason, many DCE implementations are implemented over UNIX and Windows-based systems.

6.3 DCE Security Service

DCE version 1.2.2 is based on Kerberos version 5.1 with some enhancements offered by Hewlett Packard Corporation. With DCE version 1.2.2, support is provided for authentication using public key cryptography.

The strength of the *DCE Security Service* is in its integration with the diverse components of the DCE framework and its ability to be integrated with non-DCE applications, potentially offering single sign-on across disparate applications. This allows for a much fuller, more easily managed distributed security environment. And, as most of us have learned, the easier a security measure is to implement, the more likely it is used.

The DCE Security Service is comprised of the following elements:

- Authentication Service
- Privilege Service
- Access Control List (ACL) Facility
- Login Facility
- Security API

The *Authentication Service* allows two processes executing on different machines to verify each other's identity. RPC programmers make use of Authenticated RPC. The DCE Authentication Service is based on Kerberos.

The *Privilege Service* implements authorization. It defines the resources within a server that the authenticated user has rights to. Resources include files and directories.

The *ACL Facility* is used to define lists of users authorized to access a specific resource, such as whether or not a user's access or a group of users' access to a file is read, write, read/write, or denied. This facility provides a convenient method of defining access rights for large numbers of users and resources. An ACL API is provided so that programmers can modify ACL entries for resources owned by them. DCE ACLs are based on the POSIX 1003.6 specification.

6.3.1 Tickets and PACs

When a user logs into a server, the user is first authenticated. Once authenticated, the user receives a DCE ticket. The user then presents the ticket to other services in order to prove authenticity. The user presents this ticket to the Privilege Server in order to obtain its *privilege attribute certificate* (PAC). The PAC identifies all the privileges this user has in the DCE environment, as defined through the ACL Facility. This process is illustrated in Figure 6.1.

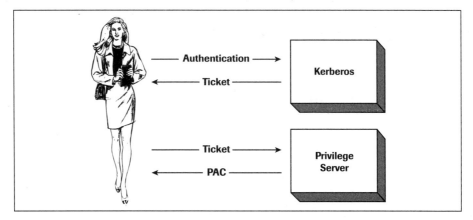

Figure 6.1 Tickets and PACs

6.3.2 Security Database

A key aspect of the DCE Security Service architecture is the *Security Database*. This database holds all of the authentication and access control information. If this database is broken into and "cracked" (decrypted), network security is compromised. This type of vulnerability is not unique to DCE, and it is a consequence of the need to keep things manageable through some sort of centralized management.

The Security Database must be highly available. If the Security Database should become unreachable, then users are forced to a default level of authentication, which in most systems will be virtually unusable. Availability is influenced by the robustness of the security server containing the database as well as the underlying network used to interconnect the client with the security server.

6.3.3 Security API

DCE version 1.1 added support for the *Generic Security Service Application Programming Interface* (GSS-API), an IETF-standard security API. GSS-API allows non-RPC applications to use DCE security features.

Version 1.1 added a feature further facilitating single sign-on when integrating DCE with non-DCE systems, providing a secure way of associating additional security information with users and groups. This feature is called *Extended Registry Attributes* (ERA).

6.4 DCE Directory Service

The *DCE Directory Service* is based on the X.500 (1988) standard. In addition to interoperating with X.500 networks, it also supports DNS.

The DCE Directory Service provides the method for resolving network addresses of resources reachable by the client. It is comprised of three components:

- *Cell Directory Service* (CDS)
- *Global Directory Service* (GDS)
- *Global Directory Agent* (GDA)

DCE supports names in either the X.500 or DNS format. A fully specified name has both a global component and a local cell component. A DCE *cell* is a collection of users and resources that routinely communicate with one another. A DCE network is usually divided into an arrangement of cells, with each cell essentially representing its own community of interest. A cell must contain a Cell Directory Server, a Security Server, and Distributed Time Servers. These services can be run on a single computer or on different ones. DCE version 1.1 allows cells to be arranged hierarchically to match the departments of your company or other organizational criteria.

The CDS stores the names and attributes of resources located in a DCE cell and is optimized in order to provide fast response for communication within the cell. This optimization is based on the assumption that users within the cell communicate most frequently with one another. All resources within the cell become unreachable if the CDS is unavailable; therefore, it should be installed on a highly reliable server and located at a highly available location. The DCE Security Database location, as discussed previously, might also be a good location for the CDS. The CDS can be replicated, thereby further enhancing availability.

The GDA acts as a middleman between the CDS and the GDS or DNS. If a name cannot be resolved by the CDS, the GDA attempts to resolve it by checking with the GDS or DNS. This process is illustrated in Figure 6.2. The GDA is actually a software process that can reside on the same machine as the CDS or on a different one.

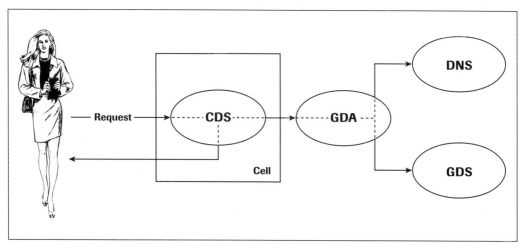

Figure 6.2 DCE Directory Service

The GDS supports access control lists (ACLs); however, these ACLs are not integrated into the DCE Security Service—the GDS ACLs are different from the DCE Security Service ACLs. Each GDS directory entry, also referred to as a GDS *object,* is assigned ACLs. These ACLs specify who may access an object and who may not. The possible ACL permissions are Public, Standard, or Sensitive. Groups of users can be assigned one of these permissions for the object. When a new object is added to the GDS directory, it inherits the security characteristics of its parent.

DCE programmers use the X/Open Directory Service (XDS) API to make all Directory Service calls. XDS uses the X/Open Object Management (XOM) API to define and manage its information.

6.5 DCE File Service (DFS)

The *DCE File Service* (DFS) is a powerful distributed file service, offering access control, file replication, concurrent file access synchronization functions, performance enhancing features such as caching, and various methods to ease system administration, including the ability to organize files and directories into filesets and then managing these filesets as a single object. It implements a superset of the POSIX 1003.1 file system semantic standard and is based on version 4.0 of the *Andrews File System* (AFS).

The original AFS was developed by Carnegie Mellon University (CMU) as part of the Andrews project. This project was aimed at providing a university wide distributed computing platform. AFS was designed with the intention of providing a worldwide networked distributed file system. AFS was so successful, that commercial products grew from it, one of them being Transarc's. AFS has enjoyed widespread deployment. A great many universities, including MIT, UCLA, CMU, the University of Michigan, the University of Grenoble in France, and Cambridge University, all use AFS.

DFS offers the following components:

- The *Cache Manager* provides a method of storing frequently used files locally rather than constantly retrieving them from the remote server on which they are stored. The Cache Manager examines every user request and determines whether a copy of the data has been cached locally. If it has, then the Cache Manager has reduced network and remote server load by servicing the request locally.

- The *File Exporter* executes on any server providing remote file access. The file exporter process services all remote client requests for files it manages. The File Exporter receives an RPC call and accesses its own local file system, which can be the DCE Local File System (the pure DCE file system implementation, discussed later) or another file system such as the UNIX File System (UFS). The File Exporter works with the Token Manager (also discussed later) to deal with the issues of concurrent file access, providing the needed file locking and synchronization to prevent multiple changes to the same file at the same time.

- The DCE *Local File System* (LFS) is the *physical* file system provided with DCE, responsible for managing disk storage on a single computer. LFS may or may not be implemented on your particular DCE server, depending upon the available options and those chosen for the server installation. In the event that it is not, the native operating system's file system, such as UFS, is used instead. LFS's capabilities include

  1. Authorization through the use of DCE
  2. Replication, backup, and moving of different portions of a file system without service interruption
  3. A logging mechanism that allows fast crash recovery
  4. Support for DCE cells allowing the owner of a file specified in an ACL to be in a foreign cell

  When UFS is used, some of the DFS functionality is reduced. There is only one fileset per UFS partition. Since partitions are usually large, this produces large filesets that are more difficult to move. Also, UFS filesets cannot be replicated.

- The *Token Manager* runs on the file server. It is responsible for synchronization required to support concurrent file access to multiple clients. The Token Manager issues tokens that represent the particular operations that can be performed by the client holding the token, such as file read or write. There are four types of tokens:

  1. Data tokens for access to file and directory data
  2. Status tokens for access to file and directory status
  3. Lock tokens for locking a portion of a file
  4. Open tokens for opening a file

The server Token Manager coordinates with the Token Manager layer in the client Cache Manager to manage tokens. The client and the server work together to guarantee that a client can perform only allowable functions, as defined by the tokens they posses at any given moment.

- The *Fileset Server* allows administrators to perform operations on filesets. This includes creating, deleting, moving, and other operations.

- The *Basic Overseer Server* (BOS) is responsible for monitoring the DFS server process. It maintains information on DFS processes and restarts them when required.

- The *Replication Server* is used by the administrator to create a copy of a fileset on another server. The Replication Server then takes on the responsibility of updating this replicated file at a specified time interval or is triggered in response to writes performed on the original file. Applications requiring up-to-the-minute synchronization must use this feature carefully since there will be periods of time during which the master file and the replica are not synchronized (the time between updates). The file being replicated (the original file) is readable and writable, whereas the copies of the file are read-only.

- The *Update Server* keeps a record of all the software revisions of the DFS process executables in the network in order to aid the administrator in maintaining compatible software releases. Anyone who has suffered through incompatibilities between different software releases of an operating system will appreciate the role of the Update Server.

- The *Scout* monitors the status of all file exporters within a file server.

- The *Backup Server,* as the name implies, is responsible for scheduling fileset backups.

- The *Fileset Location Server* (FLS) correlates which filesets are located on which file servers. The FLS is similar to the CDS except that it allows a fileset to be accessed (looked up and located) by name only. This means that a client can request a fileset by name and not necessarily be required to know the CDS/X.500 address of the machine on which the fileset resides. When a fileset is moved, the FLS database is updated; however, none of the client applications need to be updated—they can continue to use the same fileset name.

6.6 DCE Time Service (DTS)

The *DCE Time Service* (DTS) is yet another instantiation of a time-synchronization protocol. Other time protocols exist, such as the one used commonly in TCP/IP environments, the Network Time Protocol (NTP).

DTS regularly synchronizes the clocks of all computers in the distributed system. Devices that are not synchronized can cause operational and maintenance difficulties. File update time stamps on different servers can no longer be compared during troubleshooting or maintenance because their real update times are not known. Also, logs describing server events and alarms cannot be compared across servers that are not time-synchronized. Distributed applications making use of time can encounter errors in an unsynchronized system.

6.7 DCE Threads

6.7.1 A Platform-Independent API

DCE Threads provides a common platform-independent API for thread implementation. The DCE Threads implementation was originally based on a standard produced by Digital Equipment Corporation (DEC). DEC submitted this as part of the DECORUM effort. DCE Threads eventually became the basis for another threads standard, POSIX P1003.4a (pthreads). For operating systems supporting threads as part of the kernel (that is, threads integrated into the operating system), the DCE Threads API is essentially a transitional API, converting DCE thread commands to those of the underlying operating system. Where the underlying operating system does not support threads but instead is process-based, DCE Threads provides a method of emulating that functionality through the use of jacket routines that essentially offer a threads emulation layer over process functionality. By defining a common threads API, DCE enhances software portability.

DCE Threads includes functions to create and control multiple threads of execution in a single process and to synchronize access to global data within an application. Most of the DCE components make use of the threads service, including the file services, security services, RPC, directory

functions, and time servers. RPC application servers are inherently multithreaded so that they can handle multiple client RPC requests simultaneously. Both DCE clients and servers can be multithreaded, allowing for
maximal leveraging of client-side computing capability.

6.7.2 Threads Application Development

By allowing an application to execute various functions as multiple threads,
significant performance improvement can be gained; however, there is a
price—application developers have additional issues to deal with when programming multithreaded applications. Programmers must manage threads,
synchronize their access to global resources, address scheduling issues, and
manage thread priorities.

Any data, files, or other resources shared by threads require a locking
mechanism in order to guarantee that two or more threads do not attempt
to change a resource at the same time. POSIX provides a synchronization
mechanism for this known as a *mutex*. Only the thread that has acquired
the mutex can change the resource.

DCE library routines internally handle the locking for most reentrant
server functions. However, nonreentrant routines must finish before they
can be called by another thread. DCE Threads offers jacket routines for
nonreentrant routines and manages access to them. For example, jacket
routines are provided for UNIX system calls such as `fork( )` and
`sigaction( )`.

Because threads may depend upon input from other threads before
executing, it is necessary to synchronize them explicitly. For example, one
thread may need to enter a wait state until another thread completes.
Experienced application developers understand the serious problems
that can result if synchronization is not done carefully. It is usually not as
simple as waiting for another thread to complete. Complex systems can
be brought to a complete halt if a single thread stubbornly prevents the
rest of the system from continuing operation because it has not received
its input. In some cases, this might be appropriate; however, in many others,
it is not.

Little Things That Sink the Ship

A satellite-based network management system I was evaluating, responsible for managing more than 1,000 remote sites, insisted on receiving a successful acknowledgment from each of ten main controlling hubs for the network. If even one did not respond, the entire network management system would halt. This only occurred during system boot. If all ten systems were operational during system boot, there would be no problem, but if any one was down during boot, the system would hang. Obviously, in this case, the thread needed to time out rather than perpetually wait for acknowledgment. After finding this single-threaded problem, we proceeded to find hundreds more such issues. An overall system design needs to carefully map out all system dependencies in complex implementations. In some cases, it might be useful to construct a simulation model to test all possible combinations of events as part of the up-front software design process.

DCE Threads allows the programmer to implement various priorities so that some threads can get more priority than others. If priorities are used, they must be managed by the programmer.

6.8 DCE and CORBA

Relative to CORBA, DCE is both a partner and a competitor. CORBA can be implemented on top of DCE; however, a substantive part of CORBA's functionality can actually be used to replace DCE functionality. At the same time, the DCE versus CORBA argument puts software developers in a difficult position if they are attracted to the fundamentals of the DCE architecture while, at the same time, driven to leverage objects to the max. A number of vendors, including Hewlett Packard (HP), DEC, and IBM have integrated CORBA on top of DCE.

6.9 DCE Interoperability

There are three systems—UNIX, Web-based systems, and Novell NetWare—for which interoperability has been clearly defined. For your particular implementation, you will need to use the tools provided within

DCE along with those of the environments you are integrating with, along with open standards where possible, to integrate DCE with non-DCE systems.

Enhancements added in DCE release 1.2.1 include support for Novell NetWare 3.x clients, allowing them access to the DFS system. This is achieved via the implementation of a DCE NetWare gateway. DCE security services can be leveraged by NetWare users through this gateway mechanism by configuring the users within the DCE environment as well as within the NetWare environment. The ideal world would require configuration in just one of two places, not both.

DCE-Web is an Open Group advanced technology project focused on integrating DCE components seamlessly with existing Web components and technologies, the objective being to extend, rather than replace, existing Web capabilities. This work has focused on areas including the extending of DCE security mechanisms onto the Web. One DCE provider leveraging Web integration is Gradient Systems with their Web Crusader product. Web Crusader integrates the Web and public key cryptography into the DCE Security Service.

For existing UNIX application-level interoperability, DCE provides a gateway to the UNIX Network File System (NFS).

6.10 Conclusions

DCE offers an excellent example of a fully integrated standards-based distributed computing system that is designed to scale to large enterprise networks. The Open Group is looking at the possibility of adding a variety of new features and capabilities for DCE, including LDAPv3 support and the leveraging of Java as both a method to implement DCE client software and also as an extension to the DCE programming environment.

FOR FURTHER STUDY

1. J. Colonna-Romano and P. Srite. *The Middleware Source Book.* Boston: Digital Press, 1995.

2. J. M. Hart and B. Rosenberg. *Client/Server Computing for Technical Professionals: Concepts and Solutions.* Reading, Mass.: Addison-Wesley, 1995.

3. W. Hu. *DCE Security Programming.* Sebastopol, Calif.: O'Reilly, 1995.

4. J. S. Quarterman and S. Wilhelm. *UNIX, POSIX, and Open Systems: The Open Standards Puzzle.* Reading, Mass.: Addison-Wesley, 1993.

5. W. Rosenberry and J. Teague. *Distributing Applications Across DCE and Windows NT.* Sebastopol, Calif.: O'Reilly, 1993.

6. J. Shirley, W. Hu, and D. Magid. *Guide to Writing DCE Applications.* Sebastopol, Calif.: O'Reilly, 1994.

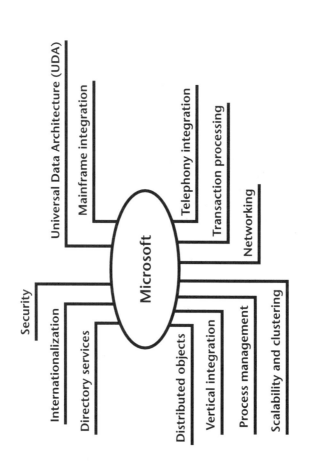

CHAPTER 7

Microsoft and WOSA

Topic	Benefits	Experience
COM/ActiveX and Active Data Objects (ADO)	COM/ActiveX and ADO provide an object-oriented component framework for the Windows environment. ADO allows for intelligent data sharing among applications and is based on COM.	COM/ActiveX is becoming an essential part of any application development geared for the native Windows environment. ADO solves the real problem of sharing data among applications and maintaining its semantic content.
Networking APIs and interprocess communication	Microsoft provides a variety of mechanisms for procedural and object-oriented applications to communicate across a network.	Support for networking APIs such as WinSock has become essential for network-enabled applications.
Microsoft Transaction Server (MTS) and Cedar	MTS provides a COM-based transaction-processing environment. Cedar allows the NT environment to be integrated with mainframe transaction-processing systems.	Transaction processing is the next evolutionary step for NT servers, and these products help to make NT a player in areas traditionally serviced by high-end mainframe technology.

7.1 Introduction

Discussing Microsoft with friends and colleagues is becoming as risky as talking about religion or politics. We enjoy passionately debating Microsoft's business practices and its role in our industry. Some enjoy blaming Microsoft for a range of afflictions, and many have argued over the years that it is monopoly and must be stopped. Some say Microsoft is a victim; others, a victimizer. One thing is for sure—Microsoft technology is systemic within us; it is everywhere. Microsoft is at the heart of our networked society. It owns the desktop, and its server market share is growing rapidly. And so, it goes without saying, understanding Microsoft's application and networking architecture and its direction is of great importance.

7.1.1 Vision

In recent times, Microsoft has committed considerable resources to object technology development. Responding to competition from CORBA and Java, Microsoft is integrating its brand of object technology, referred to as the *Component Object Model* (COM) and also known by various other names, into just about every aspect of its software environment.

Microsoft is poised to create another formidable cross-product strength—that of across-the-board integrated object technology. If you want to understand a simple benefit of object technology on the desktop, you might ask yourself why each of your applications has its own spell-checker. (My e-mail has one, my graphics program has one, and so does my word processor.) Each spell-checker takes up its own space on your hard drive, its own memory, and so forth. One solution is to put spell-checking into the operating system, but the Windows operating system is already huge. Lately, we want thinner clients that we can upgrade easily, not huge ones loaded down with everything under the sun.

What you need is to be able to install a spell-checking object of your choice and to instruct all your applications to use that one—to use just one spell-checking object that has been modified and customized to meet your needs instead of having to modify and customize each spell-checker individually. This simple example is what object technology is all about, and, while this benefit alone may seem significant, it merely scratches the surface of the wave of object technology that is now heading for us. In this chapter, we will talk about Microsoft's distributed object technology and its alphabet soup of terms, including OLE, ActiveX, COM, DCOM, and ADO.

With its object, transaction-processing, and Wolfpack-clustering technologies, it seems evident that Microsoft sees a world of rack-mounted NT servers running the core of electronic commerce someday, not the tall and mighty IBM mainframes that own that market today. In this chapter, we will review the Microsoft technologies behind its move into mainstream transaction processing.

7.1.2 Components of the Microsoft Network Application Framework

For a long time, Microsoft referred to its APIs and API architectures as the *Windows Open Systems Architecture* (WOSA). WOSA can be considered part of the Microsoft network application framework. Microsoft does not seem to use this terminology consistently or too much anymore. So, rather than talking about WOSA specifically, let's just address its technologies as part of our discussions of the broader network application framework.

Figure 7.1 illustrates major components of the Microsoft network application framework. Let's take a brief look at each of these components and then later in this chapter explore them in greater detail.

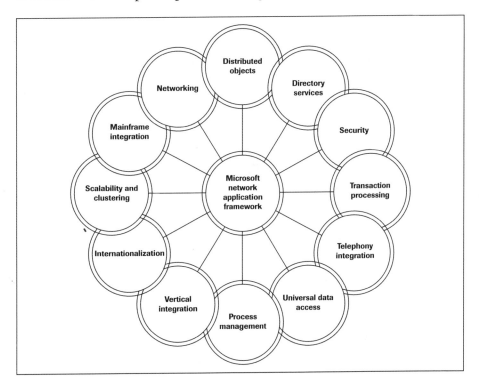

Figure 7.1 Microsoft network application framework

7.1.2.1 Directory Services

Microsoft's directory services provide the basis for the authentication and authorization mechanisms required to access services and resources within the network. NT 5 Active Directory is a general-purpose directory service providing a distributed information storage and retrieval mechanism for the enterprise. Because of the importance of this technology, Chapters 8 and 9 are dedicated to Microsoft's directory services offerings—Chapter 8 for NT 4 and Chapter 9 for NT 5 Active Directory.

7.1.2.2 Distributed Objects

Object-oriented software development techniques based on the Microsoft COM have made themselves into the heart of just about every new Microsoft product development effort and application framework enhancement. In this chapter, we will examine COM and all its related technologies.

7.1.2.3 Internationalization

The ability to take the same software and have it operate according to the language, customs, and expectations of people from a particular region of the world is known as *internationalization*. Microsoft provides tools that enable internationalization of your applications.

7.1.2.4 Mainframe Integration

While providing connectivity to IBM mainframes has long been an important and valuable function of the Microsoft network application framework, there is now considerable new development in this area within Microsoft that promises to make it a stronger contender for mainframe applications and the electronic commerce transaction-processing application space these mainframes currently dominate.

7.1.2.5 Networking

With the original release of Windows for Workgroups and NT, Microsoft demonstrated its commitment to providing strong internetworking capabilities within the operating system, including TCP/IP, a Systems Network Architecture (SNA) API, Novell NetWare, NetBIOS/NetBEUI, and WinSock.

7.1.2.6 Process Management

Microsoft's 32-bit Windows operating systems offer significant multi-processing capabilities at their core, including facilities such as threads and interprocess communication. We will review these underlying technologies since they are of prime importance to the application developer and architect.

7.1.2.7 Scalability and Clustering

As part of its initiative to expand the scope of NT servers into areas traditionally serviced by mainframes, Microsoft has developed a new technology, code-named *Wolfpack*, that is aimed at allowing separate physical NT servers to be *clustered* (grouped together) to build up performance and reliability of the overall system in a scalable fashion. However, Wolfpack, in its first release, will be aimed mainly at solving the reliability problem.

7.1.2.8 Security

Security topics are discussed throughout this book, including in Chapter 2, in which a number of Windows security capabilities, such as Kerberos and public key cryptography, were presented. Microsoft directory services themselves play a large role in security and, as mentioned earlier, are discussed within their own chapters. In this chapter, we will explore security as it relates to the various components of the Microsoft application framework, including topics such as transaction-processing security using COM objects.

7.1.2.9 Telephony Integration

Another area of importance to the desktop and server that Microsoft identified early on is telephony integration. Microsoft provides an API, the Telephony API (TAPI), that provides a standard API for integration of the PC with the telephone and its peripherals, such as modems from different vendors, fax systems, those wonderful voice-mail-enabled modems that perchance you have had the fun of installing and getting to work, ISDN adapters, and PBX systems. TAPI offers a mechanism for data to be routed to an application based on its content (i.e., fax data goes to the fax process, e-mail goes to the mail process, voice-mail goes to the voice management process).

7.1.2.10 Transaction Processing

The Microsoft Transaction Server (MTS) is Microsoft's entree into the transaction-processing services business and offers some interesting object (COM) services.

7.1.2.11 Universal Data Access

Almost 20 years ago, I sat at the terminals connected to various mainframe computers, as well as at the front of new devices that at the time were called "personal computers," and wrote software to translate data formats used by different computer programs so that people could share data between them. I wish I could say that there have been significant advances in data interoperability since that time, but I can't. By *data interoperability,* I don't mean sharing text and pictures; I mean sharing the semantic content of the data—its meaning, and the relationships between data elements. To exchange data, we still worry about some of the same exact de facto data standard formats, including the Rich Text Format (RTF), the Data Interchange Format (DIF), the dbf format developed by Ashton-Tate with their original Dbase product, and WKS pioneered by Lotus. Over the years, Microsoft has grown its suite of common APIs, allowing different applications to share data more intelligently at the programmatic (API) level, such as the Open Database Connectivity (ODBC) standard based on industry-standard SQL and the Messaging API (MAPI). Now, with the growing infiltration of object technology into the application framework, another significant event for the Windows environment, known as *ActiveX Data Objects* (ADO), is upon us.

7.1.2.12 Vertical Integration

Microsoft provides *vertical* APIs that focus on the needs of particular vertical industry segments, such as the Extended Financial Services API (XFS), which is intended to satisfy the needs of the financial industry. Others include the Licensing API (LSAPI), which provides a common means for software developers to administer licenses within the networked enterprise. In the next section, we will focus on the architecture historically used by Microsoft to introduce new services to the Windows platform.

7.2 Service Provider Interface (SPI) Architecture

Most of Microsoft's APIs are extensible. Microsoft calls the interface to do this a *service provider interface* (SPI). SPI is illustrated in Figure 7.2. SPIs abstract away the details of a particular implementation of a function, producing a common API to differing implementations. For example, there are SPIs for various communication transport mechanisms. The application may not care whether TCP/IP or Novell IPX is used to transport its data; therefore, it would rather that these details be hidden from it using the SPI architecture.

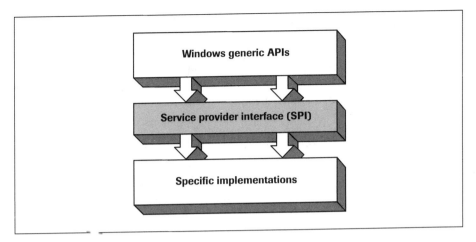

Figure 7.2 SPI architecture

7.3 Multitasking, Synchronization, and Threads

The Microsoft threads facility is built into the underlying Windows operating system. In contrast to a distributed open architecture such as DCE, the Microsoft threads facility is meant to work with Windows only. The Win32 API is designed for preemptive multitasking. Processes in the Windows environment have their own address space and manage resources such as memory, files, and threads. When a process is terminated, resource assignments such as threads are also terminated.

Multithreading in a Windows NT environment can be more effective when multiple processors are available within the computer. The multiprocessing Intel-based motherboards manufactured today support Intel's MP standard, which allows for support of multiple processors on the same motherboard.

Overuse of threads can bring an underpowered computer to its knees. It is important for the application developer to use threads carefully. While they can definitely improve performance by introducing more parallelism (less blocking) to the application, at a point, the underlying operating system may begin to "thrash" as a result of the overhead created by having to manage all those threads and the lack of CPU cycles and system resources to manage them. The Intel Pentium Pro and Pentium II microprocessors are designed to support multiprocessing environments by allowing for each CPU to have its own cache. The original Pentium architecture requires the sharing of a single cache by all Pentium processors.

7.4 Local Interprocess Communication

The Microsoft Application environment provides for the following methods of interprocess communication for communication on the local machine (i.e., not over the network):

- *File mapping* enable a process to treat the content of a file as though it were a block of memory. Different processes can read and write data to this file that they wish other processes to access. File mapping is not designed for use over a network and is not recommended for networked use, although there are various workarounds to achieve it that involve the creation of a mapped file on a remotely mounted drive.

- *Shared memory* is similar to file mapping except that the computer's swap file (paging memory) is used instead of a file, which can be more convenient for a programmer.

- *Pipes,* both anonymous and named, are concepts familiar to most UNIX programmers. An *anonymous* pipe allows a process to communicate through the logical equivalent of a pipe to its children processes. A *named* pipe, in contrast, does not require that the processes be related, as in parent and child. Anonymous pipes can be used only within a single computer, whereas named pipes can be used across a network.

7.5 Networking

7.5.1 Transports

By allowing for internetworking between applications running on different protocol stacks and by providing transport-independent APIs, Microsoft has positioned itself well for integration into heterogeneous computing environments. Windows 95 was shipped with the following transport and resource-sharing protocols built in:

- Banyan Vines
- DEC Pathworks
- IBM's Data Link Control (DLC) and Logical Link Control (LLC2) protocols

- TCP/IP
- NetBEUI and NetBIOS
- Novell IPX Client

In addition, an option for Windows NT, the SNA Server, supports the IBM APPC applications environment, including LU6.2.

7.5.2 Remote Interprocess Communication

The transports listed in the preceding section can be accessed through various methods, including

- Windows sockets protocol (WinSock)
- NetBIOS
- Named pipes and mailslots
- RPC
- Microsoft Win32 API functions (the WNet( ) functions)

Networking is illustrated in Figure 7.3. WinSock and NetBIOS allow the developer to write powerful applications that are not dependent on the underlying transport mechanism. NetBIOS, an older and less efficient

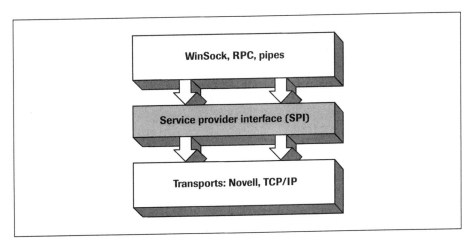

Figure 7.3 Networking

standard, is not recommended for new application development. NetBIOS is often implemented with the NetBEUI transport developed by IBM; however, use of NetBEUI is not required. The NetBIOS/NetBEUI combination should be avoided because it makes inefficient use of network resources and usually performs poorly across networks due to flow control mechanisms that are not robust. WinSock is a very significant API and will be discussed in detail in a later section.

A *mailslot* allows for the one-way transmission of messages no larger than 400 bytes and works over a network. The mailslot facility allows for message broadcast within a network domain.

7.5.3 WNet( ) APIs

The Windows Win32 API set includes APIs that allow for the establishment of network connections independent of the underlying network transport. However, this set of APIs is so sparse that the application programmer is likely to turn to WinSock, to NetBIOS, or to direct transport-specific APIs in order to develop a complex network-based application. The WNet ( ) *APIs* are useful for straightforward applications that must perform tasks such as browsing a remote file system. WNet( ) routines allow for the browsing of file systems other than Microsoft. These would include LAN Manager, NetWare, and Banyan Vines. The WNet( ) APIs are relatively simple, and their functions can be derived by reading their names:

```
WNetAddConnection( )
WNetCancelConnection( )
WNetGetConnection( )
WNetNotifyRegister( )
WNetConnectionDialog( )
WNetDisconnectDialog( )
```

7.5.4 NetBIOS

After establishment of a *NetBIOS* connection, applications exchange data using NetBIOS requests and replies. These requests and replies follow what was originally known as the *Server Message Block* (SMB) protocol. The SMB protocol was developed jointly by Microsoft, Intel, and IBM. It defines a command set used for exchanging data between computers connected by a network. SMB was recently renamed the *Common Internet File System* (CIFS), and a draft IETF RFC was issued specifying it. CIFS commands are organized into four functional area: Session Control, File, Printer, and Message.

By making use of CIFS, an application can communicate with past and present versions of Microsoft networking applications as well as internetwork with other operating systems supporting CIFS, which include the following:

- UNIX systems using Samba, a public domain CIFS implementation for UNIX
- MS OS/2 LAN Manager
- Windows for Workgroups
- IBM LAN Server
- MS-DOS LAN Manager
- DEC Pathworks
- Microsoft LAN Manager for UNIX
- 3Com 3+Open
- MS-Net

7.5.5 Berkeley (BSD) Sockets and Windows Sockets Specification (WinSock)

The first and most popular implementation of *WinSock* was that of TCP/IP stack support for Windows-based computers. Before WinSock was introduced, applications such as a Web browser or FTP client might work with a particular vendor's TCP/IP stack loaded under Windows but might not work with one provided by another vendor. WinSock provided a standard interface for all applications to write to, and, therefore, they would work with any TCP/IP implementation. WinSock was developed as a joint effort, with key participation from Microsoft and Intel. Because WinSock is such a significantly and widely used specification, we will study its history and operation in detail in the next two sections.

7.5.5.1 WinSock: Some History

The first widely implemented version of WinSock was release 1.1. WinSock 1.1 supports only TCP/IP. WinSock 2.0 allows for the simultaneous use of more than one transport.

The great strength of WinSock is its ability to shield the applications programmer from details of the underlying transport. This simplifies software development and also allows for the development of a single application that functions over multiple transports.

WinSock 2.0 is a superset of WinSock 1.1. WinSock 2.0 is fully backward-compatible with 1.1. WinSock extensions include the following:

- Support for transports other than TCP/IP. WinSock introduces transport-specific APIs, where required, to accommodate unique transport-level requirements. To the extent an application relies on these transport-specific APIs, the application becomes tied to supporting only that one particular transport. The WinSock specification currently includes extensions for the following transports (bear in mind that the SPI allows transport vendors to add theirs at any time):

  1. Novell IPX and SPX

  2. DECNet

  3. OSI

  4. ATM-specific extensions (AAL5 support only, E.164 addressing, NSAP addressing, point-to-point and point-to-multipoint connections)

- Secure Sockets Layer (SSL) extensions (Microsoft has published extensions to WinSock allowing it to utilize SSL along with the underlying transport protocol.)

- TAPI integration.

- Support for protocol-independent directory services (name resolution). WinSock provides a standard API for these different services, including DNS, Novell SAP, and X.500.

- Some improved I/O and memory management.

- Quality of service capability. An application can negotiate service levels, including bandwidth and delay characteristics and prioritization.

- Extensions for multicast. An application queries the transport for its multicast capabilities and then can use them with a common API. Multicast extensions allow an application to transmit and receive IP multicast datagrams. These extensions are based on the IP multicast extensions for BSD UNIX.

WinSock is based on the sockets implementation originally developed by researchers at the University of California, Berkeley, in order to integrate the TCP/IP protocol suite with UNIX. Their goal was to provide application developers with a networking API analogous to the standard method of performing file input and output within UNIX. WinSock 1.1 is a Microsoft implementation of the Berkeley BSD sockets implementation. In fact, if you are using Windows 95 and you look at the properties of the file WinSock.dll in your \windows subdirectory, you will likely see the following description under the Version option: "BSD Socket API for Windows."

7.5.5.2 WinSock: Its Operation

The concept of *sockets* is a relatively simple one. Applications use the WinSock function socket( ) to request networking capability. This function returns a handle. A handle is essentially a unique identification, or descriptor, used so that the application can uniquely identify the socket when it wishes to use it for communication. When creating a socket, the programmer must specify the protocol family (for example, the Internet protocol family, Novell, or some other one that is supported by your particular WinSock implementation), the type of socket (datagram or byte-stream), and the particular protocol within the family (TCP, for example, which is a member of the Internet family). An application programmer would call this function in the following manner:

```
socket_handle=socket(protocol_family, socket_type, protocol)
```

A socket does not represent a specific destination. As we will see, sockets are a place where the application goes to communicate. The destination associated with a given socket can change at any point in time. A socket should be thought of as providing communication capability, not as providing a specific connection to a specific computer, since the source and destination can always change for the same socket handle. In the remainder of this discussion, the TCP/IP protocol family will be assumed for the sake of simplicity. Note that a connectionless socket would be based on UDP, while a connection-oriented one would use TCP.

After creating a socket, a programmer fills in certain parameters within the socket data structure. Depending upon whether the application is listening to a socket (i.e., awaiting data from a client) or initiating a connection, the setting of the remote address information will differ, as we will discuss in a moment. The key data structure elements include the following:

- Protocol Family
- Type of Service
- Local IP Address
- Remote IP Address
- Local Protocol Port
- Remote Protocol Port

The process of associating a socket with a local address and port is known as *binding*.

A client may be connection-oriented or connectionless. Likewise, a server may be connection-oriented or connectionless. In order for a source and a destination to communicate via WinSock, they must both be connectionless or both be connection-oriented. You cannot mix connection types across the network.

A connection-oriented client fills out the entire socket data structure, including the remote address and protocol port. The client application then establishes a direct connection to that remote server destination.

Typically, servers do not initiate connections to clients. Instead, they sit in a passive state, waiting for client data coming in on a particular protocol port. For example, in the case of a Web server configured for the HTTP protocol, it waits for client data coming in on protocol port 80.

If the server is connection-oriented, it will wait for a client connection request and then fill out the socket data structure dynamically during connection establishment. If the server is connectionless, it merely services each datagram as an independent event.

Beyond initializing the data structures and either listening for incoming data (i.e., a server) or initiating a connection (i.e., a client), the remainder of the non-transport-specific WinSock functions are relatively straightforward. They are basically different variants of `send( )` and `receive( )` programming functions.

7.6 Open Database Connectivity (ODBC)

Open Database Connectivity (ODBC) allows for the accessing of data in a heterogeneous environment of relational and nonrelational database management systems. ODBC is based on the Call Level Interface (CLI) specification of the SQL Access Group (SAG). ODBC allows an application

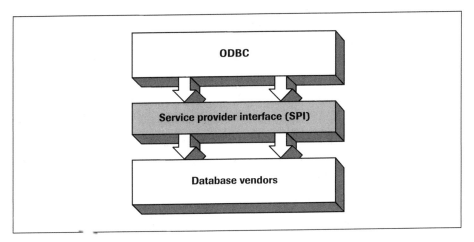

Figure 7.4 Open Database Connectivity

to be written that is independent of the underlying Database Management System (DBMS) in much the same way WinSock allows an application to be independent of the underlying transport protocol. Of course, to the extent that your application takes advantage of vendor-specific extensions to ODBC, the application becomes tied to those particular DBMS implementations. ODBC has received strong industry support; however, in its introduction, ODBC met with some performance concerns. ODBC is illustrated in Figure 7.4.

It is important to note that ODBC functionality is entirely reliant on the DBMS you choose and the thoroughness of the driver. ODBC does not represent a DBMS provided by Microsoft. It is an API to get to any compliant DBMS you choose.

We tend to take for granted the performance sensitivity of DBMS operations. However, once we add a layer or two of processing, we are immediately reminded. Efficiency is a real issue with ODBC. It seems that there is an art to writing ODBC drivers, which has created a market for premium ODBC driver providers (third-party software houses that have developed high-speed ODBC drivers for popular DBMS implementations). You would be well advised to test your expected hardware with sample ODBC-based programs, using the specific ODBC drivers you expect to deploy, before proceeding to large-scale development.

Essentially, ODBC is a generic version of SQL that everyone has agreed upon. That the underlying DBMS must be SQL, however, is not at all the case. It need only be flexible enough to allow itself to be controlled via a driver that must accept SQL commands from the application program.

The SAG CLI defines something called *core grammar* and core functions. With core functionality, an application can perform the following functions:

1. Establish a connection with a data source, execute SQL statements, and retrieve results.
2. Receive standard error messages.
3. Provide a standard logon.
4. Use a standard set of data types defined by ODBC.
5. Use a standard SQL grammar defined by ODBC.

With ODBC extensions, an application can perform the following functions:

1. Make use of data types such as date, time, time stamp, and binary.
2. Use scrollable cursors.
3. Utilize standard SQL grammar for scalar functions, outer joins, and procedures.
4. Make use of asynchronous execution.
5. Determine, through an API call, what capabilities a driver and data source provide.

Within the Windows architecture, ODBC is a *dynamically linked library* (DLL). The driver processes ODBC function calls, manages all exchanges between an application and a specific DBMS, and may translate the standard SQL syntax into the native SQL of the target data source. The benefit of a DBMS-independent API is that, in theory, the application developer does not need to modify their application if the underlying DBMS changes.

7.7 Messaging API (MAPI)

Messaging APIs allow for the integration of different electronic messaging applications and systems, such as Internet Mail (SMTP/POP), MCI Mail, SprintMail, Novell MHS, X.400 mail systems, and IBM PROFS, using a single API approach. Messaging is illustrated in Figure 7.5.

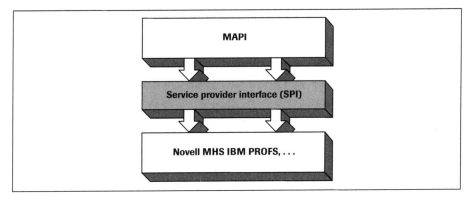

Figure 7.5 Messaging

It is important to realize that messaging covers a variety of applications beyond simple electronic mail. It includes applications like scheduling, forms, routing, and order processing. In order to integrate this functionality into a common applications environment, these APIs must support different directory system (addressing system) approaches, deal with maintaining and searching through large address books, and allow for the hierarchical storage of electronic mail.

Microsoft supports the following messaging APIs:

- Simple Microsoft Messaging API (MAPI)
- Common Messaging Call (CMC)
- Extended MAPI

These APIs essentially offer translational front-ends and required O/S services so that your application requiring messaging can work with a variety of messaging providers without modification and can also integrate messaging with the rest of the Microsoft application environment.

The architecture of MAPI is comprised of the following components:

- Messaging APIs
- Windows messaging subsystem
- Service provider interfaces (SPIs)

As with other Microsoft APIs, the messaging APIs make use of the SPI architecture. Each electronic messaging provider (e.g., IBM PROFS or the Internet) must have an SPI written for it in order for it to be programmable through the messaging APIs.

7.7.1 Simple Microsoft Messaging API (MAPI)

Simple MAPI allows you to develop simple messaging applications. It consists of the 12 most common API calls. An application can use these APIs to send, address, and receive messages. Messages can include data attachments and OLE objects. This level of functionality allows messaging applications to perform tasks such as form routing and purchase request processing. Simple MAPI includes an optional common user interface (dialogue boxes) so that developers can easily add a consistent look to their applications.

7.7.2 Common Messaging Call (CMC)

Common Messaging Call (CMC) is a standard developed in conjunction with the X.400 API Association (XAPIA) standards organization, e-mail providers, and user groups. CMC provides a set of ten API calls that are very similar in functionality to the calls offered by Simple MAPI. CMC provides the benefit of cross-platform support by an industry consortium. Extended MAPI, as we'll see in a moment, provides more flexibility; however, it is Windows-specific.

7.7.3 Extended MAPI

Extended MAPI adds strong object-oriented features and leverages the underlying messaging service's capabilities further. It is targeted toward more complex messaging applications involving the management of large amounts of information. Extended MAPI offers various object-oriented approaches to managing messaging-related information; however, it is not natively a COM interface. In fact, to create a messaging interface consistent with COM, Microsoft released a "COM wrapper" that encapsulates MAPI functions so that a developer can use a standard COM interface to access them. This COM wrapper is called *Active Messaging* and is part of what Microsoft calls *Collaboration Data Objects*.

A few observations can be made at this point. First, CMC is very similar to standard MAPI. It is arguable that, if straight MAPI meets your needs and you anticipate multiplatform requirements in the future, you might just use CMC. Note that some CMC-compliant platforms offer libraries that will convert between CMC and MAPI, which is easy enough because there is a core set of very similar functions between the two. Extended MAPI takes your software even farther away from the CMC standard by introducing its own brand of object abstraction and more functionality. Leveraging COM on top of Extended MAPI also takes you farther away from a multiplatform implementation.

Extended MAPI supports the use of hierarchically organized folders and messages. Folders contain messages. Messages contain attachments. Folder, messages, and attachments are treated as objects and therefore have their own individual properties. Extended MAPI provides a search engine function and provides tools to modify messages and store them back into their folders or into some other folder. Extended MAPI also provides the ability for event-driven notification of message arrival and storage, thereby allowing an application to receive an event notification in the event a message required by it is received from the messaging provider. Folders, messages, and attachments are all accessed through MAPI object structures. Extended MAPI address books are also structured in a hierarchy and include features for distribution lists, individual addresses, and so forth.

MAPI objects support polymorphism, so the same set of calls can be made to different objects. This reduces application development time by allowing for software reuse. For example, an application can use the same code to browse a list of messages and also to browse a list of attachments.

An important MAPI function is the MAPI Table Interface (IMAPITable) call. IMAPITable allows for the searching of an object made up of rows and columns of information. Examples of the use of this API function include searching through a large address book. The function also provides methods for sorting tables and navigating through them.

7.8 Telephony API (TAPI)

The *Telephony API* (TAPI) allows application programs to control telephony functions. It covers not only advanced services and media-stream access but also provides multiple application support and network/hardware independence:

- By allowing for the integration of services such as messaging, facsimile, and voice, TAPI enables the development of advanced interactive applications such as interactive voice-response systems and fax-back systems. Other capabilities include a visual interface to telephone features, personal communication management, voice input/output, integrated messaging, and integrated meetings.

- The underlying TAPI mechanism allows for automatic media-type switching to applications focused on a particular information type. Thus, for example, voice calls can be routed to the voice process while faxes can be routed to the fax process. This can be thought of as a data-content switching mechanism rather than the source/destination address form of switching we usually think of.

- Multiple applications can share TAPI-managed devices and cooperatively control access to incoming calls. Monitoring and logging of telephony information are supported.

- TAPI is designed to allow applications to interface with various telephone network functions, including Plain Old Telephone Service (POTS), ISDN, PBX, Centrex, Key Systems, cellular, and wireless.

TAPI functions are grouped as follows:

- Basic telephony, which supports POTS and allows for basic dialing of numbers and answering of calls.

- Supplementary telephony services, which support PBX-like features such as Hold, Transfer, Conference, and Park.

- Extended telephony services, whereby the API contains a mechanism that allows service provider vendors such as modem vendors and phone manufacturers to extend TAPI using vendor-specific extensions.

7.9 Microsoft Distributed Object Framework

7.9.1 Evolution of COM: The Art of All That Is "X"

Microsoft's object technology offers an alphabet soup of new and obsolete terminology and implementations. In this section, we will track the evolution of Microsoft's object technology. Figure 7.6 serves as a road map for this discussion.

Within the Windows operating system, objects had humble beginnings. One of the major motivations for objects within early versions of the Windows operating system was for the purpose of compound-document management and creation. This object technology provided the basis for structured storage management of multiple data objects within a document.

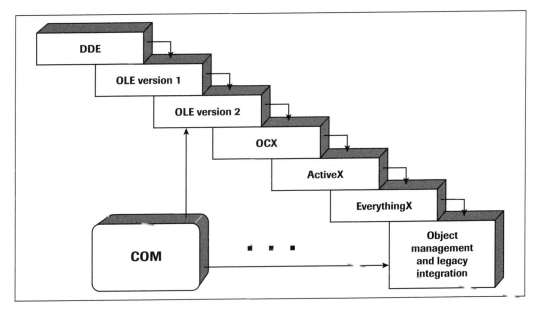

Figure 7.6 Evolution of Microsoft objects

To understand this first application, consider a spreadsheet or graph that you would like to integrate into a report. In the beginning of the Windows operating system, the solution to this, from the end user's perspective, was the clipboard. With the clipboard, you could cut and paste documents from one application into another; however, there was no link back to the original application. So, if you needed to modify your report, you had to go back to the original graphing program and modify it there. There was no way to directly modify the exact version of the graph you pasted into your word processor right there within the word processor.

Over time, though, we began to see drawbacks with this approach. What would happen if you needed to change your graph? Did you have to cut and paste that graph all over again, or could you modify it right there in your word processor? *Dynamic Data Exchange* (DDE) brought us closer to this functionality by providing a mechanism for two programs to share (link) data and to dynamically allow for changes made to the data by one program (the graphing program) to be known by the other (the word processor). DDE was a difficult facility to use, placing a heavy burden on application developers. While there are still applications supporting DDE, it is not the method of choice for new application development.

Object Linking and Embedding (OLE) version 1 was introduced in 1991 and was built on top of the existing DDE technology in an attempt to make its use easier for the programmer and more functional for the end user. Like its predecessor, DDE, it was focused on providing compound-document functionality, only this time in a considerably easier to use and more functional manner. OLE version 2 was released in 1993. OLE version 2 did not use DDE; instead, it used something new at the time—COM. In fact, OLE version 2 was the first product built on top of COM. Consequently, it is not necessarily the finest application written to COM, but it did break ground in the Windows environment and provided a reasonably robust compound-document capability.

OLE version 2 is backward-compatible with version 1. Version 2 added a number of new features, including

- In-place editing /activation, whereby a user double-clicks an embedded object and edits that document within the current application.

- Drag and drop data between applications, bypassing the clipboard altogether (from the user's perspective).

- OLE automation allowing all applications and associated data to be encapsulated and controlled by scripts and macros. With OLE automation, one application plays the role of the *OLE server* and the other as the *OLE controller,* sometimes also referred to as the *OLE client.*

Next came the *OLE Control Extension*(OCX). OCXs were supposed to replace Visual Basic controls. OCXs evolved into ActiveX controls. ActiveX objects were then positioned by Microsoft as dynamic executable content for download over the Internet.

One of the things Microsoft was forced to do early on was to establish expectations with developers that ActiveX controls should be lightweight and contain only what was needed, not the whole kitchen sink. Who wants to download a kitchen sink over their slower home dial-up Internet connection? The system's objective will always be to make such downloads no more painful than that of a small figure or a few pages of text over the average dial-up Internet connection. Later in this chapter, we will talk about ActiveX security.

COM is often described as providing *location transparency,* meaning that clients may execute a component running on a remote machine or on their local machine and they need not know the difference. Distributed

COM (DCOM), which we will discuss later, provides a mechanism for components to communicate with one another through a network by using RPC. COM objects can be written such that they are unconcerned with whether or not they are communicating with another object on the same computer or one across a network.

7.9.2 COM Wrapping: Microsoft Interface Definition Language (MIDL)

Like CORBA, COM has its own interface definition language that amounts to not much more than a wrapper around a program, as illustrated in Figure 7.7. All the options opened up by standardization of this wrapper, plus the object programming techniques that go along with such a set of wrapper agreements, make this technology not only complex but also very compelling.

The *Microsoft Interface Definition Language* (MIDL) is the programming language used to write these wrappers. MIDL provides a common ground between programming languages. While the syntax of MIDL resembles C++, it is language-independent, so you can use it with COBOL, C++, Ada, Java, or what have you.

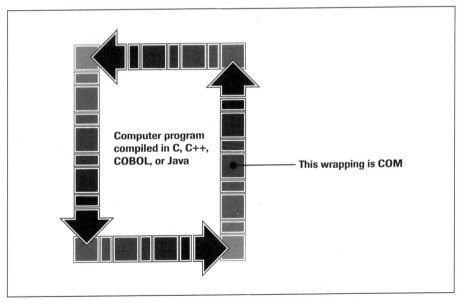

Computer program compiled in C, C++, COBOL, or Java

This wrapping is COM

Figure 7.7 COM wrapper

MIDL is based on the DCE RPC IDL we reviewed in Chapter 2. Microsoft extended the IDL to support the kind of instructions needed to specify COM interfaces (wrappers), such as COM-specific pointers to programming functions (methods).

7.9.3 COM: A Binary Standard

COM is a *binary* standard. That means COM components can be a Microsoft Windows dynamically linked library (.dll) file or an executable (.exe) file. A COM component is therefore not a collection of C or C++ source code instructions. It is a binary thing, something end users are more accustomed to. If you have Windows on your desktop, you have DLLs and EXE files all over your hard drive.

Java and COM

Microsoft allows Java applets to utilize COM through various mechanisms. These mechanisms utilize Microsoft COM extensions that allow the Java applets to run over Microsoft's Java Virtual Machine (JVM).

Note that Microsoft has extended Java beyond the JavaSoft standards in a number of areas. Some argue this means Microsoft Java is not really Java in the purest sense. The whole idea behind Java is that it can run on a variety of machines and platforms. If you add things to it so that it runs on only one machine or platform, then you are arguably defeating the purpose.

A DLL is a file that contains one or more functions that are compiled, linked, and stored separately from the process (computer program) that uses it. Windows maps a DLL into the address space of the calling process, making the DLL appear to be part of the executable—as if it were all linked up with it into one big EXE file and executed. This mapping can occur when the process is first started or even after it is started. If you go to your \windows\ system directory on your Windows desktop computer, assuming you have one, you will see all kinds of DLLs. Basically, COM DLLs are just special types of DLLs that conform to the COM interface wrapper (MIDL).

This binary component model offers some simple methods for software reuse. In fact, software reuse has been going on within Windows for a long time, even before COM was deployed. The previous paragraph mentioned the \windows\system directory. Have you ever deinstalled (removed) a Windows program and received a warning asking whether you wanted to delete a shared component? This is a DLL file that is shareable. The reason you are warned is that, in the event you installed some other software after the Windows program you are now removing, the Windows program may have noticed you had a DLL installed that it needs, so it did not install one for itself. If you now remove that shared file, this second program may stop running. So, shared components have pluses in that you can share them. They also have this downside of requiring configuration management. And, since most of the time, there is none, we are thankful that hard drive capacity is so inexpensive and is becoming less so.

COM components support *encapsulation* just as CORBA does because the client or remote component (in the case of DCOM) does not care about the implementation of the component, including what programming language the component was implemented in. If you are running an executable program on your computer, such as Corel Wordperfect or Microsoft Word, do you care whether it is written in C++ or COBOL? You care only about whether the program meets your needs. To execute the program, Windows does not pop up a dialogue box and ask, "Excuse me. Was this program written in C++, COBOL, or Visual Basic?" The same is true for COM components. If you want to upgrade a component, just make sure it implements the same COM interface (MIDL) as the older version of the component, and the client of the component, or remote object, should not know the difference. Object-literate folks sometimes refer to this as an *immutable interface*.

7.9.4 ActiveX Security

Early on, it seemed that the Microsoft marketing folks put forth the idea that you might just go to a Web page and experience it "fully" by getting *ActiveX* controls downloaded to your Web browser dynamically. People in the industry then took this as a way to posture ActiveX as being in battle with Java as the model for dynamic executable content on the Internet. There are a few problems with using ActiveX in your Web pages for visitors to "experience." One is that ActiveX is not necessarily multiplatform, so, if you have something other than Windows on the other end of the connection, such as a UNIX workstation or classic Apple Macintosh, it may not run it. The other problem is security.

As mentioned earlier, COM supports a binary model, which means that you can't tell what the program is going to do before it runs. The software is already compiled into the 1s and 0s of the machine language read by the target microprocessor, most likely one from Intel or compatible with it. You can't look at that stuff (an ActiveX DLL or EXE file) and tell whether the program is going to delete all the files on your hard drive or reboot your system, the latter being one of the first ActiveX controls made available on the Internet, not by a malicious developer, but by someone trying to prove this security vulnerability point.

Java as Dynamic Executable Content

Java capabilities-based security models such as those pioneered by Netscape allow for the Java program to be analyzed before running and for you, the user, to be given the right of first refusal for any hazardous activities the Java program might wish to undertake, such as rebooting your machine or deleting files from your hard drive. You can do this with Java precisely because it is *not* a binary model. Its byte code can be studied and forced to request permission for hazardous rights before being granted them.

A theoretical approach to solving this problem with a COM binary object is to create a separate operating environment (one restricting access to hazardous activities across the board to any applications running within this separate environment) within the client operating system whenever ActiveX components are dynamically downloaded and to force the components to run within the permissions of that environment. This is a feature that NT more or less has the groundwork for since operating environments can be started with predefined security resource permissions, but Microsoft has yet to release a shrink-wrapped desktop client version of Windows that can do that for those surfing the Internet and wanting to isolate ActiveX components to their own operating environment.

The primary solution to ActiveX security encouraged by Microsoft is *Authenticode*, which is an approach whereby you are able to identify the author of the ActiveX control and to make an "all-or-nothing" decision as to whether or not to trust the author (either complete trust or none at all, meaning you don't allow the component to run). Authenticode uses the public key cryptographic digital-signing and integrity-checking mechanisms we discussed in Chapter 2. This same kind of signing and integrity checking is implemented with a pure Java implementation also, but, in addition, Java offers the capabilities-based functions.

Experiential and Usage Patterns

The problem with the argument that Authenticode and ActiveX are fine for dynamic executable content is not as much a technical argument as it is an experiential and usage one. People do not necessarily surf the Internet and visit sites that they know and inherently trust. They just surf, finding their way from here to there, expecting the personal computer and Web browser to have security mechanisms in place to protect them from malicious Web sites. So, that might mean you could visit any site anywhere in the world today. What is the likelihood, once you get there, that its ActiveX Web page components were digitally signed using Authenticode? Many of these sites are mom-and-pop sites, people with little money or resources, language and cultural differences, governmental constraints, and so forth. Even if their ActiveX objects are digitally signed, what happens if something they give you is malicious but covers its tracks, deleting things all over the place on your hard drive, preventing you from even proving they infected you with something mean and nasty? This is the problem with using uncontrollable binary code as the thing you encounter dynamically as you surf the net.

The moral to this story is not that ActiveX components are bad. It is that downloading them dynamically over the network from sources you are not intimately familiar with (instead of from your IS department or a software vendor you know well) can be hazardous.

7.9.5 Containers

COM objects have *containers*, places where their execution is managed. Visual Basic and the Web browser (Internet Explorer or Netscape Communicator) are examples of containers on the client-side. On the server-side is the Microsoft Transaction Server (MTS), the ultimate container for COM objects involved in transitions. These container relationships are illustrated in Figure 7.8.

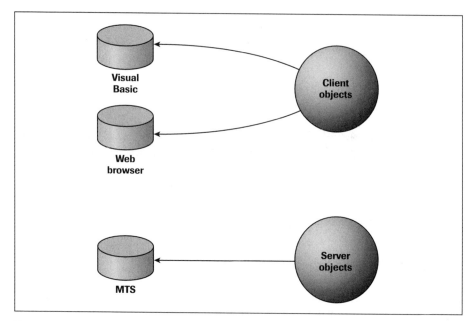

Figure 7.8 COM containers

7.9.6 COM, Clustering, and Middleware

Figure 7.9 is intended to illustrate that Microsoft's distributed architecture combines COM with a host of middleware functions that include transactions, databases, security, clustering, and multiple programming language support. It is Microsoft's ability to integrate these middleware technologies

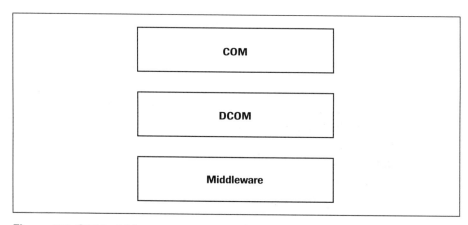

Figure 7.9 COM middleware

into shipping products that makes Microsoft's move into object technology such a significant event. Any one of these technologies alone is not so significant, but, combine them with object technology and deliver products, and you have a special occasion.

A Microsoft bid to enter IBM's home transaction-processing turf would seem to require that its clustering project, known as *Wolfpack,* succeed in one form or another. Described in the simplest of terms, *clustering* is a way of joining together computing resources (CPUs, hard drives, etc.) to enhance overall system performance (scalability) and reliability. Wolfpack would theoretically allow Microsoft NT servers to attempt to compete with the reliability and, ultimately, the scalability found in competing systems from IBM, DEC, and various UNIX operating system vendors. The first Wolfpack product does not attempt to provide the full clustering functionality (it excludes performance scalability) but instead allows a hot standby server to essentially mirror the main processing server in hot standby mode so that, if the main server fails, the hot standby can take over processing with little or no impact on the clients. We should keep in mind that clustering technology is quite complex and that companies such as IBM and DEC offer mature clustering products that have evolved over many years. Microsoft, as a relative newcomer, has its work cut out for itself.

With all the criticism heaped on IBM, much of it ends up being unfair when talking about IBM's high-end mainframe transaction-processing systems. These mainframes, which track your bank accounts and credit cards and process other high-availability transactions, are monuments to high technology and quality, offering well thought-out designs, and have years and years of testing and field experience. IBM has years of rich experience in clustering technologies. Its RS/6000 line, mainframes, and other systems offer a range of tried and tested clustering configurations. It also helps IBM that it controls both the hardware and the software, whereas, in this regard, it can be argued that because Microsoft supports a range of open hardware standards, its clustering development work is more complex.

7.9.7 Microsoft Message Queue Server (MSMQ)

COM now only supports a technique known as *synchronous messaging,* which may not optimally fit many of the real-world problems you have today, including transactional ones. *Synchronous* here means that it is assumed that messages exchanged with COM objects occur in sequence, and, if a missing message does not arrive, things wait until it does since the idea is that everything is synchronized.

An *asynchronous* event would mean that an object says something like, "OK, I haven't gotten that message yet, so instead I'll move on to this other thing I have to do until I receive that message." To deal with asynchronous messaging, Microsoft provides functionality in its *Microsoft Message Queue Server* (MSMQ). MSMQ was internally code-named *Falcon* during its development. MSMQ is not a separate Microsoft server product. Instead, it is integrated with the products that need it, which include servers such as MTS and Microsoft SQL Server, and the standard and enterprise versions of Windows NT. Without getting into detail on the mechanics of it (because that level of detail would take us outside of the focus of this book), let's just say the MSMQ enables asynchronous messaging between COM components by making up for what is missing within the current COM architecture.

7.9.8 Distributed COM (DCOM): COM with a Longer Wire

Microsoft describes *Distributed COM* (DCOM) as "COM with a longer wire." DCOM allows objects to communicate with one another through a network.

DCOM leverages a variant of Microsoft RPC called *Object RPC* to provide the communication path. As we learned in Chapter 2, Microsoft RPC itself is based on DCE RPC. DCOM operation is illustrated in Figure 7.10.

When utilizing DCOM, it is important to consider the performance implications of "chatty" exchanges between objects. It is usually best to try to group object calls and information exchanges between objects into a few large exchanges rather than many small ones. Each interaction between

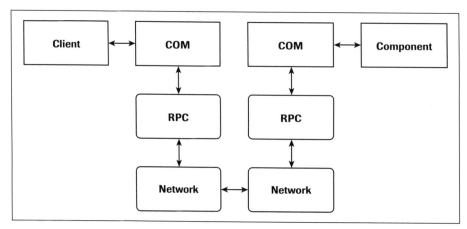

Figure 7.10 DCOM operation

remote objects consumes CPU resources on the two computers, and, as we learned in our networking studies, small packets can be a menace in your network. Since each packet has a fixed amount of overhead, it is usually best to have fewer larger packets, thereby reducing the total byte overhead for the exchange.

7.9.9 COM+

COM+ is an extension of COM and is compatible with it. COM+ includes some of the basic MTS functions within its core and adds some. COM+ provides an enhanced run time environment on top of which objects can execute.

The design goals of COM+ include simplifying the building of COM components as well as making it easier to add new COM functionality. The latter is achieved with a new extensibility mechanism called the *interceptor*. In a nutshell, the interceptor allows an application to leverage new COM functions by the setting of attributes rather than the implementation of new APIs. This can make things easier for the programmer, who now more or less throws a switch (sets an attribute) to signal the leveraging of a new service. Other features of COM+ include enhanced garbage collection capability to combat the infamous memory leak.

By incorporating the object management benefits of MTS into COM+ and then making COM+ available for the desktop, Microsoft enhances the ability to manage and develop objects on the client-side. Alternatives to MTS that are, at the same time, potential MTS integration targets, include IBM CICS, BEA's Tuxedo, Powersoft's Jaguar CTS, KIVA Enterprise server, NCR's TopEnd, and Transarc's Encina. All of these products also implement transaction processing.

7.10 Microsoft Transaction Server (MTS): Managing Objects in the Enterprise

7.10.1 MTS Services and Architecture

The *Microsoft Transaction Server* (MTS) allows a transaction to be implemented with COM objects—a very powerful combination. The services provided by MTS include

- Server-side object container, whereby MTS holds COM objects and provides an environment within which they can execute

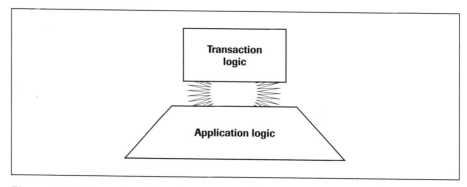

Figure 7.11 Separation of application and transaction logic by MTS

- Transaction processing (TP)
- COM interfaces for transactions
- Object pooling
- Resource sharing and efficiency
- Leveraging of MSMQ for transactional asynchronous communications

As shown in Figure 7.11, MTS separates application logic from transaction logic. You can develop your objects without worrying about the details of achieving the ACID principles because MTS takes care of the ACID part for you. This concept is a very powerful one and, if leveraged properly, can greatly reduce software development and maintenance costs.

An important part of MTS is the Microsoft Distributed Transaction Coordinator (MS-DTC). The MS-DTC is built into Microsoft SQL Server (version 6.5) and is intended to be part of NT version 5. The MS-DTC maintains the atomicity of transactions. The MS-DTC is Microsoft's TM.

Scalabilty is the challenge of MTS. It needs to scale to the processing of thousands of objects and, at the same time, meet the high availability requirements for financial institution applications and other mission-critical environments.

There are various standards for the protocols used between the TM and the RM as they work together to complete a transaction. MTS supports one developed by Microsoft called *OLE-Tx* and another from the X/Open standards group called *XA*. The MTS architecture is illustrated in Figure 7.12.

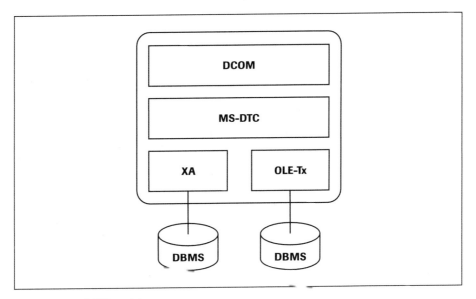

Figure 7.12 MTS architecture

7.10.2 MTS and Object Pooling

MTS implements a technique referred to as *object pooling*. Pooling is intended to make the management and execution of large numbers of objects more efficient, minimizing their resource requirements. By reusing object resources and other resources such as database connections, object pooling cuts back on the thrashing that will occur in systems having a lot of small high-frequency interactions as opposed to more efficient ones in which resource usage is grouped, or pooled together, and then shared among all those waiting in line to use them.

In order for an object to be poolable, it needs to be programmed so that it is *stateless*, meaning that it cannot keep data local to it and expect it to be around each time the object is called. This makes intuitive sense when you realize that the concept of pooling means that objects are *reused*. That's where we get the efficiency from. When an object is involved when you withdraw money from your bank account, for example, you don't want it to have data laying around from the previous withdrawal transaction (someone else's withdrawal) that might result in more money being deducted from your account than you actually withdrew. Being required to design components as stateless is the price we pay for the benefits gained from pooling. Designing components in such a way is typically more difficult up front for the average software developer, but the benefits gained here are in the long run, when the system is up and running, scaling well, and offering consistent reliability. Because MTS takes the hefty burden of maintaining the ACID properties of the transaction off the programmer's list of things to do, it also simplifies software development and maintenance.

7.10.3 MTS and Object Creationism

As mentioned earlier, MTS is a container for COM components, which means that an MTS COM component executes within an MTS server. The objects that MTS manages are within is own runtime environment, on the same machine as the MTS process itself. All MTS COM components must be DLLs, and they must implement a *class factory* to create objects. A class factory is implemented by the COM IclassFactory interface and is used to create objects of a specific class. This is the same function as carried out by the ORB in CORBA, as illustrated in Figure 7.13.

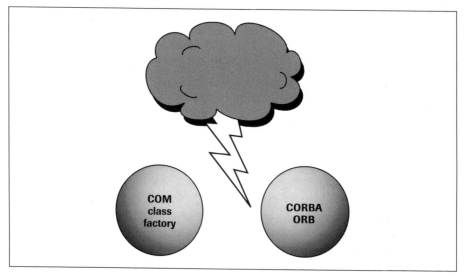

Figure 7.13 Object creationism

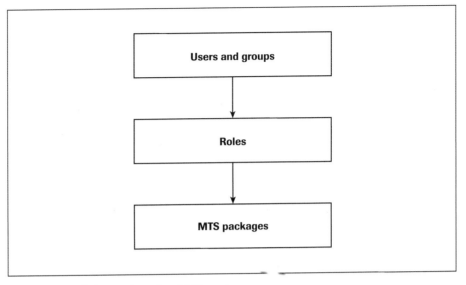

Figure 7.14 Roles assigned to MTS packages

7.10.4 MTS and Object Security

MTS leverages the same user and group directory service security mechanisms presented later in Chapters 8 and 9, so you have a common facility for managing user authentication and authorization (thank goodness). MTS extends the username/group concept by defining something called a *role*. Roles are yet another way to combine individuals and resources for the purposes of security. Users and groups are assigned roles. Objects that are part of a transaction are combined into *packages*. Roles are then assigned to packages, as illustrated in Figure 7.14. Depending upon the role you have been assigned, you will have certain permissions relative to a given MTS package.

MTS also supports another form of security called *client impersonation,* which sounds scary, and it is in the world of transaction management. Basically, with client impersonation, the MTS server adopts your username/group definition and effectively spoofs (proxies) your identity to databases and other resources within the network on your behalf. The advantage of impersonation is its ease of implementation. With impersonation, there is no need to assign and administer roles and worry about mapping them to packages or worry about the management of a new credential (the role) for all resources involved in the transaction.

While this may seem like a good and simple idea, it has its complications and drawbacks, the main one relating to performance. Here's why. If the MTS is forced to spoof each individual user to a given database, then it must dedicate a separate connection for each user it is spoofing. If 1,000 users are engaged in transactions, then that is 1,000 database connections. If, on the other hand, roles are used, then the MTS can maintain a single database connection (or more, but the point is that the decision is solely up to the MTS) with all the permissions it needs, and it remains the responsibility of the MTS, through the role-based mechanism, to control access to that database connection, not the database itself, which is what is done with the client impersonation method.

7.11 COM Transaction Integrator for CICS and IMS (Cedar): Integrating with SNA/Mainframe Technology

Cedar was the internal code name for the Microsoft project arguably aimed at moving into IBM's bottom-line business, that of transaction processing. The technology produced from this project is now called the *COM Transaction Integrator for CICS and IMS*. That's quite a mouthful, but then again, it is a reasonably powerful capability, so perhaps it deserves such a long name. Here, let's just abbreviate it as *CTI*.

CTI provides a bridge between the desktop, NT-server-based applications and the world of IBM CICS and IMS transaction-based mainframe systems. CTI allows transactions to be looked at through the eyes of the NT environment, which can choose to incorporate mainframes for certain processing requirements, which is possibly what Microsoft wants most, and as the reverse, in which the NT environment is secondary to the major horse-power, processing, and storage elements of the mainframe, which IBM might prefer. CTI does not take the more traditional screen-scraping approach to integrating with mainframe systems. Instead, it interacts directly with the applications on the mainframe environment and the transactions it manages.

CTI connects to the mainframe using the LU6.2 connectivity capabilities of Microsoft SNA Server. In accomplishing its mission, CTI acts as a generic proxy for the mainframe. Figure 7.15 illustrates the CTI system.

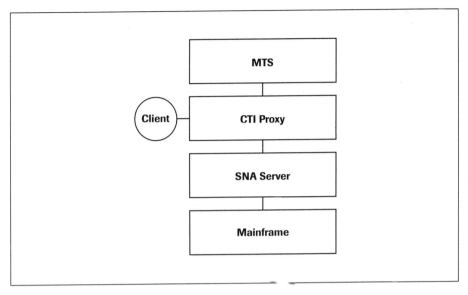

Figure 7.15 Cedar (CTI) architecture

The figure is a bit deceptive because CTI is now directly integrated with Microsoft SNA Server and MTS and is not a separate product. However, for understanding its function, it is helpful to break it out in this way.

Object calls from the client to the mainframe are intercepted by CTI. CTI then redirects those calls to the appropriate transaction processor on the mainframe or within the NT environment. CTI acts as an intermediary for all output and return values from the mainframe. CTI also handles data format (representation) incompatibilities between the NT and IBM mainframe environments. Another nice feature of CTI is that it does not require that any special software be loaded into the mainframe.

7.12 COM, CORBA, and JavaBeans: Friendly Fire and Interoperability

CORBA was produced by an organization focused on standards and open participation. COM, in contrast, evolved as a series of solutions to intermediate product requirements and did not evolve out of a standards body. So, right there are the seeds for major differences. CORBA was designed by committee as a top-down, heterogeneous standard to run across many platforms, whereas COM was primarily designed by Microsoft.

CORBA is multiplatform by design. Vendors are implementing it for many versions of UNIX, the Apple Macintosh, Windows, IBM's full line of computer systems, and others. While there have been a surprising number of product announcements relating to COM availability for some UNIX platforms, critics still argue that, when you implement your applications with COM, you are committing in one way or another to Microsoft products. Let's take a moment to compare COM with a few of its competitors.

7.12.1 COM Versus Java RMI Versus CORBA

Java *Remote Method Invocation* (RMI) is a mechanism by which Java applets can invoke one another and which allows them to function as distributed objects. Therefore, Java RMI can be viewed as a COM competitor. One important distinction to make is that the primary focus of Java RMI is on a pure Java environment, whereas component models such as COM and CORBA inherently support multiple programming languages including Java. If you are entirely sold on the Java concept, then committing to Java RMI may be right for you. However, as discussed in Chapter 2, Java can be viewed as a programming language, a middleware framework, or both. If you stick with Java as a programming language mainly and leverage component models such as CORBA or COM, you get the benefit of an environment that by its nature supports many programming languages. Of course, you can mix and match all of these if you wish. Some argue, for example, that, since it is evident that COM dominates the desktop due to Microsoft's role, the approach to take is COM on the desktop interoperating with CORBA implemented on servers. (We'll look at COM/CORBA interoperability in a moment.)

As for the COM versus CORBA debate, it may come down to religion, politics, and the importance of freedom of choice inside your organization. CORBA is open and multiplatform. COM has made some degree of progress in the UNIX area; however, its roots are with Microsoft.

On the Java RMI versus CORBA debate, it is expected that a number of RMI implementations themselves will leverage CORBA, and, therefore, in some cases, you may be actually utilizing CORBA when you choose RMI. However, in such a case, the software you write may either contain CORBA IDL or Java IDL that itself is translated to CORBA IDL. Some argue that you might as well just start with the CORBA IDL within your Java applet and skip the RMI step.

7.12.2 COM/CORBA Interoperability

On the subject of interoperability between COM and CORBA, there are a number of products available that aspire to provide this functionality. COM and CORBA are certainly close enough that interoperability is achievable. Examples include the NEO product from Sun as well as implementations of IONA's ORBIX CORBA product. There is also an OMB COM/CORBA interworking specification that provides various guidelines and approaches for interoperability.

One approach taken by some of these products is to essentially implement a CORBA ORB at the client-side, as shown in Figure 7.16, and convert COM to CORBA right there in the workstation. The weight (size) of the CORBA ORB and associated CORBA/COM interoperability bridge on the workstation-side is clearly an issue for IS managers. Those implementations that are available vary widely in this regard.

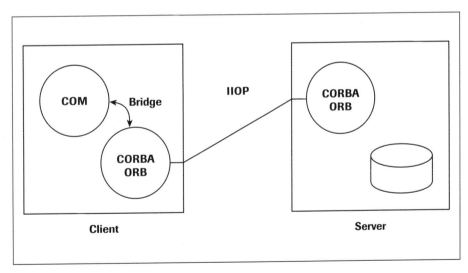

Figure 7.16 COM/CORBA interoperability

7.13 Universal Data Architecture (UDA), ActiveX Data Objects (ADO), and OLE-DB

Microsoft has integrated ActiveX/DCOM object technology into solving the problem of generalized data access and data sharing between disparate applications such as e-mail, SQL databases, and project management software. However, to date, it seems primarily focused on consolidating various Microsoft database APIs that have evolved over the years into a single homogenous COM-based API. This solution is called the *Universal Data Architecture* (UDA). UDA is illustrated in Figure 7.17.

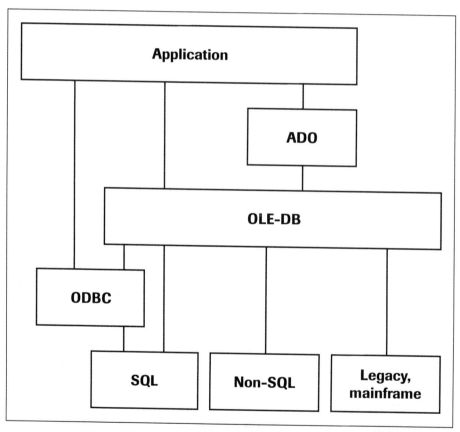

Figure 7.17 Universal Data Architecture (UDA)

Active Data Objects (ADO) and a new object-based lower-level data access API called *OLE-DB* combine to provide a generalized approach to looking at data from an object-oriented perspective. OLE-DB is a Microsoft COM-based API. Since it is COM-based and not specifically OLE, its name is somewhat confusing. These two object APIs consume lower-level APIs such as ODBC. These APIs will remain under the covers, underneath ADO.

ADO is built around the concept of recordsets. A *recordset* is a collection of records that can be manipulated as a group. You can read records from the recordset, add new records into the recordset, update records, delete records, and so forth. All these actions are translated by ADO into something the underlying data access mechanism can understand.

7.14 Internationalization

Windows allows developers to implement applications supporting international character sets using a form of data representation known as *Unicode*. Unicode was developed by Apple and Xerox in 1988. In 1991, the consortium grew to include a larger number of industry players.

Alphabets supported by Unicode include Arabic, Chinese Bopomofo, Cyrillic (Russian), Greek, Hebrew, Japanese Kana, Korean Hangul, Latin (English), and others. Unicode is a 16-bit representation and therefore can be used to represent approximately 65,000 different characters. Based on the languages defined to date, only 34,000 characters have been assigned.

While Windows NT fully supports Unicode, the initial release of Windows 95 requires the use of various workarounds that require the programmer to manage explicit buffers holding the specific character information. This is far less convenient than the NT implementation.

7.15 Conclusions

From this chapter, it is safe to conclude that Microsoft has amassed, over time, a rich network application framework. It offers a broad and reasonably integrated range of products and solutions. However, as mentioned in the introduction to this chapter, the debate for using Microsoft products and Microsoft-controlled standards usually includes a heated discussion about reliance on a single vendor and freedom of choice. It may be interesting to note that such a debate works against Microsoft in the desktop and server arena, where it dominates, and, ironically, it actually works for Microsoft in the transaction-processing large-scale electronic commerce area since companies such as IBM play such a dominant role there. At the same time, many continue to not take an "all-or-nothing" view of Microsoft technology, leveraging open standards and interoperable product offerings that allow them to maintain a comfortable enough degree of choice while recognizing and taking advantage of the strengths in Microsoft's products.

FOR FURTHER STUDY

1. D. Chappell. *ActiveX and OLE.* Redmond, Wash.: Microsoft Press, 1996.

2. D. Fleet, M. Warren, J. Chen, and A. Stojanovic. *Teach Yourself Active Web Database Programming in 21 Days.* Indianapolis, Ind.: Sams.net Publishing, 1997.

3. D. R. Grimes. *Professional DCOM Programming.* Birmingham, England: Wrox Press Ltd., 1997.

4. K. A. Jamsa and K. Cope. *Internet Programming.* Las Vegas, Nev.: Jamsa Press, 1995.

5. Microsoft. *Microsoft OLE-DB 1.1 Programmer's Reference and Software Development Kit.* Redmond, Wash.: Microsoft Press, 1997.

6. Microsoft. *Readings on Microsoft Windows and WOSA.* Redmond, Wash.: Microsoft Press, 1995.

7. Microsoft. *Microsoft Windows NT Server Resource Kit: Technical Information and Tools for the Support Professional for Window NT Server Version 4.0.* Redmond, Wash.: Microsoft Press, 1996.

8. J. Richter. *Advanced Windows: The Developer's Guide to the Win32 API for Windows NT 3.5 and Windows 95.* Redmond, Wash.: Microsoft Press, 1995.

9. W. D. Schwaderer. *C Programmer's Guide to NetBIOS.* Indianapolis, Ind.: Sams, 1988.

10. R. Sessions. *COM and DCOM.* New York: Wiley, 1998.

11. A. K. Sinha. *Network Programming in Windows NT.* Reading, Mass.: Addison-Wesley, 1996.

12. A. Dickman. *Designing Applications with MSMQ.* Reading, Mass.: Addison-Wesley, 1998.

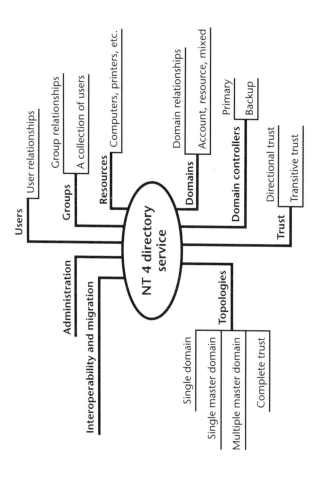

CHAPTER 8

The NT 4 Directory Service

CHAPTER HIGHLIGHTS		
Topic	**Benefits**	**Experience**
NT 4 Directory Service	To administer network-wide NT file and resource permissions in some scalable fashion, you use a directory service.	The NT 4 directory service architecture, while offering the benefit of being simple and straightforward at the start, can, without proper planning, quickly become complex and unmanageable as the enterprise grows.
Users, Groups, Resources, and Domains	Users, groups, resources, and domains provide the basis for the NT 4 organizational structure.	You need to think about how you will organize your network using these structural elements up-front to reflect the way your company is run and how it does its business, not simply in reaction to network and user growth.
Trust management	The ability to inherit permissions within the directory service is called *trust management*. It can simplify the administrator and network designer's life considerably— or make it enormously complex.	We will explore the trust management drawbacks of the NT 4 directory service. In the next chapter we'll consider how NT 5 improves upon NT 4.

8.1   Introduction

Microsoft's core *NT 4 directory service* solves two fundamental and important problems within the enterprise today: (1) that of allowing resources (workstations, servers, printer, files, directories, etc.) to be organized and located within the network and (2) that of controlling access to those resources. While relatively straightforward and workable for small-to-medium-sized companies, the NT 4 directory service does not scale well for larger networks.

Microsoft pursued a proprietary strategy with the NT 4 directory infrastructure and also did not fully integrate enterprisewide directory functions into a common framework. For example, the Microsoft Exchange e-mail directory service is separate from the core NT 4 directory service.

Still, though, the NT 4 directory service is a workable, deployable system and is simple enough for the average administrator to grasp. Other alternatives available to Microsoft engineers at the time of NT 4 architectural planning may have appeared too complex and impractical, such as X.500 or portions of the DCE architecture.

NT 4 does, however, provide APIs that allow for some level of integration with directory service products from other vendors. For example, APIs exist allowing for the integration of an external username/password scheme with Microsoft's. Netscape leveraged these APIs so that administrators could define username/passwords within the NT environment once and use those same username/password combinations with Netscape's Web HTTP basic authorization access control mechanism. This integration was performed leveraging the Netscape LDAP server. This is a welcome feature for weary IS administrators who tire of configuring the same user account twice in two different systems.

Proprietary versus open debates aside, the NT 4 directory service does indeed work and has been widely deployed across the world. In this chapter, we will explore this technology in some detail. We will even explore the parallels between human relationships and the NT 4 trust model as an added bonus.

In Chapter 9 , we will cover Microsoft's next architecture in the directory service foray, Active Directory. This architecture is slated to be part of NT 5, and it addresses many of the shortcomings found in the NT 4 directory architecture.

8.2   Directory Structure

Within an NT environment, the network is represented in terms of *users, groups* (groups of users), and *resources* (computers, printers, etc.). NT 4 allows administrators to organize users, groups, and resources into *domains.* Figure 8.1 illustrates an NT 4 domain.

Domains make it easier for users to locate and browse resources. The reason is that the Windows user interface is hierarchical and uses domains as an important part of the hierarchy. A network leveraging domains can also be easier to administer, allowing for network changes to be localized to a particular domain, for permissions to be defined on a per-domain basis, and for a great many other reasons we will explore.

It is important to note that domains are logical organizational tools, not necessarily physical ones. To prove this point, we could have, for example, one office in Tokyo, one in the United States, and another in France. We could take one user from each office and place that user into a single domain. We are not required to make the Tokyo office one domain, the U.S. office another domain, and France yet another.

{ DOMAINS (USERS, GROUPS, RESOURCES)] [allowing (RESOURCES (ws, servers, printers files, directories) To be organized and located within the network and controlling access]

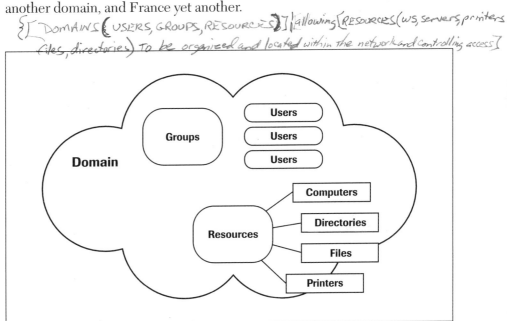

Figure 8.1   An NT 4 domain

So then, what is the basis for deciding what goes into one domain versus another? The usual approach is to put users who typically work together into the same domain. Resources accessed by a common collection of folks, say, the human resources department, are placed into their own domain. The network topology itself must also be carefully considered. We will discuss the impact of domain controllers (DCs) connected remotely through the network a few times in this chapter.

Suppose, for example, you work for a company named Speedy Skating Supply, Inc. Speedy is involved in the design and manufacture of recreational products and has three lines of business: in-line skates, snowboards, and safety equipment. You have been tasked with designing Speedy's directory infrastructure. You may find it convenient to take advantage of domains to organize people and resources. For example, you could assign a separate domain for each of the three business units, as illustrated in Figure 8.2.

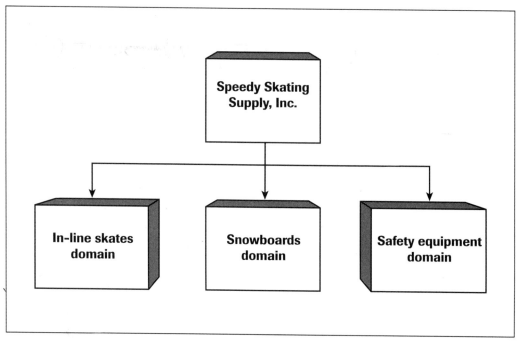

Figure 8.2   Speedy's organizational structure with one domain per business unit

Common Mistakes

A common misconception is that a user is the same as a workstation. That is, if you routinely access certain files on a remote server from your laptop PC, then you need to have that same PC with you to access those files from anywhere in the network. Not true. Instead, you can actually log in from another workstation in the network, provided permissions are set that allow you and the alternative workstation to do so (meaning an absence of route filtering or other security restrictions), and you can access those same remote server files from that alternative workstation. Therefore, your identity, defined by your username, is different from your workstation.

You have probably been wondering how user, group, and domain information is shared across the network. As you might have expected, specific network servers are assigned to perform the tasks associated with the configuration, synchronization, and distribution of this directory information. These servers are called *domain controllers* (DCs). DCs maintain directory information in the *Security Accounts Manager* (SAM) database. While a single NT server hardware platform configured as a DC can perform other tasks in addition to fulfilling its DC responsibilities, these responsibilities are sufficiently mission-critical in nature that you may choose to dedicate a server to this function in each domain.

There are two types of domain controllers: One is called a *primary domain controller* (PDC), and the other more limited version is called a *backup domain controller* (BDC). Each domain has one PDC and may be configured with one or more BDCs. PDCs from different domains communicate with one another to share information and to keep network directory information up to date. PDCs also perform user authentication. That is, when users log into their domain from their NT workstations, the PDC can verify the validity of each user's password.

BDCs are more limited in their capability. They contain read-only versions of the SAM database. Therefore, BDCs cannot be used to reconfigure a user's account, change membership in a group, and so forth. They can, however, be used for user authentication. The primary role of the BDC is to sit there, loyal and ready, in the event the PDC fails. When and if such a failure does occur, it is important to note that the BDC does not automatically take over the PDC function. Instead, the administrator must manually intervene

~~nd configure the BDC to take over and must disable the malfunctioning~~
~~PDC if it has not completely crashed already.~~

Design Tip

One little-known capability of the BDC is its ability to authenticate users—that is, to verify that a user's password is correct when the user logs into the domain. This is a nice capability to consider when you are designing large networks. While BDCs instigate traffic across the network so that they can stay synchronized with the PDC, with this authentication capability, BDCs are also capable of speeding up response time for user login requests and also eliminating the transmission of those requests across the network.

8.3   The Application of Groups Within Domains

Within a domain, we can restrict access by ~~assigning users to groups.~~ Groups ~~can be assigned permissions as a single unit,~~ which can greatly simplify things for the administrator. For example, suppose there are certain confidential files to which only the managers (Bob, Judy, and Paul) in Speedy's human resources department should have access. The administrator could address this challenge by creating an HR group and by placing Bob, Judy, and Paul into this group. The administrator could then easily assign that ~~group access~~ to highly confidential employee records as well as access to other resources to which only human resources managers should have access. Assigning these privileges individually to Bob, Judy, and Paul is three times the effort compared with configuring them just once for the entire group.

Another important characteristic of groups is that ~~one group can contain another group.~~ So, for example, we could create a World_Wide_Marketing group and include in it the following groups: European_Mktg, US_Mktg, Asian_Mktg, South_America_Mktg, and ROW_Mktg. Furthermore, European_Mktg could be comprised of groups including France_Mktg, UK_Mktg, Italy_Mktg, and so forth.

There are two types of groups: local and global. A *local* group is defined on a particular NT server only, and the group's existence is not advertised to other computers by the directory service. In contrast, a *global* group is known by the domain directory service, and, therefore, the group is known by all workstations and servers within the domain in which the global group is defined and in any other domains that trust the domain in which the global group is defined (we'll discuss domain trust later).

8.4   Domains in More Detail

One NT 4 design technique is to construct a given domain such that it contains only resources, or only users and groups, or a mixture of the two. Domains that contain only users and groups are called *account domains.* Domains that include only resources are called *resource domains.* As you may have guessed, *mixed domains* contain users, groups, and resources. This technique allows us to confine tasks such as adding and deleting users and groups to a particular domain and to focus the configuration and access control for resources in another domain. It also allows us the flexibility to define domains with fewer restrictions, allowing them to contain users, groups, and resources, where needed.

Returning to the task of designing Speedy's directory service infrastructure, we could apply this technique. In doing so, we might assign each of Speedy's three divisions two domains, one for resources and one for accounts. That would be six domains, two for each business unit, as illustrated in Figure 8.3.

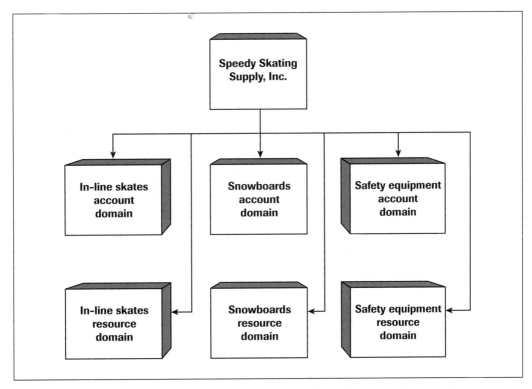

Figure 8.3   Speedy's organizational structure with two domains per business unit

8.5   Domains and Groups

Continuing with the Speedy, Inc. design example, we could define different departments within each of the account domains within each business unit. For example, the human resources department's user accounts and the product development department's user accounts might be placed in separate groups within each business unit. That would mean that each account domain (recall there are three of them in our imaginary company) would have two groups defined, one for product development and another for human resources. That would be a total of six groups for the company.

8.6   Access Control Lists

Thus far, we have alluded to resource permissions and privileges; however, we have not discussed how they are assigned. NT 4 offers an ACL facility whereby permissions can be associated with resources. For example, if you are administering the payroll-processing NT server and there is a particular file you want only the HR group to access, say, the payroll.dbf file, then you would define the ACL on the server where payroll.dbf resides.

Why Is It Done This Way?

Sometimes there are heated debates about whether an ACL should be stored on the server containing the file for which access control is being defined or should be defined at some central server dedicated to storing and managing ACLs. NT 4 implements the former. The advantage of the latter approach is that all your ACLs are available in one place, instead of on all the remote servers. By having them in one place, the argument is that things are easier to manage. The problem, however, with doing this is that the centralized ACL server needs to be synchronized with the file structures on servers in the network in some way. For example, suppose you want to define an ACL that says the file /security/marketing/press.doc on the server named PUNKSTER should be accessible only by the user Christine_W. If the file press.doc is moved to another directory, the centralized ACL server would need to know that. So, by centralizing the ACL storage, we create a more complicated synchronization challenge.

ACLs are considered a *property* of the resource. For example, a property of the payroll.dbf file is that the HR group has read/write permission to it. When you organize files into directories, you can assign ACL properties to an entire directory instead of to each file individually. For example, the HR group could be given read access to all files in the directory Employee_Health_Provider_Elections.

8.7 Trust Management

Domains are administratively separate entities, unless they are configured to *trust* each other. Similar to separate autonomous systems (ASs) on the Internet, domains need to be explicitly configured to share information with each other. Consider two domains, domain A and domain B. If A is configured to trust B, then A will allow users configured in domain B to potentially access its resources. If this trust is not configured, then A will not allow B's users to attempt to access its resources.

In case you are wondering how one domain's PDC knows whether or not to trust another, this is done via a shared secret. The administrators of the two trusting domains agree on a secret that only the two of them know. When a PDC starts up, it contacts all remote PDCs for which trust is configured and challenges each for the preconfigured shared secret. If the remote PDC knows the shared secret, then trust is established; otherwise, it is not. A shared secret can also be thought of as a password known only by the two PDCs.

8.8 Directionality of Trust and Human Relationships

In life, if you trust someone, it does not necessarily mean he or she trusts you, and vice versa. So, in life, trust is **directional**. It is also directional in the NT 4 world. For example, just because domain A trusts domain B's users does not mean that B trusts A's users.

In life, directional trust makes things more complicated for the untrusted party. If you trust someone, why can't he or she just trust you? So, too, in the NT 4 world. Administrators have to configure trust in both directions, which means twice the work. Of course, this is valuable and needed flexibility, but that still does not make it fun. Figure 8.4 illustrates directional trust.

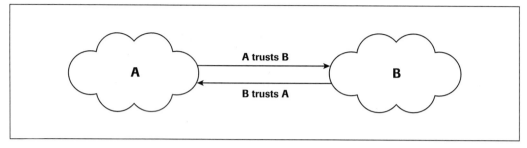

Figure 8.4 Directional trust

Now we come to the topic of **transitive** trust. Let's again consider domain A and domain B, but let's introduce domain C. Suppose that the following trust relationships exist:

> A trusts B.
> B trusts A.
> B trusts C.
> C trusts B.

Basically, what we are saying here is that A fully trusts B and B fully trusts C. The question is, does this mean that A trusts C or C trusts A? With NT 4, the answer is no, as illustrated in Figure 8.5.

In order for A and C to trust each other, this trust must be specifically requested by the administrators of A and C. This means that creating hierarchies of domains in which trust flows upward is not possible with NT 4.

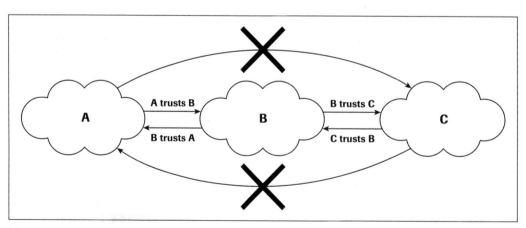

Figure 8.5 Trust Isn't Transitive

In summary, *NT 4 trust is not transitive.* This limitation is perhaps the biggest drawback of the NT 4 directory service and is why NT is referred to as "flat," meaning it is hard or impossible to elegantly configure and maintain multilevel hierarchical relationships among administrative entities. As we will see later, Active Directory solves this flatness problem.

8.9   Summary of Design Rules

Table 8.1 summarizes key design variables and rules we have studied thus far. Note that there are enough variables and limitations in the design process to get us into real trouble if we are not careful. We will be getting a little more detailed in the following sections, so a solid understanding of these rules will be helpful.

Table 8.1 Design Variables and Rules

Design Variable	Design Rule
User relationships	Users can be placed into groups.
Groups and group relationships	There are two types of groups: local and global. Groups can contain other groups.
Resources	Workstations, servers, printers, files, directories, and so forth are considered resources.
Domains	Users, groups, and resources can be assigned to domains.
Domain types	There are three domain types: account, resource, and mixed.
Domain relationships	Domains cannot contain other domains. Instead, relationships between domains are managed via the configuration of trust.
Trust relationships	Trust is directional. Trust is not transitive.
Primary domain controller (PDC)	There is one PDC per domain. It holds the read/write master version of the Security Accounts Manager (SAM) database for the domain. PDCs authenticate users.
Backup domain controller (BDC)	A domain can be configured with one or more BDCs. BDCs back up the domain's PDC. A BDC contains a read-only copy of the SAM database. The BDC is capable of performing user authentication.

8.10 Directory Service Topologies

In order to provide some order and a basic framework of examples for the directory service design process, we can think in terms of four fundamental directory service topologies: single domain, single master domain, multiple master domain, and complete trust. Let's now explore these topologies.

8.10.1 Single Domain

With *single domain* topology, everyone and everything is placed into a single domain. This method of organization is exactly what it seems, which is not much organization at all. If you have a small network to deal with, say, less than 50 users, this approach may work. For anything larger, chaos can ensue.

The advantage of single domain architecture is that you need not worry about managing trust relationships between domains. Here are the disadvantages:

- In terms of performance, you have one PDC servicing all users, which means that it is burdened with processing all directory service functions for all users. So, this amounts to a potential performance problem.

- As for reliability, you are fully dependent on a single PDC. If it fails, the switch-over to the BDC had better go well; otherwise, you don't just have one division of your company out of work, you have the whole company twiddling its collective thumbs. It is important to note that this switch-over must be done manually.

- With regard to changes and growth, since you don't have any domains, you have no means of organizing resources by department or what have you. So, as your network grows, as pride of ownership and control grow between the various departments in your company, and as arguments break out along the lines of "That's *our* color printer—we bought it with *our own* engineering budget, and marketing is *not* allowed to use it!", you have no quick solution because you have not created separate domains.

8.10.2 Single Master Domain

With *single master domain* architecture, we maintain one special domain called the *master domain*. All other domains are configured to trust this domain, but not vice versa. That is, one-way trust relationships are defined. An example implementation of this architecture is illustrated in Figure 8.6.

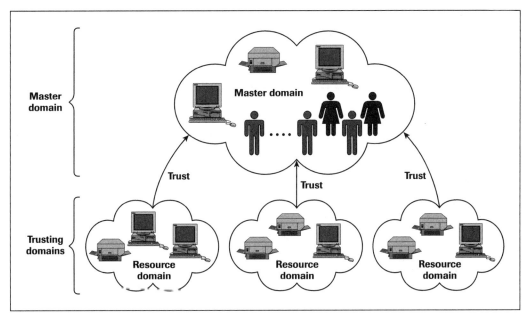

Figure 8.6 Master domain model

With this configuration, all users are defined in one domain, the master domain. This allows all accounts to be administered within the same PDC—that is, centrally. Let's look at some of the key characteristics of this topological approach:

- If global groups are defined within the master domain, then all domains will know about the global groups since all other domains trust the master domain.
- All users are authenticated within the master domain.
- Users defined in the master domain can access the resource domains since these resource domains have been configured to trust the master domain.
- Note that, if one of the resource domains is converted to a mixed domain, meaning that one or more users are defined in that domain, then those users will not be able to access resources in any of the other domains since none of them have been configured to trust the mixed domain.

Under what conditions might the master domain model be considered? The most obvious one is where users are administered by one central IS department. The next topology we will study, multiple master domain, is suited for distributed IS departments.

8.10.3 Multiple Master Domain

The *multiple master domain* model is illustrated in Figure 8.7. Instead of having just one master domain as we did with the single master approach previously discussed, we have many. All master domains may be configured to fully trust each other (two-way), as shown in the figure. Within this architecture, if the domain is not a master domain, then it is therefore considered a trusting domain. Trusting domains can be configured to trust one or more master domains. As we can see from all the arrows in Figure 8.7, the maintenance of trust relationships can get quite complicated.

What are the applications of such an architecture? In your company, the IS department might be distributed, meaning that each division might have its own collection of administrators. Returning to our Speedy, Inc. example, the in-line skating division might have its own IS department, the snowboards division another, and the safety equipment division yet another. In this case, you could use a separate master domain for each business unit, and the IS staff for each business unit could have control over their division's domain but not over any other division's domain.

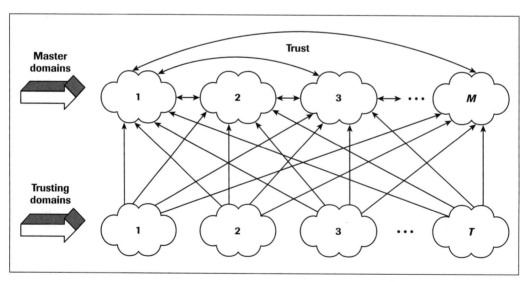

Figure 8.7 Multiple master domain model

One benefit of the multiple master domain approach is that network performance within a division's domain does not degrade as more users are added to some other division's domain. The reason is that each domain has its own PDC, so only that PDC is affected by the burden of processing an additional user.

8.10.4 Complete Trust

In life, complete and unbridled trust can be a dangerous thing. This is also true for directory architectures. With the *complete trust* approach, there are multiple domains in the network, but each domain is configured to trust every other domain. With this approach, separate IS administrators can manage their individual kingdoms (domains), and, because all domains trust each other, users can potentially access resources in every other domain subject to the ACL definitions of each individual resource. The problem with this architecture is that all those trust relationships have to be maintained. If you have M domains, then you have $M\times(M-1)$ trust relationships to manage. To see this, you might draw some domains, interconnect them with arrows in each direction, and count up all the arrows.

8.11 Interoperability and Migration

Other than for integration with SAM username/password mechanism, an example of which was given relative to Netscape's LDAP server, NT 4's approach to integrating with competing directory services, such as Novell's NDS, is to more or less displace them, not coexist with them. This means that Microsoft provides a migration tool that allows the administrator to transfer data configured within NDS to NT 4 . The idea is that, after you complete the data transfer, you would remove NDS from your network. This approach is not practical for many organizations due to their heavy investment in Novell-based applications. Third-party products are available from companies such as NetVision and others that allow the NT 4 directory service and NDS to interoperate in various ways, thereby allowing real-time coexistence of both directory services.

Microsoft has stated that it intends to include native NDS support in Windows 98, meaning that a Windows-98-based workstation could directly access an NDS server. This would alleviate the need to integrate NDS directly with the NT directory service and would instead place the burden on the client to work with different directory services. In Chapter 10, the NDS for NT product from Novell will be discussed. Another approach to solving the same problem will exist when Active Directory and NT 5 are released. Because Active Directory and NDS both support LDAP, they could be integrated via LDAP, in which case the existence of multiple directory services would theoretically be able to be made more transparent to the Windows workstation client.

8.12 Conclusions

The NT 4 domain directory service solves the fundamental problem of organizing users, groups of users, and resources within the enterprise network. Though Windows-proprietary, the NT 4 directory service technology offers the advantage of being simpler and easier to grasp than some of the more open approaches available to Microsoft at the time NT 4 was designed. The NT 4 directory service architecture does not scale well as the organization grows and changes, and it offers administrative complexities that can increase the cost of managing the network as well as increase the probability of the introduction of a trust configuration error, which can be viewed as a security problem. If you are not careful, you could end up with the network illustrated in Figure 8.8. Is this organization?

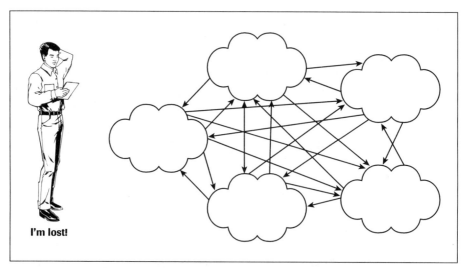

Figure 8.8 Organizational chaos

A summary of the drawbacks of the NT 4 directory service follows. You might use this summary as the basis for understanding the advantages of Microsoft's next architecture, Active Directory, as well as the other alternatives:

- The domain model, because it is essentially flat, is limiting and increases network management cost and complexity as the organization grows in size and changes in structure. Much of this centers on the transitive trust issue and the inability to nest domains.

- Complexity breeds errors. As we saw, it is very easy to make an error when configuring trust relationships. So, it could be argued that the probability of a security vulnerability being introduced into the network increases as directory configuration complexity increases.

- The BDC has a read-only copy of the SAM database. You cannot perform administration at a BDC.

- Note that, while the BDC replicates the SAM database, other files are important for operation, such as scripts and so forth, that require replication but that are not automatically replicated. The administrator must remember to configure replication for these files as a separate step. It is not out-of-the-box automatic.

- Microsoft Exchange Mail Server uses a separate directory service for e-mail addressing. Therefore, the network administrator must maintain multiple directory services inside the organization.

FOR FURTHER STUDY

1. K. Siyan. *Windows NT Server 4: Professional Reference.* Indianapolis, Ind.: New Riders Publishing 1996.
2. S. A. Sutton. *Windows NT Security Guide.* Reading, Mass.: Addison Wesley Longman, 1997.

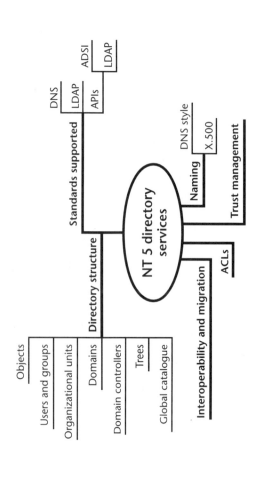

NT 5 directory services

Standards supported
- DNS
- APIs
  - LDAP
  - ADSI
  - LDAP

Directory structure
- Objects
- Users and groups
- Organizational units
- Domains
- Domain controllers
- Trees
- Global catalogue

Naming
- DNS style
- X.500

Trust management

Interoperability and migration

ACLs

CHAPTER 9

NT 5 Active Directory Services

CHAPTER HIGHLIGHTS		
Topic	**Benefits**	**Experience**
NT 5 Active Directory	NT 5 Active Directory significantly improves upon the NT 4 directory service offering. Active Directory will increasingly play an important role in a broad range of Microsoft products and technologies since it is a general-purpose directory service.	Directory services are becoming the lifeline of corporate networks and the Internet. When Microsoft decides to expand the scope of its technology in an area such as this, it is more than worth knowing about.
NT 5 Naming and enhanced Organizational Capabilities	NT 5 Active Directory introduces DNS natively into the NT naming scheme. Also, an X.500-like tree-based approach is used for organizing information, significantly improving scalability and trust management.	NT 5 Active Directory represents a significant advancement over previous NT directory service offerings. At the same time, there are alternatives available as discussed in this book, including LDAP, X.500, and Novell NDS.

9.1 Introduction

Microsoft's *NT 5 Active Directory* addresses most of the shortcomings of the NT 4 directory services product. It provides for trust inheritance, is more scalable, and is expected to maintain support for a wider range of standards.

Active Directory is an X.500-like product; however, it is not an X.500 directory service. There is support for other important standards including LDAP, DNS, and X.500-style naming. As a result, Active Directory is considerably more standards-based than its predecessor. By integrating with Kerberos, Active Directory provides a scalable single-user logon solution, while offering general-purpose directory service capabilities such as those offered by Novell NDS and X.500.

9.2 Standards Supported

Perhaps one of the most distinguishing characteristics of Active Directory is its support for a wide range of standards. These include the LDAP client access protocol and API, Kerberos, and DNS. Microsoft has thrown in an API standard of its own called the *Active Directory Service Interface* (ADSI), which it pitches as a proprietary, higher-level, easier-to-use API than the standards-based LDAP API. In addition, Active Directory provides support for MAPI. Figure 9.1 illustrates standards supported by NT 5.0 Active Directory. Let's briefly review each of these standards, starting with Domain Name Services (DNS).

9.2.1 DNS

Active Directory leverages DNS in a few ways. First, it is the means by which LDAP clients locate an Active Directory server. Next, Microsoft has used the DNS style of naming as the basis for its naming alternative to the X.500 address format. For the basic things that administrators want to do, Microsoft's alternative may prove appealing. By providing support for DNS naming in addition to X.500 naming, Microsoft's approach is similar to that taken by DCE.

Also, DNS itself is integrated with Active Directory as a mapping mechanism between domain names and IP addresses. Furthermore, Microsoft has indicated its intention to implement Dynamic DNS, thereby replacing the proprietary WINS approach followed by earlier Microsoft products.

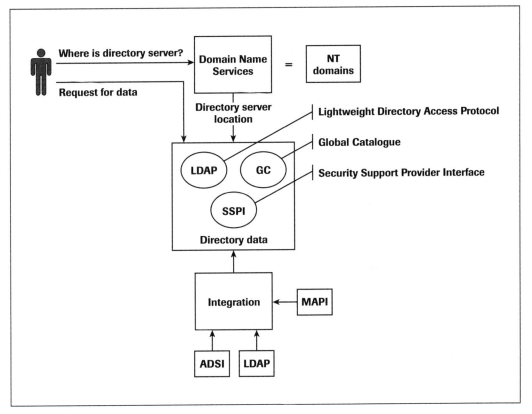

Figure 9.1 NT 5.0 Active Directory services

9.2.2 Kerberos and SSPI

For the management of trust, Active Directory strongly leverages Kerberos as its underlying trust management system. An overview of Kerberos was provided in Chapter 2, and a few Active Directory Kerberos specifics will be discussed in this chapter.

As part of NT 5, Microsoft introduces a valuable feature that allows the specific security mechanism used by the directory, server, and clients to be replaced with some other. This interface is called *Security Support Provider Interface* (SSPI). Without going into great detail on SSPI, let's just say that it allows you the flexibility to use different security mechanisms in your enterprise that meet your specific needs, without tossing the whole thing out just because your security requirements change. The value of such a capability is clearly very high.

9.2.3 X.500

Active Directory supports X.500 naming, but is designed to heavily leverage DNS. It is important to understand that, when you make the decision to go with DNS-style naming instead of X.500 naming in your organization, it is a big decision and, potentially, a long-term commitment. Users, administrators, and application developers will all begin to think and work in terms of the chosen style of naming. Applications, administrative processes, and scripts may be tailored specifically to the particular naming standard, despite attempts to keep things generic and independent of one naming style or another. DNS has its benefits—mainly simplicity. One drawback, which we'll discuss later, is possible interference of your IP DNS namespace with your NT enterprise DNS namespace.

9.2.4 ADSI, LDAP, and MAPI

With regard to integrating Active Directory with other directory service implementations, ADSI and the LDAP API are both supported by Active Directory, and both provide a means for integrating external directory services. In addition, to the extent you are bought into the Microsoft object strategy, ActiveX and DCOM add more value in the integration area when coupled with these APIs. Of course, so would CORBA, an open multiplatform alternative. And finally, Active Directory maintains support for applications written using MAPI. However, for new applications, it is probably wise to avoid using MAPI and instead choose one of the other APIs supported by Microsoft.

9.3 Directory Structure

Like NT 4, Active Directory makes use of users, groups, resources, and domains for location of resources, and access control. In addition to these, Active Directory offers the following new methods of organization: *organizational units* (OUs) and *domain trees*.

Just as it was the case with the NT 4 directory service, these organizational elements are logical, not physical. These methods of organization are illustrated in Figure 9.2 and will be discussed in more detail in the next section.

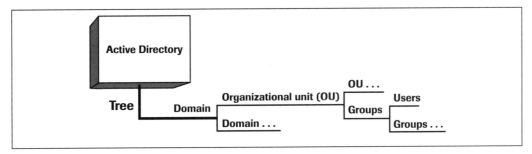

Figure 9.2 An Active Directory domain tree

9.4 Objects, Users, Groups, Resources, and OUs

Active Directory is a true general-purpose directory service. That means it can store *objects* of any kind. Users, groups, and resources are the three most obvious objects and the ones with which most administrators are immediately concerned. So, users, groups, and resources are simply objects from the directory service's perspective.

Users, groups, and resources can be placed into OUs. OUs are, generally speaking, *object containers.* OUs are an administrative tool so that rights and so forth can be assigned to an entire set of objects as a whole rather than to the objects individually. We need not get that abstract, though. Just look at OUs as a convenient means of organizing users, groups, and resources. OUs can contain other OUs and can be arranged in a hierarchy of OUs through which trust can be inherited. That is, *trust is transitive between OUs.*

It is important to note that Active Directory OUs are not necessarily the same as X.500 OUs. These OUs are part of the Microsoft DNS-style naming convention and should not be confused with the X.500 organizational unit of the same name.

OUs, as containers of objects, are themselves objects. Access rights to container objects can therefore be managed within the directory service. What that means is that one network administrator may be allowed to give you permission to a specific container object, say, one referencing certain confidential files, while another administrator may not.

With regard to ACLs, the ACL approach used with NT 4 is architecturally similar to NT 5. That is, permissions can be associated with resources, and you can assign ACL properties to an entire directory instead of to each individual file.

.. **Naming, Domains, and Trees**

Active Directory utilizes domains as the core organizational unit, just as the NT 4 directory service docs. However, Active Directory offers considerably more flexibility in the organization of these domains, as we will see. Any given domain can be organized into organizational units (OUs). A domain can contain users, groups, resources, and OUs.

Whereas NT 4 trust relationships are not transitive, with Active Directory, they can be. Domains can be organized into a *tree,* and trust flows through the tree. A tree is a hierarchical structure of domains. None of this will make much sense to you unless we get into how naming is done within Active Directory.

First, a domain is given a DNS style of name. For example, Speedy, Inc. might have a domain name of speedy.com. Then, if we have other domains that we wish to form into a tree under speedy.com, we merely make sure they appear underneath the speedy.com namespace. For example,

        speedy.com
            division.speedy.com
                group.division.speedy.com

Note that speedy.com is called the *root domain.* The root domain's name is also said to be the name of the entire tree. So, the name of the tree is speedy.com. Note also that division.speedy.com can inherit trust relationships from speedy.com and that group.division.speedy.com can inherit them from division.speedy.com. You cannot inherit trust with NT 4 directory services, but you can with Active Directory.

Usernames within Active Directory also follow the DNS naming style. For example, John Fastenberg, a Speedy, Inc. employee in the division.speedy.com domain, might have the following e-mail address: johnf@division.speedy.com.

Note that domain names are contiguous. That is, we just kept adding prefixes onto the root domain and maintained those prefixes as we grew the tree. Here is an example of an invalid namespace for a tree:

        speedy.com
            wheels.com
                fast.wheels.com

9.6 Kerberos: Guarding the "Forest"

[The Active Directory domain is equivalent to the Kerberos realm.]The
Kerberos KDC is integrated directly with the Active Directory domain controller's (DCs) security services. Users can authenticate to domains anywhere
in the tree because authentication services (KDCs) in each domain can trust
tickets issued by other KDCs in the same tree.

The default Windows NT 5 domain logon uses the Kerberos security
provider to obtain an initial Kerberos ticket. Windows NT uses the authorization data in Kerberos tickets to carry Windows NT security IDs representing
user and group membership.

Other Options

Microsoft also lets you authenticate yourself to the Kerberos server with a smartcard. The user might have a smartcard with his or her certificate and private key on
it, and the Kerberos server can be set up to challenge the smartcard to prove ownership of the private key. So, the smartcard serves as an authentication mechanism,
replacing the username/password. Note that, in this case, we would still be using
the Kerberos ticket as the means within the enterprise to authenticate to the
individual servers, not the X.509 certificate. The X.509 certificate is used only to
authenticate to the Kerberos server, not to all other servers in the network. This
strategy is different from a purely certificate-based authentication mechanism
implemented among all systems in the network.

9.7 The Global Catalogue: Make It Snappy

Active Directory also introduces a new architectural component known as a
global catalogue (GC). The GC improves performance and efficiency by
acting as a cache for commonly accessed information searched for within the
Active Directory infrastructure. As such, it is focused on offering higher performance by limiting the size of the database that must be searched to those
most frequently requested directory objects.

Domain Controllers

While at the same time providing support for certain NT 4 directory functions for migration purposes, Active Directory's new architecture does away
with the NT 4 PDC/BDC model and replaces it with a far more sophisticated *peer-to-peer* model whereby there is no longer a concept of a backup
or primary domain controller but only domain controllers (DCs) themselves
that are all peers, all with the same capabilities. DCs are still assigned to
domains and are said to be authoritative for those domains. These DCs
can be used to add/delete/modify directory entries for the domain as well
as propagate changes to other DCs. If a DC is down, another DC within the
domain can be used. In order to allow changes to be made at any DC and
also retain integrity of directory service data, it is necessary to implement a
reliable distributed update mechanism, which, for Active Directory, is the
use of *update sequence numbers* (USNs).

USNs provide a means of version control for directory service information. USNs are stored as properties of directory service objects, providing
a record of revision status. By analogy, if you ever had to keep track of many
documents and their versions (such as I had to do in writing this book),
then you would have had to track various revision numbers and attach
them to each document. That is effectively what USNs do for directory
service objects.

DCs that must be synchronized exchange USNs among one another
for directory service information shared (replicated) among them. A DC with
the highest USN value for any given directory service object is considered to
have the latest and most up-to-date version of that object. This most up-to-
date object is then shared with all DCs replicating that data.

The replication process just described is proprietary, and the protocol
used to implement it is proprietary. Therefore, in order to allow such replication and synchronization with external directory service devices, the external
directory service would need to implement this proprietary protocol and
process. Otherwise, you would need to use one of the Microsoft-provided
APIs or use LDAP.

9.9   Name Interference

A consequence of using the DNS-style naming convention is that it can conflict/interfere with anything you are doing in the Web world. For example, if your company is speedy.com on the Web and you choose to use speedy.com in Active Directory, how are you going to differentiate things so that you can tell whether someone wants to reach "speedy.com the Web server" or "speedy.com the root domain" of the corporate tree? On the other hand, if the addresses are maintained as different, then a user's e-mail address, say, johnf@speedy.com, may be different from the user's NT login, say, johnf@speedys_active_directory_domain.com.

9.10   Trust Management

Active Directory provides a means for interoperating with existing NT 4 networks while allowing for migration to a significantly more capable Active Directory trust management facility. As previously mentioned, a transitive trust relationship exists among the domains in an Active Directory domain tree. This eliminates the need to explicitly maintain and manage two-way trust relationships between all of the domains on a corporate network. Domains that are members of the same domain tree automatically participate in a transitive, bidirectional trust relationship with their parent domain. If there are specific domains where transitive trust is not appropriate, explicit one-way trust relationships can still be defined.

9.11   Interoperability and Migration

With regard to interoperability with existing NT 4 directory service installations, a Windows NT 5.0 domain controller can play the role of a Windows NT 4.0 BDC and receive domain account replication from an existing Windows NT 4.0 PDC. This allows NT 4 user workstations to send username/password authentication requests to a Windows NT 5.0 domain controller acting as a BDC in the Windows NT 4.0 domain.

With regard to integrating with other directory service offerings, there are more than a few approaches. Here are the most obvious ones:

- Don't integrate them at the server-side. Instead, enable the client to speak to more than one directory service. For example, enable your clients to speak both NDS and Active Directory. Microsoft has included an NDS client as part of Windows 98. One of the disadvantages with this approach is that two directory services must be configured to support the same users, which doubles the configuration fun.

- Use LDAP to integrate the directories with one another.

- Write software using the ADSI and/or LDAP APIs to join up the disparate directory service implementations.

9.12 Conclusions

Compared to the NT 4 directory service, Active Directory's trust management features enable it to scale to significantly larger organizations. Active Directory supports important open standards and a few enticing proprietary features as well. Choosing to implement the proprietary features may limit your interoperability options but may also simplify your management and deployment burden in the short term.

Because Active Directory can potentially carry large amounts of data, such as when it is integrated with Microsoft Exchange or another mail infrastructure, and because changes can be made from any DC, network designers must carefully consider the impact on their network of data required to replicate and synchronize DCs interconnected via a wide area network.

The directory infrastructure should be designed to minimize the moving of objects from one domain tree to another. Also, the changing of the structure of domain trees should be avoided due to the impact on the naming scheme.

Features such as peer-to-peer synchronization, the GC, and Kerberos trust management contribute positively to Active Directory's manageability and performance. Active Directory interoperability is facilitated by support for LDAP.

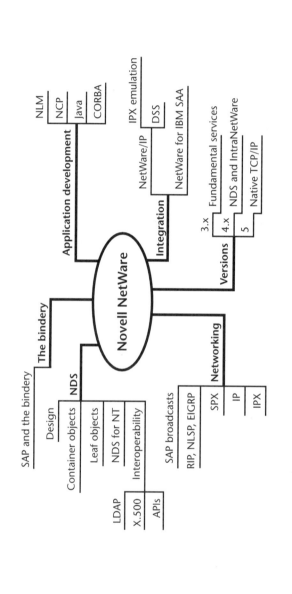

CHAPTER 10

Novell NetWare

CHAPTER HIGHLIGHTS		
Topic	**Benefits**	**Experience**
Multiple versions of NetWare(3.x, 4.x, and 5)	Design and architectural information is provided for mixed NetWare networks.	Most corporations today have a mix of various NetWare versions deployed, not just one.
Service Advertisement Protocol (SAP) and the bindery	SAP is a broadcast protocol that needs to be controlled and minimized in your network. It plays a fundamental role in 3.x networks as part of the bindery services.	SAP, as a broadcast protocol, has caused serious challenges in some large networks. There are opportunities to control it in 3.x networks and to deemphasize it with release 4.x and NDS.
NetWare Directory Services (NDS)	NDS is one of the most comprehensive directory services available. With the exponential growth in services and information embedded within networks today, directories are becoming the pillars upon which enterprise networks are built.	Without a powerful enterprisewide directory service, you are forced to manually configure service availability information in individual servers and clients throughout your network. As we have seen with the Internet and the power of DNS, directory services offer many benefits. They are now going to the next level, well beyond simple address resolution.

CHAPTER HIGHLIGHTS		
Topic	**Benefits**	**Experience**
NetWare application development	NetWare provides robust networking services, and it is natural for developers to want to leverage them within their applications.	Application-level protocols such as the NetWare Core Protocol (NCP) provide performance challenges across networks. Novell is improving its application development tools to include Java and CORBA. Integration of important CORBA services such as the Trader Service with NDS offers a powerful combination.

10.1 Introduction

In an era where even power strips for your home computer are labeled "Internet-enabled," it is natural to ask yourself what relevance Novell's technology could have going forward. Critics have argued that Novell, the company that revolutionized low-cost highly functional enterprise networking in the 1980s, was swept over by the Internet and TCP/IP. What, then, of Novell NetWare?

While it could perhaps be argued that Novell initially underestimated the Internet and its open standards, collaborative nature, and explosive business opportunities, as did many others, it did remain focused on some very important work. During this time, Novell designed, implemented, protected, and nurtured significant technology that corporations sorely need today, Novell Directory Services (NDS). NDS, introduced with NetWare 4.x, is a very strong directory service offering for the enterprise, providing a highly scalable and manageable global namespace, single-user logon, service management, and administration infrastructure. Many argue that Microsoft's NT 4 domain functionality does not compete with NDS's broad object-based, tree-based distributed architecture and that NT 5 Active Directory is Microsoft's first attempt at realistically matching what Novell has accomplished with NDS.

Today, Novell maintains a huge installed base. It claims over 79 million users, and, in 1996, International Data Corporation (IDC) reported that Novell supplied 41% of all server operating systems shipped. This kind of installed base cannot be ignored.

Novel NetWare is comprised of (1) a stand-alone server operating system coupled with networking facilities, such as file and print services, and (2) multiplatform client-side software that augments existing operating systems such as Windows, empowering them to leverage NetWare services. NetWare provides development tools so that client- and server-side applications can be written to take advantage of NetWare services.

There are three major releases of Novell NetWare deployed throughout corporations today. They are **NetWare versions 3.x, 4.x, and 5.** Versions 3.x through 5 are covered in this chapter as well as **IntraNetWare,** which is NetWare 4.x bundled with various Web and connectivity value-added products. Why cover so many versions? The answer is that most networks have a mix of these deployed, and there are implications, in terms of network and application design, as a result. We will learn, for example, that having 3.x servers in the network can undo some of the network efficiencies gained from NDS.

In this chapter, we will consider the networking implications of the NetWare protocol suite. NetWare is a serious networking protocol suite and has been around for quite some time. As with all the frameworks we have studied, routing among applications on a LAN is not where the challenges and issues show themselves so clearly. It is when we add a wide area network (WAN) to the equation that we begin to see the issues with ad hoc broadcasting, inefficient flow control methods, and so forth.

We will briefly study NetWare/IP, Novell's stopgap effort at meeting the need for a common protocol suite, TCP/IP, in the enterprise. While NetWare 5 promises native TCP/IP support, NetWare/IP is what is available for version 4.x users. As we will see, NetWare/IP offers some complexity and overhead, as well as the risk of doing neither TCP/IP nor native NetWare particularly well, depending upon the needs of your organization.

We will also take a look at NetWare applications development. NetWare 4.x and 5 offer some exciting Java and CORBA platform capabilities of interest to application developers. And, of course, we will discuss NDS, including the NDS schema and various design approaches.

10.2 NetWare 3.x

The major distinction between NetWare 3.x and 4.x is in the availability of NDS, as well as the value-added IntraNetWare Web-based products. In this section, we will study the predecessor to NDS, called the *bindery,* and various core protocols that form the basis of NetWare versions 3.x and 4.x. Because your networks will likely maintain some 3.x servers, at least for some period of time, it is important to understand the networking implications of the bindery and its related protocols.

10.2.1 Core Protocols and Functions

The Novell protocol suite can be viewed in terms of transport protocols, routing protocols, and application-layer protocols. The two Novell transport methods are the Internetwork Packet Exchange (IPX) and the Sequenced Packet Exchange (SPX). At the routing layer, there is RIP, essentially the same as TCP/IP RIP; the NetWare Link Services Protocol (NLSP), similar to the TCP/IP OSPF protocol; and EIGRP. At the application layer are the NetWare Core Protocol (NCP) and the Service Advertisement Protocol (SAP). Note that SAP is primarily a broadcast protocol (we'll explore that topic in a bit). These protocols are illustrated in Figure 10.1. The figure is intended to illustrate that IPX is the transport vehicle for the protocols shown above it. Let's take a closer look at each of these protocols.

10.2.2 Internetwork Packet Exchange (IPX)

The *Internetwork Packet Exchange* (IPX) is a connectionless protocol similar to IP, but it does not share all of its functionality. The IPX packet format is shown in Figure 10.2. A discussion of important IPX packet fields follows.

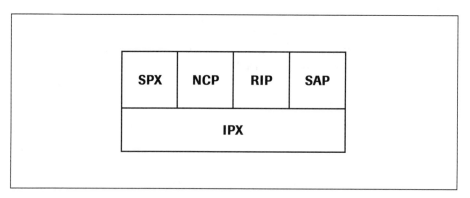

Figure 10.1 NetWare 3.x protocol suite

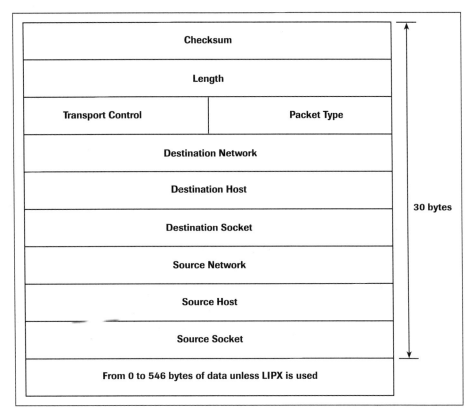

Figure 10.2 IPX format

10.2.2.1 Destination Host

Like the TCP/IP protocol suite, Novell NetWare has the concept of unique host addresses. However, Novell uses the device's physical (MAC layer) LAN address, such as the 48-bit physical Ethernet address, as the device's IPX host address. It just inserts that address into the IPX packet.

10.2.2..2 Destination Network

Clients and servers on the same LAN are administratively assigned a common network number. Unlike TCP/IP, where the analogous subnet address is numerically related via a masking mechanism to the host address, IPX keeps the host address and network number numerically separate (that is, you cannot, for example, apply a mask to the host address to get at the network number). Administrators must take great care when assigning network numbers in order to guarantee they are unique. NetWare RIP routers use the network number to locate the LAN to which an IPX packet is destined.

10.2.2.3 Transport Control

Routers make use of the Transport Control field to prevent an IPX packet from perpetually looping through the network due to a routing error of some kind. This field indicates the total number of routers (hops) traversed by the packet from source to destination. Each router through which the packet passes increments this value by 1. When the hop count reaches 15, the next router in the path will discard the packet.

10.2.2.4 Destination Socket

The Destination Socket field defines the destination software process for the IPX. Example socket numbers are given in Table 10.1.

Table 10.1 Example IPX Sockets

IPX Packet Destination Socket	Value (Hexadecimal)
RIP	0001
Echo protocol packet	0002
Error handler packet	0003
File service packet	0451
Service advertising packet	0452
Routing information packet	0453
NetBIOS packet	0455
Diagnostic packet	0456

10.2.2.5 Packet Type

Example IPX packet types are shown in Table 10.2. Note the similarity between the IPX packet type field and the IP Protocol number field. Both signal the type of protocol (for example, TCP for IP, NCP for IPX) being carried.

Table 10.2 Example IPX Packet Types

Packet Type Field Value (Decimal)	Packet Type
0	Unknown, used if no type is defined for this packet (sometimes IPX uses this or type 4)
1	Routing Information Protocol (RIP)
4	Packet Exchange Packet (PEP), used by SPX and IPX
5	Sequenced Packet Exchange (SPX)
17	NetWare Core Protocol (NCP)
20	Propagated packet, used by NetBIOS over IPX

10.2.2.6 Byte Overhead

When you add up all these packet fields, you discover IPX offers a reasonably sized 30-byte header, and, when we add NCP (discussed later), we will be up to 40 bytes. As with IP, this 40 bytes of overhead for every IPX/NCP packet must be considered during network design because bandwidth must be available for it and response times can be influenced.

10.2.2.7 Maximum Packet Size

One of the problems that Novell hit with IPX was its original maximum packet size of 576 bytes (546 bytes of data + the 30-byte IPX header). This packet size may not be efficient for some applications involving larger transfers. This small/large packet trade-off has been touched upon a number of times in this book, including in Chapter 1. If your analysis indicates larger packets are better, then you may find the Novell *Large IPX* (LIPX) feature, more recently referred to as *Large Internet Packet* (LIP), useful. To enable it, you need to load a special LIPX module on your NetWare server and to make sure all of your NetWare client software is ready for those larger packets.

10.2.3 Sequenced Packet Exchange (SPX)

The *Sequenced Packet Exchange* (SPX) is a connection-based protocol that layers a packet retransmission mechanism on top of IPX, providing guaranteed delivery. Because of the overhead of implementing the retransmission mechanism, SPX is a bit slower than IPX. However, if you are running over links with higher error rates, as is the case in some areas internationally, and if you fail to run a link-layer error recovery mechanism underneath NetWare (such as a full HDLC) over parts of your routing infrastructure (between routers), then you may need to write your application to use SPX. Note that, because of the extra information needed in each packet to handle retransmission, the SPX header adds 12 bytes of overhead on top of IPX.

In general, most of your applications will use IPX, and some important utilities will make use of SPX. A number of Novell's system utilities are based on SPX, including RCONSOLE, RPRINTER, and PSERVER. There are other utilities that also make use of SPX, including data backup programs and various gateway products.

Blame It on the Network

Worldwide networks with low-speed links or highly congested networks offer many challenges. When you start having problems with them, the last thing you want is to be locked out from using any of your SPX-based management tools, or any application for that matter.

Sometimes, SPX-based applications run into trouble over slow networks. Why? Because each end of the SPX connection sets various maximum-valued timers (retransmission timers) whenever they send a packet. If one end of the connection repeatedly does not receive a response from the other end within the timer's duration acknowledging receipt of the packet, then the connection may fail. These retransmission timers can typically be extended as needed by using system utilities and configuration files on the client- and server-sides.

10.2.4 Service Advertisement Protocol (SAP) and the Bindery: Precursor to a Directory

10.2.4.1 SAP and the Bindery

The *Service Advertisement Protocol* (SAP) is used by NetWare 3.x servers to advertise the services they offer, such as file, print, gateway, or other networked services. This information is broadcast around the network via SAP, so that all servers, in the 3.x server-centric world, know what services are available and where. The servers then are able to provide that information to clients that log into them. In addition to this broadcast mechanism, clients are capable of broadcasting SAP requests for a specific type of service.

The SAP packet contains the IPX network number, host address, and socket number of the server along with the Server Type field, which identifies the service available from the server. Example server types include file server (4), job server (5), and gateway (6).

In a NetWare 3.x network, SAP combines forces with and provides information to the bindery. The *bindery* is a database maintained by every server that tracks the services available on the network and manages resources. In addition to SAP information, the bindery also contains information manually configured by the server administrator. Figure 10.3 illustrates how the bindery is populated dynamically by SAP and manually by the administrator, on a per-host basis.

Users take advantage of the bindery every time they log into a NetWare server. Upon login, users are provided a view of the services available in the network. The bindery within the server is used to provide this view of service availability.

The bindery carries information about services available, as previously discussed, and, in addition, information about access rights to those services and their resources. Once a user logs into a server, the bindery is used by the server to determine what rights the user has.

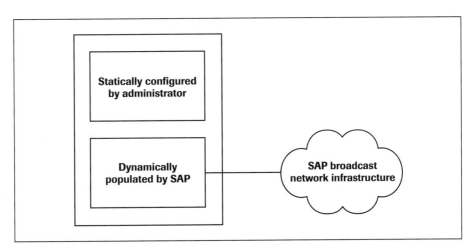

Figure 10.3 The bindery

Entries in the bindery are essentially objects, and these objects have properties. An individual user or a group of users can be defined in the bindery, and these users and groups of users may be assigned permissions to bindery objects. For example, there are access properties defined within the bindery for files and directories controlled by the server.

The bindery does support a form of access-right inheritance. You can assign trustee rights to a user at a given point in the file directory tree, and that user will have access to all files and subdirectories below that directory in the tree. This access-level information is stored in the bindery. These permissions can be modified programmatically or via NetWare administrator tools.

Bindery APIs are available to developers that allow them to manipulate the bindery. These APIs allow developers to search the bindery and also modify it.

NDS, part of NetWare 4.x and discussed later, does away with the need for the bindery and much of the need for SAP. Servers no longer need to maintain their own persistent database of services available in the network. They can get it dynamically from NDS. NDS holds an administratively managed view of the entire network, its services, resources, and so forth.

In an NDS environment, reliance on SAP is heavily reduced. For NDS, the main role of SAP is reduced to that of providing a protocol for time synchronization between NDS servers (important since they use time as a factor in the replica synchronization process and for other purposes) as well as advertising the existence of NDS servers themselves. In a pure NDS network, SAP is no longer needed as the primary vehicle to communicate service availability among all servers in the network—NDS itself provides this information for servers that attach to it.

10.2.4.2 Controlling SAP Broadcasts in the Network

SAP can be thought of as providing directory service functions in which the directory is broadcast around the network every 60 seconds, which is not too efficient. Trying to replicate the entire service namespace for the network through a broadcast protocol works fine on local LANs and small networks, but if you get beyond five or so sites and a few hundred users, things get complicated. Removing the reliance on SAP for all but a few basic functions is a big advantage of NDS. Of course, if you keep older systems around that are not integrated into the NDS infrastructure, then you must maintain SAP.

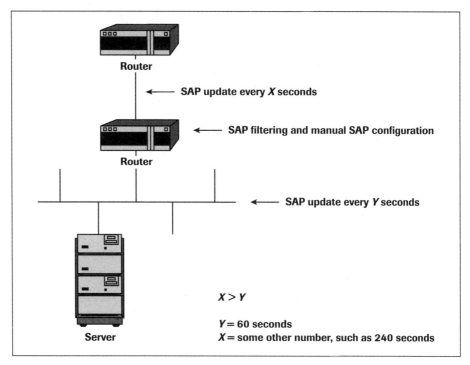

Figure 10.4 SAP broadcast control

There are a few methods for controlling SAP broadcasts in your network. One is to filter the broadcasts in your routers so that the network sees only those services that remote users need to know about. Another is to configure your routers to use a different rate of broadcast among themselves, one greater then 60 seconds, as shown in Figure 10.4. In the figure, the routers transmit RIP updates at the rate of X, for example, every 240 seconds, while devices on the LAN transmit updates at the Novell default rate of once every 60 seconds, denoted as Y in the figure.

A third method is to employ a routing protocol adapted to support SAP. We discussed EIGRP in Chapter 4—it is one protocol that controls SAP broadcasts. We also have NLSP, which is an OSPF-like protocol and also offers controls for SAP broadcasts. These protocols focus on sending only changes in SAP information through the network, as opposed to allowing to continually broadcasting SAP information.

10.2.5 Routing Protocols: RIP, NLSP, and EIGRP

Novell offers two routing protocols for IPX: NetWare RIP and NetWare Link Services Protocol (NLSP). Cisco's EIGRP is also capable of routing IPX and of controlling SAP broadcasts by forwarding only changes to the SAP table.

NetWare RIP operates very similarly to the TCP/IP RIP we discussed earlier, except that it uses a broadcast timer of 60 seconds, as opposed to the 30-second default used with IP. RIP with IPX suffers from all the same challenges it has with IP. It does not scale well to large networks.

NetWare Link Services Protocol (NLSP) operates very similarly to the OSPF protocol we discussed in Chapter 4. NLSP has the added benefit of working to control SAP broadcasts. Because of this, NLSP is quite attractive.

10.2.6 NetWare Core Protocol (NCP)

NetWare's server-side operating system makes extensive use of the *NetWare Core Protocol* (NCP) for fundamental networking operations. Typically, applications written for NetWare servers rely on NCP. NCP processes client requests, for file or print services, for example, and passes a response back to the client. In this regard, NCP offers an RPC-like mechanism for requesting NetWare services.

A great deal of what you do will make use of the NCP application protocol. NCP supports file server functions, printers, name servers, file locking, and so forth. The NCP header adds 10 bytes to the 30 bytes in the IPX header, bringing the total to 40. Many of your applications will make use of NCP to, for example, mount the disk on a remote machine in order to access a database there. From a networking standpoint, we need to recognize that the NCP protocol executes a flow control mechanism between the client and server that can wreck your day if you are not familiar with it.

NCP is available in two flavors from NetWare: the original nonburst mode NCP and the newer burst mode NCP. The *nonburst mode* NCP will provide you, in most cases, with unacceptable performance over your WAN because it is a stop-and-wait protocol, meaning that one acknowledgment is required for every packet sent. It is difficult to do any worse than this from the perspective of throughput and still use any type of data acknowledgment scheme. The maximum achievable throughput you can get with this protocol, provided LIPX is not used, is roughly equal to (546 bytes × 8 bits/byte) ÷ (round-trip delay through your WAN). For example, if you have a round-trip delay of 600 milliseconds and have a 64-Kbps access link, then your maximum throughput is 7.28 Kbps, which is 7.28/64=11% of the total available bandwidth on your link. That is bad, and if your users are not happy with their service level and you choose to use nonburst mode NCP, don't necessarily run to your communications carrier to help you solve a WAN problem—the problem is, unfortunately, likely to be yours.

Fortunately (very), Novell responded to this problem by providing *burst mode* NCP, which allows for a number of packets to be outstanding before an acknowledgment is required. If you install burst mode and you configure it properly to provide you a reasonable number of outstanding packets for your application, then you will get significantly better performance. For example, if you configure it so that five packets can be outstanding, your throughput will be increased approximately five times the nonburst mode case, so you would achieve 36.4 Kbps, or 56% utilization, which is much more respectable.

10.2.7 Application Development

The NetWare application development environment has, in recent years, had a difficult time keeping pace with those offered by competitors, including, of course, Microsoft Novell's strengths, however, are broader than just providing a server operating system for application development. They are in providing highly manageable and robust core file and print networks that network applications developed under a variety of operating systems can leverage.

The server provides two classes of functions: (1) functions we might think of as fundamental, which include a file server, printer services, security services, gateway services, and management of other resources in the network, and (2) added functions offered by *NetWare loadable modules* (NLMs) installed on the NetWare server. NLMs are any applications you write or purchase for running on your NetWare server. With NetWare 4.x and 5, NetWare framework applications can be written in Java, can leverage CORBA, and can bypass the NLM mechanism (more on that in a later section).

The NetWare 3.x server operating system is not particularly application development friendly. If you are a programmer developing applications for it, then you will feel the pain of crude memory management and protection from rogue applications, scant multitasking, prioritization, and threading capabilities.

Through the NLM APIs, programmers can leverage NCP as previously discussed, can internationalize their applications using Unicode, and can provide transport access via the WinSock version 2 API. In addition to NCP, Novell provides emulation functions for NetBIOS applications for applications written specifically to the IBM and Microsoft NetBIOS interface specification.

10.3 NetWare 4.x/IntraNetWare

The most significant advancement with the release of NetWare 4.x was the
availability of NDS. Along with NDS, Novell introduced a number of other
significant advancements, including

- IntraNetWare, which is NetWare 4.x bundled with Web server capability whereby the Web server is an NLM running on the NetWare
  server, along with a few other value-added products. Through this
  Web server, Java and CORBA services are provided. Touting
  improved integration with the Novell framework, the Novell Web
  server still did not catch the attention that similar products from
  Netscape and Microsoft did. In response, Novell formed an alliance
  and a new company named *Novonyx* specifically to bring Netscape
  products into the NetWare environment.
- A broad server-side Java, CORBA, and NDS software development
  kit and strategy.
- The vision of clients that request object services universally, through
  a universal directory infrastructure, by seeing the wisdom of offering
  CORBA trading object service (Novell Trader) and beginning the
  process of providing integration with NDS.
- Improved operating system fundamentals like server-side memory
  management and multitasking.

10.4 NetWare Directory Services (NDS)

The *NetWare Directory Services* (NDS) technology is patterned after the
X.500 standards, but it is still a proprietary directory services offering. That is
not all bad since to do everything that Novell wanted to do, there were not
always standards available at the time that were either functional enough or
practical enough to implement a quality product. Still, NDS does convey the
feel and spirit of X.500:

- The X.500 Distinguished Name (DN) format and NDS's are essentially the same.
- The NetWare Directory Service (NWDS) APIs are patterned
  directly after the X.500 XDS APIs.

- NDS does not use any of the protocols defined between X.500 components, so interoperation with X.500 requires development of a gateway function, either around LDAP or through use of APIs.
- NDS uses its own security authentication scheme. While proprietary, it is quite practical and leverages public and private key cryptography.

NDS provides a number of powerful enterprisewide functions:

- As we'll discuss later, the user need only log in once to the NDS infrasructure, and, after that, everything is transparent to the user, regardless of the server being visited. Single-user logon is a great feature, and, combined with the richness of NDS and its ability to broadly manage services and resources in the enterprise, quite powerful.
- The administrator deals with NDS, not each and every one of the servers in the network, to manage services, resources, and users in the network, which is a lot different from version 3.x, where each individual server's bindery must be administered.
- NDS is essentially a distributed database. It consists of objects, each of which has properties (attributes). These objects can be organized in a treelike fashion.
- NDS allows the administrator to improve performance and reliability by partitioning the directory service (the object tree), shielding details of one part from another, and replicating it for higher-performance local access and redundancy.
- LDAP clients can access NDS information. Note that LDAP compatibility does not automatically mean that any two LDAP-compatible directory services can just gateway between each other and synchronize everything with a flick of a switch. LDAP is, as currently specified (LDAPv3), a client-access protocol, not a server-server one (more on this later).
- NDS for NT is an interesting capability allowing for NDS integration with NT domains.
- Directory information needs to be kept replicated for reliability and performance across multiple directory services. These replicated directories need to be synchronized. The manner in which this is done greatly affects performance and reliability. The two different approaches, master/slave and peer-to-peer, were introduced in Chapter 2. NDS uses the peer-to-peer model for directory synchronization.

- As we discussed earlier, NetWare 3.x is server-centric. From the perspective of each server, it is a free-for-all with regard to learning the global namespace—the SAP broadcast protocol and the manual bindery configurations are all server-centric. NDS changes all of this.
- A broad set of APIs extend NDS functionality.
- NDS is capable of emulating bindery functionality, allowing 3.x servers and clients to interoperate with NDS.

10.4.1 Containers and Leaf Objects: Organizing People, Resources, and Services

NDS *leaf objects* are stored in *containers.* Containers are the organizational elements of the X.500 name. An administrator creates leaf objects for users, services, and resources within the network and assigns them to containers. An administrator can simplify things by assigning properties, such as security

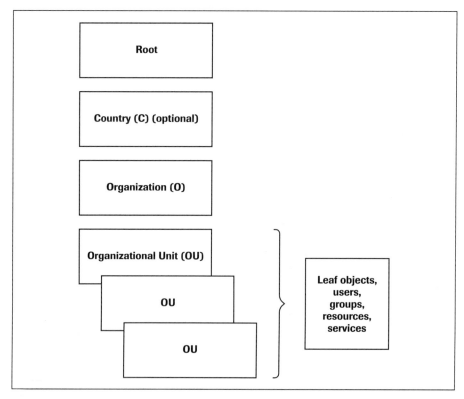

Figure 10.5 NDS objects

access rights, to containers rather than to individual leaf objects. Figure 10.5 illustrates the four NDS container types, a description of which follows:

1. The *root* contains everything in your network. Your network can have only one root. It is the top of the tree, period.

2. The *country* (C) container is optional and is often not used. It is a throwback from the X.500 roots of NDS, whereby public networks would often benefit from thinking about things in terms of countries. Locality and state container types, under country, are also defined; however, the current NDS utilities do not support them, and their benefit is not obvious. The country container can only be defined directly underneath the root; it cannot be defined underneath an O or OU.

3. Typically, right under the root, you have the *organization* (O). It is usually your company's name. All NDS trees require at least one O. A large corporation could divide separate companies that might be completely autonomous by assigning them separate O's under the root. Typically, though, if there is any level of integration, you will want to put them under the same O. O's are not allowed beneath other O's. O's can contain leaf objects or an OU object.

4. The *organizational unit* (OU) is your primary container for organizing leaf objects in the network. OUs can be nested underneath each other as needed. An OU is defined beneath an O or beneath another OU only.

NDS leaf objects include the following:

- *NetWare Server* represents the services offered by the NetWare server, including the NetWare Core Protocol (NCP) services.

- *Volume* represents data storage devices within the Novell network that are referred to as *volumes.*

- *Printer* represents the network printer itself, Printer Server represents the software services offered for the printer, and Printer Queue represents all print jobs waiting to be printed.

- *User* represents the user account. Users are granted or denied rights to access resources (such as file directories, printers, etc.) and services. Group represents, you guessed it, the group account. Users can be placed into groups, and these rights can be assigned to groups instead, which makes things easier. This facility is similar to the Microsoft NT user/group capability discussed in Chapters 8 and 9.

- *Organizational Role* can be quite useful, allowing for the assignment of so-called role-based security. Rather than simply assigning rights to individual users or to groups of users, this object allows you to define a particular type of role, for example, human resources (HR) administrator, and then grant or deny that role various rights. So, when you have a new HR administrator join the company, all you need to do is assign that person the role of HR administrator, and, in one shot, all the appropriate permissions are assigned to his or her account. You could have done a similar thing by creating an HR administrators group and assigning the new employee to that group. The advantage of Organizational Role is that you need not form groups and groups of groups for the purposes of basic role assignment. You can perform role assignment and then communicate other relationships with groups as needed.

- *Bindery* and *Bindery Queue* are used by NetWare as part of providing the bindery emulation feature.

- *Distribution List* is used to represent things like e-mail distribution lists.

- *AFP Server* allows a server compatible with the AppleTalk Filing Protocol (AFP) to be represented within NDS.

- *Alias,* as the name implies, allows an object to go by more than one name. One of the problems with uniquely naming objects and then giving those objects names out to people and programmers is that, if you change the object name, sometimes people and systems do not react well since they may have hard-coded that object name into their brains or their program or script. With an alias, the NDS administrator can change the name of an object while, at the same time, keeping the old name.

- *Computer* is used to represent a computer other than a standard NetWare server. You can, for example, represent a UNIX workstation, an IBM mainframe, or a network router.

- *Directory Map* is a special kind of alias dedicated to network drives (network-connected storage devices). NetWare allows clients to use storage devices (drives) on servers as if they were directly connected to the local workstation. For example, you (the client) might want to mount a drive on, say, remote server Bob, and since your machine already has a drive *c:,* when you mount this drive, called *mapping* in NetWare terminology, this drive would be drive *d:.* From that point forward, you need only reference drive *d:* and need not worry that the drive is located remotely on Bob. When you issue the mapping command at your workstation, you can either explicitly configure the NDS path to the drive on server Bob or you can use an intermediate name, configured with the Directory Map object. If the drive ever moves from server Bob to elsewhere, you do not need to modify the mapping commands you issue at your workstation.

- *Message Routing Group* is used as part of NetWare's messaging product to represent a group of messaging servers that can communicate with one another.

- *External Entity* is used to import non-NDS objects. For example, you could import users from an X.400 directory in order to provide a common e-mail address book that includes both NDS and non-NDS (in this case, X.400) addresses.

- *Unknown* is used by NDS when it receives an object that it cannot comprehend. This can happen if the database has been corrupted in some way.

With all this organizational flexibility, it is easy to get into a gridlock trying to decide how to organize the directory service. One approach, based on organizing the tree according to the company's WANs, LANs, and departments, is illustrated in Figure 10.6. This is the most straightforward approach for the majority of applications. Figure 10.7 illustrates the other consistent principle, which is that the likelihood of changes to the tree should decrease as you get nearer to its top.

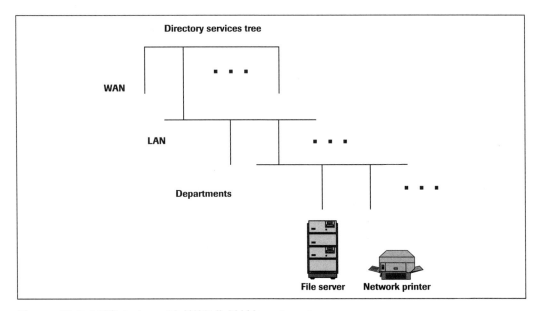

Figure 10.6 NDS design with WAN/LAN/departments

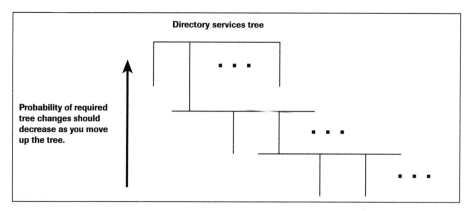

Figure 10.7 NDS design with fewer changes at the top

10.4.2 Trust Management and Inherited Rights Filter (IRF)

NDS supports *inheritance,* meaning that container objects inherit the rights of their parent container objects and leaf objects inherit the rights of their containers. The *Inherited Rights Filter* (IRF) allows the administrator to disallow specific rights that would otherwise be inherited at any point in the tree. The IRF is illustrated in Figure 10.8.

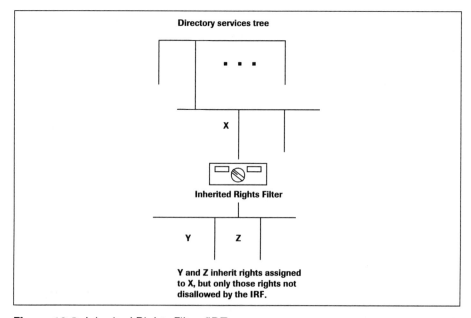

Figure 10.8 Inherited Rights Filter (IRF)

10.4.3 Security: Authentication and Authorization

Novell brewed up its own authentication and authorization mechanism for NDS. It leverages RSA public key cryptography while allowing the private key (the signing key) to be dynamically delivered to the client. This offers the benefit of private key portability without requiring the use of a token, such as a smartcard, as discussed in Chapter 2. The downside is that, by not bonding the private key entirely to the individual by keeping it completely with the user and, instead, storing it on a server where an impersonator can get to it, you lose the nonrepudability characteristics of the private key. Figure 10.9 illustrates the NDS mechanism, with each step described as follows:

1. Alice uses her username/password to authenticate to NDS.
2. NDS gives Alice her private key.
3. Alice requests file services from Bob.
4. Bob requests Alice's public key from NDS.
5. Alice authenticates herself to Bob using public key cryptography.
6. Bob gives Alice a session key to use when communicating with him. The session key expires at some point.

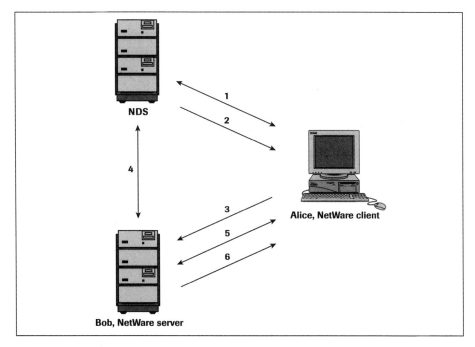

Figure 10.9 NDS authentication and authorization

Note that the public key cryptographic authentication Alice does with Bob is transparent to Alice the user—she just entered her username/password once and was done with it. All the other steps happened automatically, under the covers, from the perspective of the end user (Alice). If Alice wants to visit another server, say, Miller, for example, then Alice does not need to enter anything new to authenticate to Miller—she need only request to access Miller's resources. Thus, NDS allows for *single-user logon,* meaning that Alice need only enter her username/password once, after which she can access any services and resources she has permission to access.

This authentication and authorization approach offers many benefits. It is just not a standard approach, such as that offered by SSL/TLS, and so, when we integrate with standards like LDAP, we need to address that. SSL/TLS was not available to the NDS developers during its design, and, besides, SSL/TLS itself does not yet define a mechanism for dynamic delivery of the private key, but NDS does.

10.4.4 Partitions and Replicas: Designing for Reliability and Performance

NDS allows the directory to be divided up into partitions, as illustrated in Figure 10.10. Different partitions can be placed on different servers. So, for example, you could take the New York office's partition and put it on a server located remotely, in the New York office. That way, user NDS requests are all

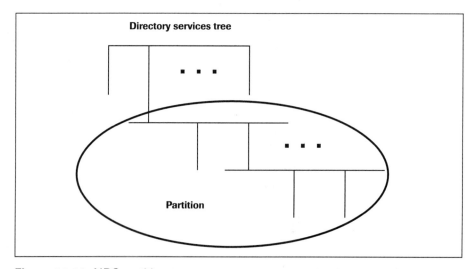

Figure 10.10 NDS partition

serviced locally rather than consuming wide area network resources and slowing things down waiting for responses from across the network.

Partitions themselves should be backed up. What happens if the server in New York carrying the New York partition fails? NDS supports replication to allow you to protect against this. Replication is illustrated in Figure 10.11.

If you replicated that partition onto another server, say, in the New York office, then users will barely miss a beat. You could also replicate it at headquarters, across the network. The only downside with this is that the data updates required to synchronize the New York partition with its replica at headquarters must traverse your network, consuming resources. And, if the

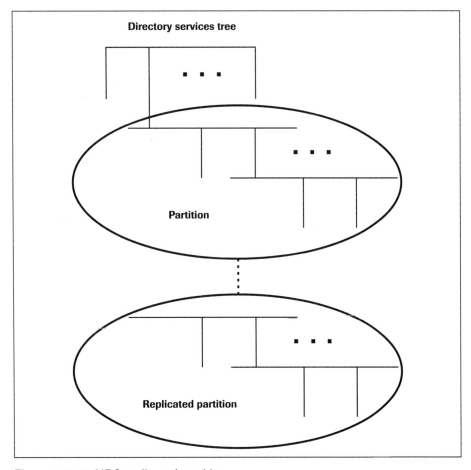

Figure 10.11 NDS replicated partition

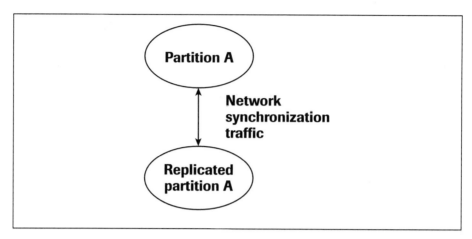

Figure 10.12 NDS replication traffic

network goes up/down, so will the synchronization process between your partition and it replica, as illustrated in Figure 10.12.

Partitions have the added benefit of not requiring synchronization. So, if you replicate one big tree, you need to synchronize the entire tree. However, if you divide it into two partitions and replicate only one of the two partitions across the network, for example, then you reduce your replication traffic to only the synchronization traffic required to keep that particular partition up-to-date, as illustrated in Figure 10.13. The point to be made here is that you should use partitioning and replication to maximize network performance by minimizing network traffic, while at the same maximizing

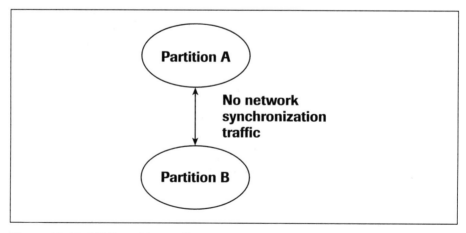

Figure 10.13 NDS partition traffic

reliability. Also, by partitioning, we can simplify administration, by assigning individual administrators their own partitions, allowing roles and responsibilities to be clearly understood and enforced among administrators.

10.4.5 NDS for NT: Integrating with Microsoft NT Domains

If you have a mixed NT and NetWare environment and you like working with NDS, then the *NDS for NT* feature set from Novell might be for you. NDS for NT allows NT 4 Microsoft domains to be administered from NDS. It is not as easy as flicking a switch, and, wham, everything is integrated. You do have to think about exactly where in the NDS directory tree you want your domains to be. Once in NDS, you get some of the benefits of NDS when working with domains. For example, your domain information can now be replicated with the NDS replication facility.

Within NDS, each NT domain is reborn as a *domain object.* Domain objects are similar to the NDS group object. It is important to note that group membership in NDS is a property—a group is not a container. So, an object can be a member of a group but also exist anywhere else in the tree inside a container. That allows you to take the domain user and assign that user rights elsewhere within the directory tree, as either a member of the domain or not.

NDS for NT includes software that is installed on an NT server, allowing it to act as a primary or backup domain controller, as shown in Figure 10.14. This software communicates with the Microsoft Security Accounts Manager

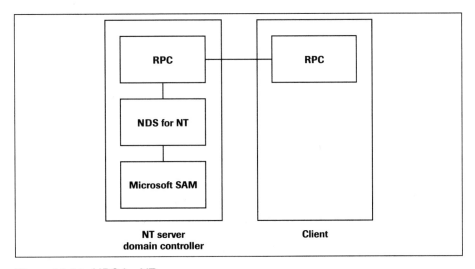

Figure10.14 NDS for NT

(SAM) database, the holder of usernames and passwords within the NT environment. NDS for NT then uses RPC to communicate with the client.

NDS for NT does not require that trust relationships be configured between domain objects. Instead, things are simpler—you merely assign the group rights and properties, and these properties are inherited.

Note that NDS for NT still requires that Microsoft PDCs and BDCs be maintained for the purposes of holding the NT username/password. NDS keeps its own password, but the idea is for NT and NDS to have the same password. This complexity is required because of the way NT authentication works—it assumes that you integrate with it, not displace it.

10.4.6 LDAP Services for NDS

LDAP services for NDS allow an LDAP-compliant client to access NDS information. However, there is a catch. NDS offers a reasonably advanced authentication and authorization access control mechanism, whereas LDAP has been a bit in flux in this area (through LDAPv3). Therefore, an LDAP client still must be authenticated via the NDS authentication method, either directly or through a program that proxies on its behalf.

10.5 NetWare 3.x/4.x Integration with TCP/IP

With the introduction of *NetWare/IP*, Novell introduced a more consistent method of integrating TCP/IP into the NetWare environment. However, as mentioned in the introduction to this chapter, none of this is particularly easy.

The main motivation for routing NetWare using IP rather than IPX would be either of the following:

1. To utilize a pure IP routing infrastructure for NetWare, keeping SAP and IPX routing off of it. Large networks can certainly benefit from such a move since supporting multiple routing protocols on the network (IP, IPX, and SAP) offers operational challenges by requiring people to understand and manage more protocols than they might otherwise need to.

2. To allow the NetWare client to access an IP-based service. The argument for this is weakening considerably since most desktop machines have no problem running a pure TCP/IP stack and IPX at the same time (for example, Windows 95). That being the case, the easiest approach would be to access IP services with the IP stack and routing infrastructure and IPX services with the IPX infrastructure. This has

been a popular approach to date. Having TCP/IP enabled on the desktop is almost like making sure you have a floppy drive. It is becoming ubiquitous.

Critics argue that the problem with NetWare/IP is that it attempts too many things. Plus, add to it your client-side installation burden and need for new servers and organizational concepts (NetWare/IP domains), and you have some challenges.

When NetWare/IP is used to provide access to IPX- based applications, it can use what NetWare refers to as *IPX emulation.* In this case, the entire IPX packet, with all 30 bytes of overhead, is added to an IP UDP-based packet, which adds another 28 bytes (20 for IP + 8 for UDP), giving a total of 58 bytes of routing overhead per packet. NetWare/IP is illustrated in Figure 10.15. Take that overhead and send it down a 64-Kbps link, and you will feel it, or simply compute the average data packet size for your applications and note what percentage of overhead gets sent along with every packet—you can translate that to dollars in monthly bandwidth costs and network capacity requirements.

So, for IPX-based applications, NetWare/IP is, in fact, encapsulation approach. Still, though, Novell added some functionality on top of this by providing a way to map the IP routing environment into the IPX and SAP environment.

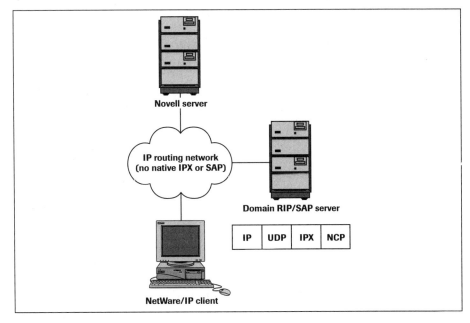

Figure 10.15 NetWare/IP

NetWare/IP clients rely on the old SAP mechanism as the way to obtain service information. However, IP does not support SAP, and, at the time Novell developed NetWare/IP, there was no IP standard that offered equivalent functionality to SAP. Furthermore, there needed to be a way for client applications to know about IPX connectivity in the network since they were written with the assumption that such information was available to them.

So, Novell developed a new kind of server, one that had to be installed for each NetWare/IP domain in your network (domain is an IP domain in this context), called the *Domain SAP/RIP Service* (DSS). DSS is used to share SAP service availability and IPX connectivity information with NetWare/IP clients and servers. NetWare/IP clients and servers send queries to the DSS server to obtain service availability information. The DSS server is an additional administrative burden that can extend across your network. And, since NetWare/IP clients and servers must regularly communicate with it, you cannot just have one server for your whole network—you need to distribute DSS servers nearest to your NetWare/IP clients and servers and manage traffic to and from them. Finally, don't forget the importance of DSS redundancy—you will therefore need multiple DSS servers for backup purposes.

NetWare 5 will be the first NetWare release to natively rely on TCP/IP, which will offer relief from the challenges associated with approaches such as those offered by NetWare/IP. We will discuss NetWare 5 in more detail in a later section.

10.6 NetWare and IBM SNA Integration

Novell offers a gateway product, jointly developed with IBM and called *NetWare for IBM SAA,* that allows NetWare clients to access Systems Network Architecture (SNA) hosts. Other approaches include those discussed in Chapter 11, such as the use of TCP/IP-based Web client and 3270-based emulation.

Historically, Novell has done a reasonably good job with its gateway products. The most commonly implemented configuration is based on using 3270 emulation software on the desktop that uses IPX as the transport mechanism. This software communicates with the NetWare SAA gateway, which converts IPX to SNA SDLC and/or token ring protocols (see Chapter 11 for details on SNA protocols).

The NetWare SAA gateway supports LU6.2, allowing PU2.1-based functionality between the gateway and the IBM SNA system. By supporting a full range of LU6.2 APIs, the application developer can write NetWare client-side applications that leverage advanced functions on the IBM mainframe.

10.7 NetWare 5: The Dawn of Native TCP/IP over NetWare

NetWare 5 represents the coming together of a number of core efforts inside Novell, including native TCP/IP support and a robust server application development environment, all tightly integrated with NDS. NetWare 5, with its strong directory services offering and commitment to Java and CORBA, can offer considerable benefits to the enterprise. Here is a summary of key NetWare 5 features:

- This release is based entirely on TCP/IP. No more must you rely on IPX and SAP, unless, of course, you require them to interoperate with earlier versions of NetWare in your network. NetWare 5 offers full-out TCP/IP support, including an implementation of the IETF-standard Service Location Protocol (SLP), essentially an IP-based version of SAP. Also, NDS has been integrated with DNS and DHCP.

- Well-behaved legacy applications written to leverage NCP through standard NetWare APIs, unless "dirty-hooked," as Novell puts it, into IPX, can natively leverage TCP/IP without IPX encapsulation. This is achieved through what Novell refers to as *compatibility-mode* drivers. New applications written to standard NetWare APIs will use TCP/IP natively. For anywhere that IPX is still required, Novell will provide *migration gateways* that allow both protocols to be managed and translated between each other. Applications that are dirty-hooked will still require IPX encapsulation when run over TCP/IP.

- As discussed in the next section, NetWare 5 offers a rich Java and CORBA application development environment.

- Offering an alternative to the Microsoft Wolfpack effort, NetWare 5's clustering support allows multiple servers to be connected to form a more powerful system, subject, of course, to the ability of the application to be modular enough to be able to be decoupled and run across several servers.

10.8 Modern Novell Application Development: Java, CORBA, and the Directory Service

Historically, NetWare has suffered in the application development area, forcing software developers to rely on the NLM model, providing a lack of stability due to poor memory protection from misbehaving applications and a shallow set of generalized development tools when compared with other competing operating systems. The core file and print services offered by NetWare ended up being NetWare's main draw. These services were then augmented with the bare number of server-side NLMs needed for a particular application. Associated client-side applications, developed in the native desktop environment (for example, Windows), leveraged these services through calls to NCP.

With the release of IntraNetWare and NetWare 5, Novell offers more attractive server-side application development technologies based on many of the open multiplatform approaches discussed in Chapter 2. In doing so, NetWare better competes with NT 5 as a server-side development platform. Note the use of the word *server-side* here. It is not such a grand story to talk about the NetWare client supporting Java and CORBA, for example. Numerous Web browsers are available today, bordering on free, that do just that. What is exciting is that these development tools are available to run within the NetWare server itself, a place heretofore being a relatively unfriendly place for application development.

Here is a summary of key next-generation application development tools available as part of IntraNetWare and NetWare 5:

- The object infrastructure allows networking and management services available within the NetWare environment, both core file and print services as well as third-party applications, to be exposed as methods within a rich object infrastructure. Novell has based its CORBA offering on the VisiBroker for Java product by Visigenic Software, Inc. The OMG has defined, as part of CORBA, the *trading object service,* which is one of the most fundamental and important services needed for object technology to fully proliferate within the enterprise. This service allows a client or server to query it to determine the availability of objects capable of performing a certain service. So, for example, if you need a Russian spell-checker, then you can query for an object capable of that, and, if it is available, you can invoke it. Now, what you really want to do is go to global directory service, a.k.a. NDS, to make this query, not to a secondary information source. Fortunately, Novell is taking steps toward this by providing tools that integrate its trading object service, called *Novell Trader,* with NDS.

- Support for a platform-independent language and APIs (Java and JavaBeans) allows for accessing equivalent NCP functionality using open multiplatform programming standards. Java provides an alternative to the NLM software development approach.

- Support for the NWDS API (an X.500-like API specified by Novell), for LDAP, and for Java makes NDS quite an appealing platform for building value-added directory-service-based applications. Novell offers a JavaBean that provides NDS edit/add/create/delete object functionality using standard Java development tools.

- Planned support for Java Distributed Printing Services (JDPS) allows NetWare's rich printing services to be accessible via Java. Novell worked on JDPS along with Sun, Hewlett Packard, and Xerox to extend Java so that it can be used to manage print jobs and queues, deal with status information, and so forth.

- Server-side languages and tools include Perl, JavaScript, Dynamic HTML, and NetBasic (a Visual-Basic-compatible language for server-side applications).

10.9 **Conclusions**

Novell NetWare offers a comprehensive network application framework for the enterprise and has an extremely large installed base. NDS is one of NetWare's greatest strengths. Novell has taken serious steps in moving toward a pure TCP/IP environment. Novell's decision to focus on open multiplatform technologies such as Java and CORBA, combined with the strength of NDS and its existing installed base, make the latest versions of Novell NetWare a potentially compelling solution for the enterprise.

FOR FURTHER STUDY

1. R. A. Hanley. *NetWare Migration: Methods, Tools, and Techniques for Migrating to NetWare 4.* New York: John Wiley, 1996.

2. J. F. Hughes and B. W. Thomas. *Novell's Four Principles of NDS Design.* San Jose, Calif.: Novell Press, 1996.

3. M. A. Miller. *LAN Protocol Handbook.* Redwood City, Calif.: M&T Books, 1990.

4. K. Siyan. *NetWare Professional Reference, Fourth Edition.* Indianapolis, Ind.: New Riders Publishing, 1995.

5. C. Malamud. *Analyzing Novell Networks.* New York: Van Nostrand Reinhold, 1992.

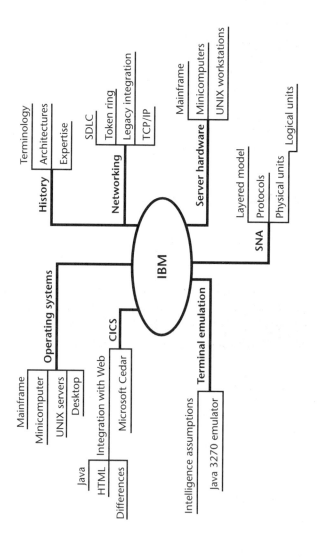

CHAPTER 11

IBM

CHAPTER HIGHLIGHTS

Topic	Benefits	Experience
IBM computer hardware, including mainframes and minicomputers	Because of IBM's long history there is an "alphabet soup" of IBM products deployed in the enterprise. Being able to work with IBM networks and associated applications requires knowledge of different hardware systems and their roles.	IBM owns the top end of the data food chain. Find yourself in a crowd of IBM-conversant folks, and you will be quickly lost if you lack knowledge of IBM hardware naming, roles, and evolution.
Systems Network Architecture (SNA)	SNA is one of the first fully architected network application frameworks. It is still widely deployed across enterprise networks in larger companies.	Do you know what a PU2, PU4, PU5, or LU6.2 is? How about LLC2 or DLSw? If not, then you may have difficulty managing integration with legacy IBM networks.

CHAPTER HIGHLIGHTS		
Topic	**Benefits**	**Experience**
SDLC, token ring, and LLC2, including spoofing techniques and DLSw	SDLC and LLC2 are challenging protocols from a networking perspective. They are "chatty" and do not respond well to delays within the network. Techniques such as spoofing and converting legacy SDLC devices to token ring/LLC2 devices allow us to deal with these challenges. DLSw allows us to integrate SDLC and LLC2 devices with TCP/IP.	Understanding the networking issues associated with SDLC and token ring/LLC2 is make-or-break kind of knowledge. Either you have some exposure to it and its issues, or you are a sitting duck for a wide range of networking headaches. We will go into detail on these subjects because they are fundamental to understanding how to bring IBM legacy systems into our modern networks.
IBM CICS transaction processing and Web integration	CICS is one of the most widely deployed transaction-processing systems today, in spite of the fact that its origins date back to the 1960s. Transaction processing is a main staple of our expanding era of electronic commerce. Integrating it with the Web is fundamental.	It is not at all uncommon to be requested to make certain data residing within an IBM mainframe available on the Web. Much of this mainframe data is handled by CICS. We will explore CICS and techniques and technologies for integrating with it.

11.1 Introduction

Electronic commerce, the Internet, the Intranet, and Extranet applications will not, as a whole, meet their expectations if we ignore the fact that much of the mission-critical data at the core of businesses today resides on IBM mainframe technology. It is not just a harsh reality or a complication to us that this data resides on these mammoth systems. IBM has earned, in many respects, its reign at the top of the data food chain. IBM products offer noteworthy scalability and reliability.

It is in vogue at the moment, although perhaps temporarily, to turn one's nose up at the thought that it is necessary to understand mainframe fundamentals. With exception of those working deep within the bowels of mission-critical IS departments, many IS professionals have evolved without much mainframe experience. They are mainly Windows and UNIX experts. More and more, though, these folks are finding themselves pushed up against blue steel (IBM, that is) when it comes time to take their applications to the next level.

This chapter is intended to help guide you to this next level by providing a straightforward architectural view along with practical exposure to key IBM mainframe technologies and standards, as well as workgroup and workstation computing designs. With this information, you will be able to understand the role of legacy mainframe applications within your overall information system design and plan their future, as well as consider where IBM architectures and products might play a role in new application and networking system development.

IBM offers its own world of communications and application development standards. IBM essentially wrote the book on the fundamentals of distributed computing, and IBM products reflect a long history of work in the development of architectural frameworks and networking protocols. Because of this long history and legacy proprietary architectures, integrating with IBM applications can often introduce a variety of performance and functional challenges, as with any integration effort. In this chapter, we will explore key integration challenges.

11.2 An IBM Time Line and Computer Systems Overview

As a result of IBM's long history, and because of the rich technical work that has evolved during it, one of the largest stumbling blocks for those wishing to understand IBM products and their evolution is the deciphering of complex terminology that has accumulated throughout this history, including the manner in which this terminology has adapted over time, and understanding where a particular product family or architecture fits within the overall IBM scheme of things.

This whole topic of legacy IBM hardware and history is very important. There is still a tremendous amount of installed (existing) legacy IBM equipment deployed today—equipment, in some cases, dating back, either in architecture or manufacture, to the 1970s. It is especially prevalent in the financial services industry, an industry where IBM's reputation for rock-solid reliability is not in the least bit taken for granted, but you will see it all over. Some may not believe this, justifiably, perhaps because they have been raised on a steady diet of new technology (that displaces technology that came before it) every 12 to 18 months, the kind of change that has been served up across the industry especially over the last ten years. You will, however, become a believer the first time you walk into a room full of blue water-cooled mainframes and controller equipment, and you want to know where to begin. You will quickly learn the value of understanding IBM history. If you are required to work with networks and applications leveraging this installed legacy base of equipment, you will need to understand the names, roles, relationships, and timing of IBM hardware and architectures.

11.2.1 The Time Line

So, let's open here with the time line and nomenclature overview provided in Table 11.1. You should review this table before continuing with this chapter. Most of these terms will be discussed in more detail as we proceed.

Table 11.1 Key IBM Advancements

IBM Advancement	Key Elements	Date
S/360	First comprehensive mainframe architecture. Note that number "360" came from all the points of a compass (360 degrees) and was intended to symbolize the universal applicability, full range of performance and price, and "whole company" focus of the 360 project.	1964
S/370	Expanded memory address space, allowing for greater memory, dual-processor support, virtual storage capability, and enhanced channel communications capabilities.	1971
Systems Network Architecture (SNA)	One of the original fully architected network application framework architectures.	1974
370/XA	Further expanded address space (31 bits), allowing for backwards-compatible support for S/370 and enhanced multiaccess channel support.	1981
First IBM personal computers	First IBM-architected and -produced "PC-compatible" machines. While IBM does not own the market now, its designs are the basis for the majority of desktop PCs in use today.	1981

Table 11.1 (continued)

IBM Advancement	Key Elements	Date
Advanced Peer-to-Peer Networking (APPN)	Added dynamic capabilities to the IBM-architecture. The original approach IBM took with its communications and applications architecture was based on predefined connectivity as opposed to dynamically discovering the route to a destination, its capabilities, and so forth.	1985
OS/2	Originally a joint development effort between IBM and Microsoft but never hit the desktop as a mainstream operating system. Continues as a viable desktop component within an enterprise SNA network and is also appreciated by die-hard technologists knowledgeable enough to appreciate the goals to which OS/2 has aspired and its hidden technical strengths.	1987
370/ESA	Compared to 370/XA, offered further enhanced data storage architecture with up to 16 terabytes of addressability.	1988
AS/400	Typically positioned as a workgroup minicomputer, larger than a desktop server but smaller and less expensive than a mainframe. Newer models use Reduced Instruction Set Computer (RISC) technology.	1988
S/390 with ES/9000-series processors	Compared to 370/ESA, offered more powerful ES/9000 CPU processor options, parallel processing capability, higher-speed fiber optic channel communication, enhanced LAN connectivity, and other advancements.	1990
RS/6000	PowerPC RISC-based UNIX workstation and server products based on IBM's AIX UNIX operating system.	1989: RS/6000 1993: PowerPC-based RS/6000

Table 11.1 (continued)

IBM Advancement	Key Elements	Date
S/390 parallel sysplex	Parallel processing support with the S/390. Up to 32 servers can be coupled together to execute as a single machine, enhancing performance and reliability.	1994
OS/390	All-encompassing operating system architecture that includes existing technologies like MVS and DCE security services, as well as more recent parallel processing advancements.	1995

11.2.2 Processors and Architectures

11.2.2.1 Mainframes

Let's begin our education in IBM nomenclature with a study of how IBM names its mainframe products. IBM's mainframe processors are based on an architecture:

- A *processor series* is designated by a *series number.* Examples of such numbers include 3090, 4300, and 9000, which are not particular processor models but represent a series of processors based on a particular design. A particular processor model, based on one of these designs, is identified by a *model number,* such as 4381. For an analogy, we might consider how we often refer to the standard Intel processor architecture upon which Windows and DOS are based as "x86." The designation x86 is something like a processor series. Specific processor models within this series include the 80386, the 80486, and the Pentium.

- Mainframe *architectures* include the 370/XA, 370/ESA, and so forth. An architecture defines the way a particular series of processors work together with the operating system and input/output devices.

A mainframe configuration is therefore designated by architecture, by processor series number, and by processor model number.

11.2.2.2. Parallel Processing

Microsoft's entree into parallel processing is through its Wolfpack product, which was briefly discussed in Chapter 7. While Microsoft is relatively new to this game, IBM has been in the parallel processing business for quite some time. The 3090 mainframes support highly advanced multiprocessing, as does the RS/6000. The RS/6000 SP supports up to 128 parallel processing nodes.

Parallel processing can offer reliability and performance benefits. For reliability, by using more than one processor, it may be possible to protect the mainframe or RS/6000 server from a total failure in the event that one or more individual processors fail. And, with regard to performance, it may be possible to increase performance for your particular application by adding processors operating in parallel to your configuration. Note that, in order to get this performance benefit, your application must be modular enough so that different parts of it can be broken out and run in parallel. Before investing heavily in a parallel processing configuration, it would be wise to conduct benchmark tests to see whether adding more processors does in fact increase performance.

11.2.2.3 AS/400 and RS/6000

IBM introduced the *AS/400* as a workgroup computer, It was intended to fill the gap between mainframe and desktop computers. The AS/400 is considerably less expensive than a mainframe computer setup and is easier to maintain. The AS/400, as introduced, took on more of a mainframe feel with regard to its applications than the next midrange computer line introduced by IBM, the *RS/6000*.

The AS/400 runs an operating system called *OS/400*. The RS/6000 offers a UNIX-based operating system called *AIX*. From a hardware standpoint, both the AS/400 and the RS/6000 processors have roots in the PowerPC RISC architecture.

11.2.3 **Mainframe Operating Systems and Applications**

IBM's mainframe operating systems include the following:

- Multiple Virtual Storage (MVS)
- Virtual Machine (VM)
- OS/390

Multiple Virtual Storage (MVS) is an early example of a multiuser, multitasking operating system. The basis of the naming was that, at the time, the multiuser, multitasking problem was seen primarily as a challenge of sharing the storage (address) space of the machine by different users and tasks such that each one did not have to worry about the other—that is, that the machine and its storage would appear as belonging entirely to the user, from the user's individual perspective.

MVS/XA supports the 370/XA architecture, *MVS/ESA* supports the 370/ESA architecture, and so forth. Notice that the architecture designator, XA, for example, is appended to the operating system name, MVS, for example, yielding MVS/XA.

Virtual Machine (VM) was intended to allow a single machine to run multiple operating systems and, for itself, to act as an operating system. This is quite a feat, even by today's standards. This capability allows companies to keep an older version of an operating system and, at the same time, run a new one in parallel. As they gain familiarity with it and leverage the new operating system, they can maintain their existing operations without disruption. Like MVS, there is a VM/XA, VM/ESA, and so forth.

OS/390 is an all-encompassing operating system. It combines MVS support with enhanced Open Group DCE security services and parallel processing advancements.

When reading about IBM mainframes and working with them, you are bound to run across the *Virtual Telecommunications Access Method* (VTAM). VTAM provides the method for applications to communicate with terminals, storage devices, other computers, and so forth. Applications therefore leverage the underlying operating system but, at the same time, leverage VTAM for communication services. Figure 11.1 illustrates VTAM for two common mainframe applications, the Time Sharing Option (TSO), sort of an interactive command-line shell environment for the mainframe, and the Customer Information Control System (CICS).

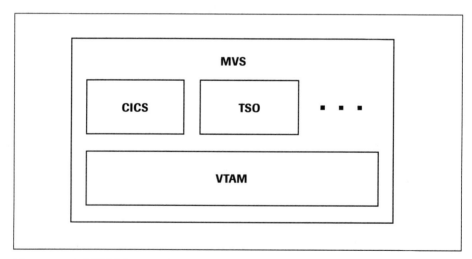

Figure 11.1 VTAM for two common mainframe applications

11.2.4 Mainframe Access with Terminals

Historically, the way for a user to interact with an IBM mainframe has been with a computer terminal such as the popular *3270 terminal.* So, you might walk into a room and see rows and rows of these things lined up, one after another, with busy workers typing away, entering in customer orders, checking status, or doing whatever else their business required. As desktop personal computers became more popular, IS departments moved to *3270 emulation software,* which allowed a personal computer to perform the same functions as a dedicated 3270 terminal.

As we will discuss later, you can now integrate the 3270 style of terminal handling straight into a Web browser interface, complete with Java, and not even be required to modify the back-end mainframe application. Note that 3270 is actually a "data stream" format and protocol and not a particular hardware product.

3270 terminals can be connected to another hardware component called the *3174 establishment controller.* We will discuss the 3174 and similar devices in the next section.

11.3 SNA Components: Physical Units and Logical Units

The IBM *Systems Network Architecture* (SNA) is full of its own complex and redundant terminology, as with any advanced technology. We will focus on getting up to speed on this terminology in this section.

Stand-alone intelligent computing devices are referred to as *physical units* (PUs) within the SNA framework. A PU is designated by a *type*, a number that denotes its role within the SNA architecture. As we build our knowledge of SNA physical units in the following discussion, you should refer to Figure 11.2, which provides a summary of key PU architectural components.

The mainframe processors, or *hosts*, are considered *type* 5 physical units. Mainframe processors typically off-load CPU-intensive communication processing to devices referred to as *communication controllers* or *front-end processors* (FEPs). Within the SNA architecture, these are considered *type* 4 physical units. For simplicity, we usually drop the word *type* and refer to a particular physical unit by its abbreviation (PU) plus the type number. For example, we refer to a type 4 physical unit as a PU4 device and to a type 5 as a PU5. Using our newly established terminology, we can say that PU4 devices perform communications processing for the host (PU5).

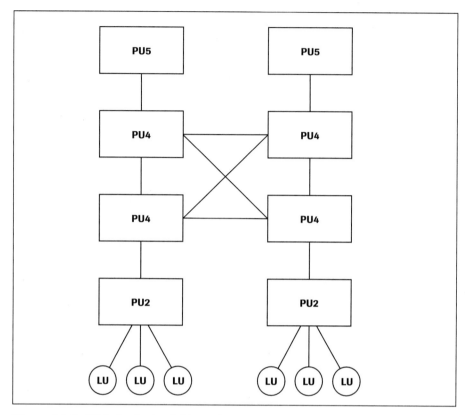

Figure 11.2 IBM physical unit hierarchy

Let's look at the PU4 in a little more detail. A PU4 is functionally, for the most part, a packet switch conforming to the protocol architecture and configuration requirements of SNA. PU4s can route traffic to one another and can therefore form a switching network. Figure 11.2 shows PU4 devices interconnected in a mesh configuration. PU4 devices provide connectivity to hosts and to *type 2 nodes* (PU2).

PU2 devices, also called *cluster controllers,* provide access to terminals and printers. Under the SNA architecture, terminals and printers are referred to as dependent *logical units* (LUs). Figure 11.2 also shows LUs.

We can match up our newly learned PU terminology with particular IBM products. For example, an IBM model S/370 is an example of a PU5, a model 3745 is an example of a PU4, and a model 3174 is an example of a PU2. LU examples include IBM 3270 and 5250 terminals.

Let's examine the relationship between PUs. SNA imposes a *master/slave* relationship between PU2 and PU4 devices. This means that the PU4 determines when the PU2 can send data and when it cannot. This is enforced through the underlying communication protocol. Later, we will discuss SDLC and LLC2, which are two SNA protocols providing mechanisms to control the flow of data between a PU4 and a PU2 in a master/slave fashion.

The hierarchical form of SNA is essentially based upon the assumption that the host PU5 device has practically all of the intelligence and that PU2s and LUs are input/output devices, advanced as they may be with regard to performing input/output functions, as is the case of the more advanced IBM terminal products. Later, we will see a newer form of SNA, called *APPN*, that modifies some of these assumptions.

11.4 The Systems Network Architecture (SNA) Layered Model

The SNA layered model for communications and applications is similar to, but not the same as, that of OSI. Figure 11.3 provides a summary of the SNA model.

Transaction services	**User services (DIA, SNA/DS, DDM), management, translation**
Presentation services	**Application programming interface, data formatting**
Data flow control	**Request/response, chaining**
Transmission control	**Session management, pacing, sequencing, encryption**
Path control	**Routing, trunk groups**
Data link control	**SDLC, IEEE 802.2/LLC2, X.25/QLLC**
Physical control	**Dedicated leased lines, LANs**

Figure 11.3 IBM SNA model

Let's explore each SNA layer:

- The *physical control* layer is the same as in the OSI model. It simply specifies the physical interface (RS-232, V.35, RS-449, LAN connectors) and the physical cabling used to carry the signal, such as token ring or Ethernet cabling.

- The *data link control* layer is essentially the same as the link layer in the OSI model. Its purpose is to provide an error-free link between two PUs within the SNA framework. The legacy technology for this layer is the Synchronous Data Link Control (SDLC) protocol. The equivalent, though different, protocol used on LANs for SNA is specified in an IEEE standard, the IEEE 802.2 Logical Link Control protocol (LLC2). Later sections are devoted to SDLC and LLC2, as well as to their interoperability with TCP/IP.

- The *path control* layer is responsible for routing between PU devices. Path control handles features such as load sharing across multiple SDLC links. Load sharing is enabled by configuring communication links as part of an SNA *transmission group*, which is a collection of individual transmission facility elements, such as SDLC leased lines, that act as if they were a single larger transmission facility.

- The *transmission control* layer handles management of LU sessions and provides LU-to-LU sequencing and flow control via a method known as *pacing*, as well as SNA security services such as encryption. The pacing function, illustrated in Figure 11.4, can have a significant impact on system performance. Pacing is a method by which each LU communicates to the other the number of packets at any given time it is willing to receive. Clearly, if this number is low, then throughput performance for the particular LU session will suffer. The maximum pacing value for a session is an SNA configurable value, and network engineers are strongly advised to tune the value of this for their application, with bigger often meaning better performance, especially when the underlying communication network offers significant propagation delay, such as in the case of a satellite-based network.

- The *data flow control* layer is responsible for LU-to-LU data flow control. LU communication is formatted in *request units* and *response units* (RUs). Sometimes, it is necessary to chain RUs together. For example, an entire screen update needs to happen as a single event since a user does not really know how to react to half a screen that is updated and another half that is not, other than to assume the system

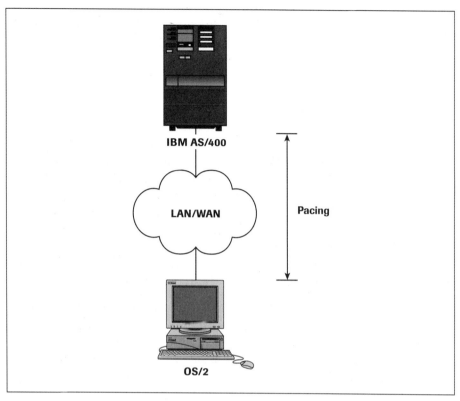

Figure 11.4 SNA pacing

has crashed. So, while the individual update elements of the screen might constitute separate RUs, they are chained so that they are performed as a single action, from the perspective of the host. If there is an error during the screen update, then the entire chain is re-sent; therefore, chaining provides a means of logically correlating RUs that represent, from the perspective of the action being performed, essentially one action, such as a complete screen update.

- At the *presentation services* and *transaction services* layers, the syntax and presentation of data are handled, and facilities for distributed database management and transaction processing are provided. LU6.2, and important SNA feature we will discuss later, are defined within these layers. At these layers, you will find data-synchronization functions such as checkpointing and backout procedures that are used in transaction processing. For example, if a database is being updated, both peer applications may need to update their databases simultaneously. They will likely perform checkpointing during the update process, meaning that each application verifies the other is at essentially the same point in the database update process before moving to the next point. If there is an error, then both applications will attempt to back out of the change.

Other services defined at the transaction layer include the Document Interchange Architecture (DIA) for electronic mail and documentation librarian services, SNA/Distribution Services (SNA/DS) for store and forward networking, and Distributed Data Management (DDM) for remote file and remote database access.

11.5 IBM Networking

TCP/IP, as a nonproprietary interconnection standard, offered a long-awaited alternative to the large and expensive proprietary systems IBM pioneered, and the Internet has revolutionized the way business and government institutions alike communicate, as well as the general public.

IBM has had, during its development of SNA over the years, the burden of providing a full and complete solution, from the application layer to the physical layer, for corporate information systems and the networks that support them. IBM SNA is a fairly complete solution for each class of application, providing a specification up to and including the application-layer programming interface, as is the case for LU6.2.

Today, IBM products continue to be found almost everywhere. They now require integration with open technologies such as TCP/IP, require migration to LAN technologies, and require a migration either to IBM's newer SNA architectures or to other application frameworks.

11.5.1 The First Networking Intelligence Assumption: The Desktop Has None

In its beginnings, SNA was built on the assumption that the device in front of the user was a simple display device with a keyboard, such as the 3270 emulator we discussed earlier. Obviously, with the availability of inexpensive but powerful personal computers, it is no longer necessary or correct to assume this is the case, though it is sometimes shocking to see how much software exists today, both old and new, based on exactly that assumption.

With the introduction of *Advanced Peer-to-Peer Networking* (APPN), SNA introduced capabilities allowing the desktop to become more of a peer in the computing experience, moving SNA away from the dumb terminal assumption.

11.5.2 Making It Dynamic: APPN

The problem with SNA as we have described it thus far, with its PU2s and PU4s and its preconfigured master/slave relationships, is that it is difficult to maintain and not particularly flexible. With this earlier form of SNA, typically referred to as *subarea SNA*, everything is predefined, and the computing intelligence is assumed to be centralized—remote devices are not assumed to be capable of much in the way of dynamic route discovery, directory services, and so forth. There is nothing dynamic about much of anything with this form of SNA. From the routes through the network to the decision of who is master and who is slave, there needs to be a human being who manually configures it and, if things change, someone to administer the change.

What is missing from this earlier form of SNA is the ability to dynamically learn about other devices on the network, to dynamically determine the best possible route to the destination, to dynamically resolve addresses (dynamic directory services), and so forth. These dynamic features reduce the burden on the administrator and make it easier to add and remove services. And, besides, we have all come to expect such features since the TCP/IP protocol suite combined with IP routing provides all of these capabilities at a low cost. The old statically defined way of doing things just won't cut it for a generation of IS people raised on TCP/IP.

APPN does away with the master/slave relationship between devices and instead treats them all as peers. APPN assumes intelligence within the LUs themselves by no longer assuming there is just a dumb terminal on the other end of the connection. To achieve this, APPN introduces a new logical unit called *LU6.2* as well as a new physical unit called *PU2.1*. An LU6.2 is an intelligent, independent logical unit, not necessarily a terminal or printer but instead an intelligent device such as a desktop computer, that can communicate on a peer-to-peer basis with other LU6.2 devices. This newer architecture, based upon the LU6.2 standard and a PU2.1, assumes peer-to-peer communication between PU2.1 devices.

11.5.3 Networking Media and Methods

Let's now turn our attention to the methods by which PU4 and PU2 devices communicate as well as PU2.1 devices. We will study the legacy SNA method of communication based on leased lines, typically operating at speeds of 56 Kbps and implementing the Synchronous Data Link Control (SDLC) protocol. Next, we will study token ring technology and its associated protocols, as well as the performance challenges associated with designing networks with these mechanisms, including interoperability between SDLC and token ring networks and their integration with TCP/IP.

11.5.3.1 Leased Lines: Synchronous Data Link Control (SDLC)

Synchronous Data Link Control (SDLC) is a communications protocol designed to run over leased lines. On one end of an SDLC connection is PU4. On the other end is a cluster controller that concentrates traffic from one or more PU2s onto the SDLC link. From an operational standpoint, SDLC is similar to other link-level protocols such as HDLC. SDLC detects errors, requests retransmission for errored frames, offers an addressing mechanism, and so forth. SDLC also offers a mechanism for the master PU4 to poll individual PU2s.

Figure 11.5 illustrates an SDLC link. As shown in the figure, PU2s service LUs, as we previously discussed. The figure illustrates that a given SDLC link can carry multiple PU2s wishing to communicate with the host PU4, and each of these PU2/PU4 connections can carry multiple LU sessions. This is the most important part of SDLC to understand—that it provides a multiplexing mechanism for LUs to communicate with the host connections between it and downstream PU2 devices. Also, of course, we must not forget that SDLC provides an error-free link through its detection and recovery mechanisms and that this is fundamental.

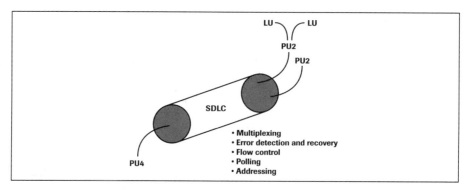

Figure 11.5 An SDLC link

A single SDLC link can support connections between on PU4 and many PU2 devices. The number of these connections in the real world may range from a few, sometimes fifteen or so, and sometimes even more. Performance on the link degrades as more PUs are added since each one incrementally increases bandwidth and communication processing requirements.

Each PU2 on an SDLC link has a master/slave relationship whereby the PU4 device *polls* the PU2 device when the PU4 wishes to receive data from it. The overhead associated with polling (i.e., the poll packets stating that the PU2 is allowed to send) is very large. The transmission of these polling packets, which can add up to hundreds every few minutes depending upon the configuration, can wreak serious havoc on your wide area network. Therefore, SDLC polling packets are often *spoofed* by the router or other communications hardware whenever a wide area network exists between the PU4 and its PU2s.

Spoofing means that polling and acknowledgment traffic are handled locally and not passed end-to-end through the network. Straight tunneling of SDLC, with all of its overhead and without any form of spoofing, tunneled into another protocol such as IP and sent end-to-end through the network, will often result in a very poorly performing application, not to mention excessive expense in terms of network bandwidth usage, network switching processor utilization, and staff required to keep the thing running. The difference between allowing the end-to-end transmission of polling and SDLC acknowledgment frames versus spoofing, or local acknowledgment, is illustrated in Figure 11.6.

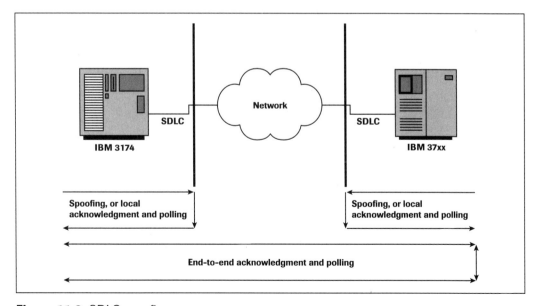

Figure 11.6 SDLC spoofing

11.5.3.2 Token Ring, IEEE 802.5

The *IBM token ring* is based on the IEEE 802.5 standard. The token ring standard calls for two operating speeds: 4 Mbps or 16 Mbps. Token ring is a more advanced and modern method for interconnecting physical units.

All devices on the token ring share a common medium (the ring itself), and, therefore, there needs to be an arbitration mechanism so that everyone does not try to communicate at the same time. In other words, all devices connected to the token ring LAN must take turns transmitting. In order to control which device can send and which cannot, token ring LANs utilize a token to manage contention. A device on the LAN cannot transmit unless it holds the token. Devices on the LAN must take turns acquiring and then releasing the token so that all devices get a fair chance to transmit. This basic operation is illustrated in Figure 11.7.

The acquisition and relinquishing of tokens, as well as other details associated with making this mechanism workable for all operating conditions,

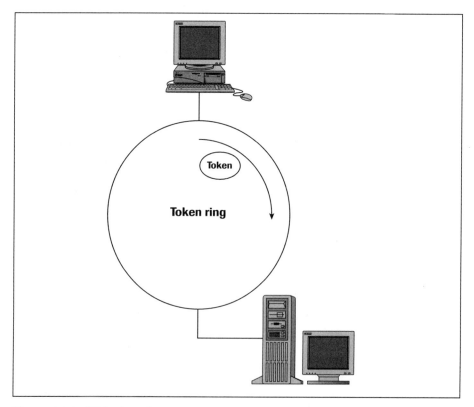

Figure 11.7 IBM token ring operation

are managed by designated devices on the LAN called *ring monitors.* Any device on the LAN is capable of being a ring monitor. Devices on the LAN can vote over which device will be the ring monitor and which will back up that device. All this can occur in a relatively transparent fashion, from an administrative standpoint.

So, we have covered communication between devices on a single token ring LAN. What about devices connected to separate token ring LANs? How do they communicate?

The first method developed for such communication—and one still widely used, though not without its challenges—is called *source route bridging* (SRB). With SRB, individual token rings are interconnected by devices called *bridges,* which are essentially communication switches that aid in finding paths from one token ring to another. From the perspective of a device attached to a token ring LAN, the bridge or bridges that must be traversed to reach a destination token ring address are learned by using a broadcast explorer mechanism based upon its broadcast of a special explorer token ring control frame. This frame is broadcast by the device on the token ring wishing to send data to all reachable token ring LANs. Responses are sent back to the device (the originator of the explorer frame) indicating the path taken by the frame. The originator then looks at all responses and typically chooses the path with the fewest number of intermediate LANs to reach the destination, Most SRB devices will support only seven or fewer token ring bridges along the path from source to destination. If you have more than seven bridges, you may require a routing approach (we'll discuss this later), or you may need to reduce the number of token rings required to be traversed to reach the given destination by redesigning your network.

One of the biggest problems with SRB, aside from the traditional seven-hop limitation, is that of the flooding caused by *SRB explorer* packets. These packets are generated frequently by token ring devices in order to learn routes to a given destination. They can produce significant network traffic and bandwidth overhead in large token-ring-based networks. For these and other reasons, many people are moving away from bridging and into routing approaches that we will look at later. However, to use these other approaches, it is still usually necessary to spoof the SRB behavior within the router.

11.5.3.3 SDLC and IEEE 802.2 Logical Link Control 2 (LLC2) Token Ring Legacy Integration

Just having a means to arbitrate communication across a token ring LAN, which IEEE 802.5 specifies, is not enough to accommodate SNA sessions on the LAN. There needs to be a protocol that provides some of the same fundamental error detection, recovery, and multiplexing functionality that

SDLC provides, plus some new features needed to accommodate LAN interconnection. This capability is provided by another protocol called *Logical Link Control 2* (LLC2). LLC2 is defined in the IEEE 802.2 standard. Let's explore key differences and similarities between LLC2 and SDLC.

11.5.3.3.1 Polling   The LLC2 protocol does not enforce a polling mechanism; it does not require that one end of the connection be predesignated a slave and the other a master. However, it is quite talkative and

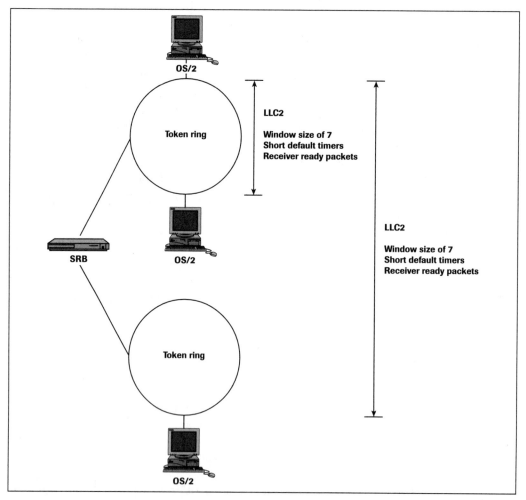

Figure 11.8 LLC2 overhead across the network

generates large amounts of acknowledgment traffic, used by the recipient of data to signal to the sender that the data has been received correctly. Acknowledgment traffic comes in the form of *receiver ready* (RR) packets. LLC2 also has relatively short default data acknowledgment timers, thereby producing time-out and retransmission scenarios between devices communicating across lower-speed networks. Therefore, like SDLC, LLC2 benefits from spoofing when two devices are communicating across a wide area network. LLC2 acknowledgment operation is illustrated in Figure 11.8.

11.5.3.3.2 Window Size   Because SDLC and LLC2 both enforce a window for error recovery and flow control, the configured maximum window size (the maximum number of data frames that can be outstanding before the source of the data frames must receive an acknowledgment) significantly influences performance since frames cannot be transmitted until they are acknowledged, and you can transmit only as many frames as the window size will allow at any given time. Many LLC2 default configurations are set for a maximum window size of 2. For many applications, this can be increased to a default maximum of 7, offering much better performance.

11.5.3.3.3 A Dynamic Window Size   The LLC2 window size is dynamic, meaning that two devices can negotiate a lower value if they choose, as opposed to relying on one configured by the administrator. However, in most implementations, if both devices are set for a maximum value of 7, they will use this value. While LLC2 and SDLC both provide for modulo 128 operation (maximum window size of 127), these options are not available on a great deal of available equipment and are not commonly used. A larger window size, if it were supported by the token ring devices, could potentially produce better throughput on low-bit error links.

11.5.3.3.4 Multiplexing   An SDLC link and a LAN can both carry traffic from multiple physical units. That is, they provide multiplexing.

11.5.3.3.5 Networking   Token ring devices support SRB functionality whereby, if a destination becomes unreachable, a new explorer frame is broadcast to determine whether the destination is still reachable by some other path through the network, whereas with SDLC, there is no analogy. In this regard, token ring can offer greater session-level reliability by automatically responding to changes within the interconnecting LAN infrastructure. At the same time, as mentioned earlier, the SRB explorer frames generated as part of the token ring device's effort to discover a new route can place a significant load on the network.

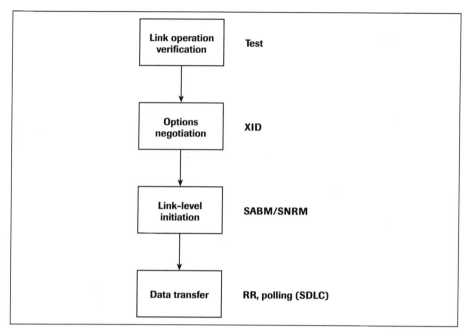

Figure 11.9 Link setup

11.5.3.3.6 Link Setup   With regard to link setup, SDLC and LLC2 operate quite similarly. Figure 11.9 shows the four basic states of these protocols. This level of detail is included here because a number of operational and installation challenges can be solved by understanding the fundamental states of this connection setup and where the failure may be occurring.

Both SDLC and LLC2 employ the *test* frame, which we have thus far referred to as the "explorer" frame for simplicity. SDLC uses it to verify the PU is up, whereas token ring uses it to find different paths to the destination for optimum path selection and the discovery of new paths to the destination in the event of a failure along the currently used path. The options negotiation phase identifies one PU to another, using unique identifiers, IDBLK and IDNUM, that are manually configured within the PUs themselves, and also supports the negotiation of window size, data field size, and various other information elements between the two communicating PUs. This identification and negotiation phase is called the *XID exchange.* If the XID exchange is successful, the link level is brought up. While it may seem like a detail, the XID exchange tends to become very important when trying to understand compatibility issues, wide area networking connectivity issues, and so forth. It is thus a valuable function to understand.

11.5.3.3.7 A More Advanced Addressing Methodology   With regard
to data link control addressing, SDLC uses a simple physical unit identifier
number, whereas LLC2 uses a more advanced approach based upon a *destination service access point* (DSAP) address, *source service access point* (SSAP)
address, *destination token ring address,* and *source token ring address.* Token
ring addressing is illustrated in Figure 11.10.

DSAPs and SSAPs identify the type of application being accessed. SNA
generally uses an SSAP of 04 (hex), meaning that you will often see SSAP and
DSAP set to 04 and 04. Some SDLC/LLC2 conversion devices will vary the
SSAP over the range 04 through EC (hex) in 04 increments in order to create
an overall unique address to the host for each PU2 device connecting to it.
This is done by the SDLC/LLC2 conversion device because all other aspects
of the address (the source token ring address, destination token ring address,
and DSAP) remain fixed and, for the host to tell one PU from the next, the

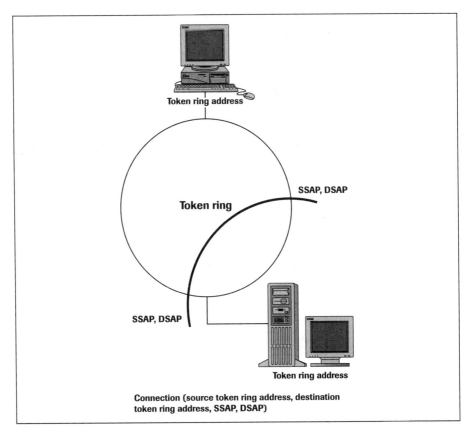

Figure 11.10 Token ring addressing

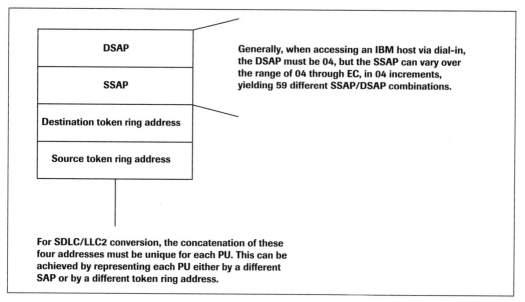

Figure 11.11 SDLC/LLC2 conversion addressing issues

SSAP must be varied. An alternative approach used by other SDLC/LLC2 conversion devices is to fix the SSAP and DSAP to 04 and to assign a separate source token ring address for each SDLC PU. This latter approach makes each SDLC PU appear as a separate token-ring-attached device instead of appearing as a different SSAP on the same token ring device. Figure 11.11 summarizes these addressing issues.

11.5.3.4 Legacy SNA Integration with TCP/IP: Data Link Switching (DLSw)

Earlier, we discussed SRB as a method for interconnecting token ring LANs. Now let's take a look at an alternative approach called *data link switching* (DLS or DLSw). IBM produced the DLSw specification and first implemented it in its IBM 6611 multiprotocol router. It is now available in a number of different router vendor products and has become an Internet Engineering Task Force (IETF) RFC standard.

In a nutshell, DLSw converts SRB to IP routing by converting LLC2 sessions to TCP/IP sessions controlled by a special DLSw transport protocol. Destination token ring addresses are mapped to IP addresses, and LLC2 sessions are spoofed at the IP router supporting DLSw, allowing a token ring frame to be routed as an IP datagram. This allows SNA to be routed over the same dynamic routing infrastructure used by TCP/IP applications. For example, if your router network uses OSPF or EIGRP, SNA with DLSw is routed through the network just like any other IP datagram. TCP/IP is more efficient across the WAN than LLC2 because its retransmission timers are variable and longer, it produces less acknowledgment traffic, and it provides an advanced, larger, variable-length, sliding-window retransmission mechanism. Another big advantage of DLSw is that the number of SRB explorer broadcast frames are now significantly limited because the routers cache the mapping of IP addresses to token ring addresses, greatly reducing the amount of broadcast traffic. This improves system performance and stability significantly by reducing the probability of broadcast storms that occur when a large number of token ring devices are forced to issue explorer broadcast frames. Such a broadcast can occur in response to failure of a primary communications path. Figure 11.12 summarizes basic DLSw operation, showing how DLSw spoofs the LLC2 protocol and transports data via TCP/IP.

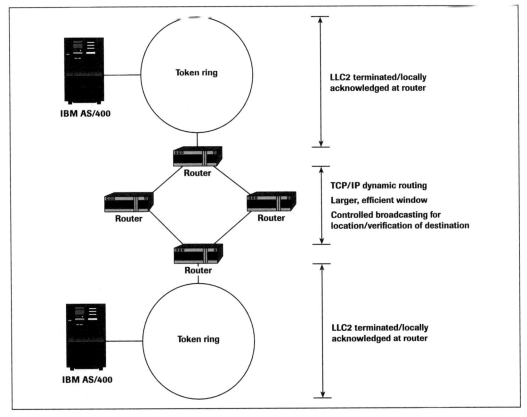

Figure 11.12 SNA and data linking switching (DLSw)

11.6 IBM Transaction Series Systems: The Customer Information Control System (CICS)

Historically, the IBM *Customer Information Control System* (CICS) has played a core role in making IBM mainframe computers transaction-friendly, capable of handling the kinds of activities and user interactions required to automate business. It is amazing when we consider that CICS, a highly relevant technology today, was originally introduced in the late 1960s. Also amazing is that its evolution and current product state put it into such a strategic technical position today.

IBM's advantage with transaction processing is rooted in its architectural premise, dating back to the 1960s, that most interactions with the computer are best viewed in terms of transactions. Just about every interaction with the computer, whatever it was, was viewed as a transaction. IBM then evolved the CICS facility to handle broader types of transactions.

Why is this robust transaction technology that has evolved over 30 years important to us today? The answer is that not only does so much legacy code exist written to CICS, but this technology also is quite viable for the growing challenges of electronic commerce. Now that we have achieved ubiquitous connectivity with our networking advances, everyone having anything to do with anyone else—customers and corporations, corporations to corporations, corporations with government—all want to do business with each other electronically in ways never before imaginable. In the early days, you required a private network to do this and a means to connect private networks, which was all expensive and complex. Today, get an inexpensive Internet connection, and you are well on your way. The problem you hit, though, is that there are cast amounts of fundamental information stored on IBM mainframes today as well as mission-critical transaction processing that is actually being handled quite well (thank you, says the devout IBMer) by a number of existing and newer mainframes. Microsoft has recognized the importance of mainframe integration and transaction processing through the introduction of Cedar, MTS, and COM technology, as we discussed in Chapter 7.

CICS is available on all major IBM operating systems, including OS/400, MVS, OS/2, AIX, and so forth. It is also available for Microsoft Windows. CICS has both client and server software components and offers a number of capabilities and APIs:

- It offers distributed computing in the form of the *Distributed Program Link* (DPL), which allows one CICS program to invoke another CICS program running on another computer interconnected across the network in the same way it might be invoked if both CICS programs were running on the same computer. This concept should sound familiar, being similar to capabilities offered by Java RMI, RPC, and CORBA (not in the object-oriented sense, but in the remote invocation aspect mainly, very roughly speaking). For example, like RPC and CORBA, different data formats are automatically handled (marshaled) by DPL, such as the conversion between ASCII character representation and the EBCDIC representation used by IBM mainframes.

- It offers two legacy integration APIs:
  1. The *External Call Interface* (ECI) allows a non-CICS program to invoke a server CICS program either synchronously or asynchronously. Note that the availability of asynchronous support differentiates CICS from other offerings. Asynchronous support matches the realities of the way most transactions actually occur. Note also that the server-side CICS program does not know or care if the invocation request is local or via DPL.
  2. The *External Presentation Interface* (EPI) allows non-CICS programs, even those that are not 3270-based, to emulate a 3270-based terminal and interact with an existing unmodified CICS application.
- CICS supports full two-phase commit transaction functionality, allowing transactions to be rolled back if there is a failure of an individual component of the transaction.
- CICS is protocol-transparent. It is independent of the underlying transport, be it SDLC, token ring, or what have you.
- CICS message queues provide a mechanism to pass data between CICS transactions.

11.7 Integrating CICS with the Web

When we think about integrating CICS and the Web, we should probably start by identifying the two key differences between CICS and Web technologies:

  1. CICS is stateful; however, the main protocol of the Web, HTTP, is stateless. Therefore, there must be a software layer above HTTP that implements state when integrating CICS with the Web.

2. There is no error recovery mechanism at the Web HTTP level. This is not at all compatible with transaction processing, which is totally reliant on error recovery for its usefulness. Therefore, error recovery must be accommodated in some way during the integration.

In terms of CICS facilities, we might ask ourselves which ones help us with this integration. One straightforward approach to integrate with the Web would be to use DPL to invoke the CICS server program and then to use ECI to handle the user interface issues. IBM leveraged some of this functionality in the CICS integration products we will review in a moment. Note that, while we will only look at products from IBM here, many companies other than IBM are offering similar integration products.

Two products from IBM for integrating CICS with the Web include the *CICS gateway for Java* and the *CICS Internet gateway.* You could, using the approach previously discussed for example, do the integration on your own, without these products, if, for some reason, this were desirable. Let's take a quick look at each of the IBM products.

11.7.1 CICS Gateway for Java

As illustrated in Figure 11.13, the only requirement with this approach on the client-side is a Java-capable Web browser. Clearly, this offers significant

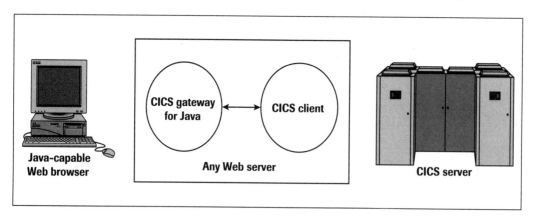

Figure 11.13 CICS gateway for Java

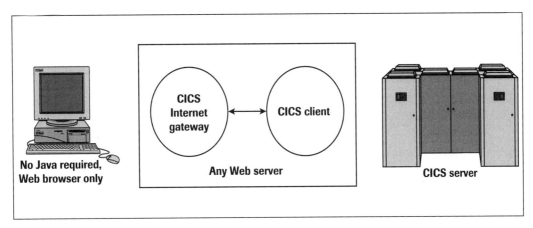

Figure 11.14 CICS internet gateway

advantages for the IS manager, eliminating the need for special software or hardware installation or new networking software on the user workstation. The CICS server application does not require modification; from its perspective, it is talking to a standard CICS client. The CICS client within the Web server is capable of emulating multiple clients, each one representing a CICS Web user.

11.7.2 CICS Internet Gateway

As illustrated in Figure 11.14, with this approach only HTML is used on the client-side to exchange CICS data with the user workstation. The CICS Internet Gateway converts between HTML and the CICS client running on the Web server. The CICS client emulates a normal CICS user in its communication with the CICS server. The CICS server application does not require modification; from its perspective it is talking to a standard CICS client. The disadvantage to this approach is that, with only HTML, you cannot do much in the way of error recovery or sophisticated real-time session management as you can with Java. Java gives you more options and more control over what is going on at any moment within the CICS session.

11.8 The IBM 3270 Java Emulator

To close this chapter, we can ponder a nice example of the technological clash of old and new—the *IBM 3270 Java emulator*. This product produced by IBM that allows a Java-capable Web browser to emulate a 3270 terminal. Java 3270 emulators are also available from other companies. Java 3270 emulators are usually written entirely in Java. The benefits of this are obvious. You get 3270 access from anywhere within your TCP/IP network, and, if your Web browser is multiplatform, then you can offer 3270 emulation to all your clients, be they Windows-, Macintosh-, or UNIX-based.

11.9 Conclusions

IBM's role in electronic commerce cannot be ignored, not only because of its legacy installed base but also because it offers certain core areas of expertise, such as in large-scale transaction processing, that command respect and a careful eye when designing new applications and modifying existing ones. Integrating with legacy SNA technology and communication methodologies including SDLC and token ring is fraught with performance risks that need to be understood and planned for up front. Spoofing techniques play an important role in networking of traditional SNA devices.

FOR FURTHER STUDY

1. A. Kapoor. *SNA: Architecture, Protocols, and Implementation.* New York: McGraw-Hill, 1992.

2. R. K. Lamb. *Cooperative Processing Using CICS.* New York: McGraw-Hill, 1993.

3. A. Meijer. *Systems Network Architecture: A Tutorial.* London/New York: Pitman/Wiley, 1988.

4. J. Ranade and G. C. Sackett. *Introduction to SNA Networking: A Guide for Using VTAM NCP.* New York: McGraw-Hill, 1989.

5. S. J. Randesi and D. H. Czubek. *SNA: IBM's System Network Architecture.* New York: Van Nostrand Reinhold, 1992.

6. W. Stallings. *Handbook of Computer-Communications Standards,* 2d ed. New York/London: Macmillan/Collier Macmillan, 1989.

7. E. Taylor. *Demystifying SNA.* Plano, Tex: Wordware, 1993.

8. E. Taylor. *Integrating TCP/IP into SNA.* Plano, Tex: Wordware, 1993.

9. J. Young. *Exploring IBM's New Age Mainframes.* Gulf Breeze, Fla.: Maximum Press, 1996.

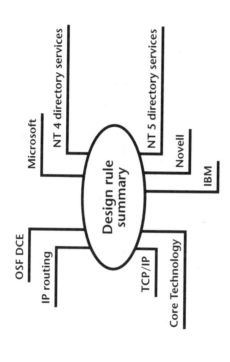

CHAPTER 12

Design Rule Summary

12.1 Introduction

Each of the frameworks and technologies we have studied evolved from different requirements and at different points in time, and all have their strengths and weaknesses. They are perhaps best characterized as a complex collection of neurally interconnected concepts and ideas, not linear ones easily divided and conquered. Putting all the material we have covered in this book into a nice neat package, in which we have tied up all the loose ends and have drawn bold sweeping conclusions, does not seem particularly practical. Attempts at doing so defy the very nature of the beast. It is like trying to herd cats. Try as you will, cats typically do not respond to such tactics.

As mentioned in the Preface, there is an art—a Way—to sifting through the mountains of information and zeroing in on the observations, be they byte-level details or broad implementation characteristics, that influence the design and architecture of your network application framework implementation. In this spirit, this final chapter of the book provides a summary of design observations, rules if you will, that we have discussed throughout this book, not in a nice neat package, but as near to that as seems realistic. Read straight through, these tables may appear to contain random bits of information, just as a road map or complicated collection of wires appears when looked at from a distance. When combined with the rest of this book and some reflection and perspective, however, they work together to convey a way of looking at these technologies that hopefully works for you.

12.2 Tables

Tables 12.1 through 12.9 are organized alphabetically by chapter subject matter, and technology topics within each chapter are themselves listed alphabetically. The tables are designed for quick reference, allowing you to look up information on a particular topic. Consequently, all key information is not included in the tables—that is what the book is for. Instead, the tables provide information that is easily summarized yet important to include here. Note that the tables contain the following abbreviations: directory service (DS), transaction processing (TP), parallel processing clustering (PP), and operating system (OS).

Table 12.1 Core Technology

Topic	Observation
CORBA	■ CORBA defines an Interface Definition Language (IDL) to describe object interfaces. The CORBA Object Request Broker (ORB) is used by objects to share interface information, to communicate with one another, and to leverage common services.
	■ CORBA is open, is multiplatform, supports multiple programming languages, and is standards-based. It is a broad-based object framework supporting a full range of services including naming, trading, event, time, transaction, and security services.
	■ The Internet Inter-ORB Protocol (IIOP) provides a standard method for ORBs to communicate across a TCP/IP network.
	■ CORBA supports dynamic invocation. The CORBA Trader Service allows for the searching of objects by function.
IPSEC	■ IPSEC offers network-level IP-centric security. It is retrofitted to IPv4 and integrated with IPv6.
Kerberos	■ Users, servers, and resources can be organized into a Kerberos realm.
	■ Kerberos provides authentication and facilitates authorization. It is most applicable within the enterprise (Intranet). Microsoft NT version 5 as well as DCE incorporate Kerberos.
	■ Each realm contains one master key distribution center (KDC). The KDC holds all client and server keys (numerically related to passwords) within the realm and therefore must be heavily secured and highly available.
	■ Kerberos requires that all servers run a time-synchronization protocol, which may be an incremental administrative and engineering burden if a time-synchronization protocol was not previously required in your network.
LDAP SASL	■ Simple Authentication and Security Layer (SASL) is a very simple specification defining a mechanism to negotiate an authentication protocol but does not itself define one.

Table 12.1 (continued)

Topic	Observation
LDAP SSL	■ There are implementations of LDAP leveraging Secure Sockets Layer (SSL). SSL and LDAP can be combined to offer single-user logon based on X.509 certificates.
LDAP versus X.500	■ The Lightweight Directory Access Protocol (LDAPv3) offers open multiplatform standards-based directory services over TCP/IP networks. LDAPv3 is, by definition, a client-access protocol. It is patterned after the X.500 Directory Access Protocol (DAP). X.500 is a broader but considerably more complex and difficult to implement specification addressing issues not specifically defined by LDAPv3 at this time, including server-to-server protocols for shadowing/replication (DISP), peer-to-peer protocols (DSP), and management protocols (DOP).
Public key cryptography	■ X.509 certificates are digitally signed by certificate authorities (CAs).
	■ Symmetric key encryption is more efficient than public key encryption, so we combine the two approaches.
	■ Private-key(data) = Signed data
	■ Public/private key reciprocity → Public-key(private-key(data)) = Data
	■ The private key must be kept secret.
	■ MAC = Hash(data) = Unique number corresponding to data for integrity checking
	■ Instead of digitally signing the entire message, we often simply sign its MAC.
	■ Public-key(data) = Encrypted data
	■ Asymmetric encryption employs two different keys: a public key and a private key. Asymmetric encryption is also sometimes referred to as *public key encryption.*
	■ The public key is public knowledge. Public keys are contained in X.509 certificates.
RPC	■ Remote Procedure Call (RPC) is a standardized method of executing a remote program on a remote computer across multiple operating systems and hardware platforms. RPC defines a standard Interface Definition Language (IDL) for use by programmers. In spite of the standardization, differences between RPC implementations must be considered.
Security, general	■ Security fundamentals include authentication, authorization, privacy, integrity, and nonrepudiation.

Table 12.1 (continued)

Topic	Observation
SSL/TLS	■ The Secure Sockets Layer (SSL) version 3.0 protocol is widely deployed today and is built into all major Web browsers. The Transport Layer Security (TLS) protocol is the IETF standardized version of SSL. ■ SSL is a transport-layer security protocol. It is coupled with the application protocol, such as HTTP, yielding HTTPS. ■ SSL supports both client and server authentication. ■ SSL can be integrated with your application in a variety of ways. ■ SSL and firewalls present challenges because SSL is a two-way protocol. SSL with HTTP (HTTPS) uses TCP port 443.

Table 12.2 IBM

Topic	Observation
Network	■ Traditional SNA is administratively intensive due to extensive manual configuration requirements. APPN offers more dynamic capabilities. ■ SDLC devices can be integrated onto LANs. ■ Relatively newer APPN offers peer-to-peer capabilities. ■ LLC2 has a dynamic window size and short timers. ■ Traditional SNA (PU2/PU4) relies on a master/slave relationship. ■ LLC2 replaces SDLC for devices communicating via a LAN. ■ APPN leverages PU2.1 and LU6.2. ■ The network can benefit from spoofing of SDLC and LLC2. ■ DLSw converts SRB to IP routing. ■ SRB typically supports the traversal of a maximum of seven bridges.
OS	■ VTAM provides core communication services. ■ MVS is an early version of a multiuser, multitasking operating system. ■ VM runs multiple operating systems.
PP	■ IBM has experience with clustering (parallel processing). For example, the RS/6000 supports up to 128 nodes.
Terminal emulation	■ The 3270 terminal emulation standard is very popular. There is a Java 3270 emulator product.

Table 12.2 (continued)

Topic	Observation
TP	■ There are CICS APIs that aid integration. ■ IBM mainframes offer powerful transaction-processing capabilities. ■ CICS is a popular transaction-processing platform. ■ There are approaches to integrating CICS data with the Web.

Table 12.3 IP Routing

Topic	Observation
ARP	■ Endpoint IP devices within the same subnetwork use ARP to map IP addresses to physical addresses. For devices in different subnetworks, IP routers and associated routing protocols can be used.
ASs	■ Autonomous systems allow the network designer to shield one part of the network from another. ASs can potentially improve routing performance and efficiency, enhance security, and allow network administration to be partitioned. There are two classes of IP routing protocols: inter-AS and intra-AS.
BGP-4	■ CIDR reduces routing table size and makes more efficient use of address space by allowing routing paths to be advertised and recording in routing tables based on collections of Class C addresses, as opposed to solely relying on Class B addresses, which are scarce. ■ BGP-4 can be viewed in terms of IBGP and EBGP. Protocols such as OSPF are often used to provide routing for IBGP TCP connects. ■ BGP-4 allows for the enforcement of policy-based peering and transit routing relationships. This can be achieved through the static configuration and dynamic exchange of routing preference and discriminator mechanisms supported by BGP-4. ■ Routers running BGP-4 share their full routing table upon initialization and then issue incremental updates as needed. ■ BGP-4 is designed for routing between ASs and has been used extensively by ISPs. It can also be useful within large corporate networks benefiting from AS partitioning. BGP-4 is a path vector protocol. ■ BGP-4 uses TCP/IP for the reliable exchange of routing information between routers.

Table 12.3 (continued)

Topic	Observation
EIGRP	■ EIGRP utilizes the DUAL algorithm to allow for the communication of routing updates on an as-needed basis, as opposed to protocols such as RIP and IGRP, which continually rebroadcast their routing tables.
ICMP	■ ICMP allows the network (IP routers) to notify endpoint IP devices of problems.
IGRP	■ IGRP rebroadcasts its routing table every 90 seconds (default configuration).
IGRP/EIGRP	■ IGRP and EIGRP are proprietary distance-vector routing protocols developed by Cisco. IGRP addresses critical shortcomings of RIP. EIGRP advances the protocol further and more favorably compares to open protocols such as OSPF. EIGRP routes IP but also supports the routing of other protocols, including Novell NetWare and AppleTalk.
OSPF	■ External AS routes can become a problem in large OSPF networks if not carefully managed.
	■ OSPF supports load sharing over equal-cost links.
	■ Routers interconnected by virtual-circuit-based protocols such as frame relay can utilize either the OSPF PTP or NBMA methods or some combination of them. As the number of routers increases, the number of required adjacencies required with the PTP approach is dramatically higher then that required with the NBMA approach. Each adjacency increases router CPU and memory load.
	■ OSPF area border routers should be powerful enough to accommodate all the adjacencies they manage. Typically, these routers are equipped with faster processors and larger amounts of memory than, for example, remote access routers and are often deployed in redundant (hot standby backup) configurations.
	■ OSPF offers significantly more functionality and flexibility than RIP. OSPF is standards-based intra-AS protocol supporting VLSM, hierarchical routing, a shortest path first routing algorithm, and it is optimized for nonbroadcast multiaccess technologies such as frame relay.
	■ When you add routers to an OSPF area, the CPU utilization of routers participating in adjacencies with other routers can increase at a faster rate than you might assume. CPU utilization will typically increase logarithmically, not linearly.

Table 12.3 (continued)

Topic	Observation
OSPF (cont'd)	■ Routers running OSPF exchange information using a reliable protocol supporting error detection and recovery. RIP routers, in contrast, share routing information without a reliable protocol. OSPF routers exchange information on an as-needed basis, as opposed to RIP, which rebroadcasts routing information at fixed time intervals. ■ The OSPF BDR is a hot standby version of the DR. The BDR and DR should be isolated from one another as part of the design so that they do not fail together due to a common failure, such as a power outage in the same building facility. ■ OSPF NBMA networks do not require a full mesh; however, when you do not fully mesh the routers, then devices at sites within the NBMA not connected via virtual circuits will be unable to reach one another (unable to exchange IP data) unless some other routing mechanism is implemented. ■ Routers within the OSPF NBMA are required to form adjacencies with the DR and BDR only. The other virtual circuits used to connect non-DR and non-BDR routers within the NBMA to one another typically will not place a computational burden on the OSPF routing processes unless they are for adjacency connections to the DR and BDR.
Ping	■ Ping provides important statistics and troubleshooting capabilities.
RIP	■ The RIP maximum hop count is 16. ■ Three significant improvements offered by RIPv2 over the original RIP include VLSM, security authentication, and route tagging. ■ RIP is implemented by servers for LAN access but less frequently as the routing protocol for the network backbone, due to its limitations. ■ RIP is a distance-vector protocol. ■ A device running RIP rebroadcasts its routing table every 30 seconds by default. ■ The three most commonly used methods used with RIP to prevent routing loops and reduce convergence delay are split horizon, poison reverse, and triggered updates.

Table 12.3 (continued)

Topic	Observation
Route flapping	■ A single router can potentially flood the network with a stream of updates caused by some rapidly oscillating malfunction. This can bring a network to its knees either instantaneously or over time, dramatically affecting response time, available network throughput, and reliability. This phenomenon is referred to as *route flapping*.
Routing errors	■ Routing errors can cause datagrams to loop within your network, consuming bandwidth and router CPU resources. Gathering and analyzing SNMP statistics on traffic can be helpful in detecting routing errors.
Routing protocols	■ There are three fundamental routing protocol characteristics: path selection, convergence delay, and cost.
Security	■ Hackers can use ICMP redirects to override intended routing.

Table 12.4 Microsoft

Topic	Observation
ADO	■ The Active Data Objects (ADO) specification provides a modern object-oriented alternative to direct ODBC API programming. ADO can itself leverage ODBC.
COM	■ The evolution of Microsoft COM technology is DDE, OLE version 1, OLE version 2, OCX, and ActiveX. COM was introduced with OLE version 2. OLE version 2, OCX, and ActiveX are based on COM.
	■ OLE automation allows applications and associated data to be encapsulated and controlled by scripts and macros.
	■ There are significant security risks associated with using ActiveX on the open Internet without the use of Authenticode. Authenticode makes use of digital signing.
	■ Distributed COM (DCOM) uses RPC for communication between COM components.
	■ The Microsoft IDL (MIDL) is used to wrap your program, making it a COM component.
	■ COM is a binary standard, meaning that COM components are DLLs or executable (.exe) files.

Table 12.4 (continued)

Topic	Observation
COM (cont'd)	■ COM objects have containers. On the client-side, there is Visual Basic or the Web browser such as Internet Explorer or Netscape Communicator. On the server-side, there is the Microsoft Transaction Server (MTS). ■ The Microsoft network application framework combines COM with a rich set of middleware functions, including transactions, databases, security, clustering, and multiple programming language support. ■ The Microsoft Message Queue Server (MSMQ) enables asynchronous messaging between COM components. ■ When utilizing DCOM, it is important to consider the performance implications of "chatty" exchanges between objects. It is best to try to group object calls and information exchanges. ■ COM+ is an extension of COM and simplifies the building of COM components. ■ CORBA was produced by an organization focused on standards and open participation. COM, in contrast, evolved as a series of solutions to intermediate product requirements and did not come out of a standards body.
Interprocess	■ Microsoft local interprocess communication mechanisms include file mapping, shared memory, and pipes.
Java	■ As an alternative to ActiveX, capabilities-based object signing makes Java a good model for dynamic executable content on the open Internet. The Java program is analyzed before running, allowing the user to refuse any hazardous actions that the Java program may be requesting.
MAPI	■ The Messaging API (MAPI) provides a common interface to heterogeneous messaging systems. ADO can itself leverage MAPI, allowing you to use ADO as a higher-level alternative to MAPI.
Network API	■ Microsoft's networking APIs and remote interprocess communication methods include WinSock, NetBIOS, named pipes and mailslots, RPC, and the WNet( ) Win32 API functions.
ODBC	■ The Open Database Connectivity (ODBC) API provides a common API for accessing heterogeneous databases. The performance of the ODBC driver for your particular database should be well understood.

Table 12.4 (continued)

Topic	Observation
PP	■ Microsoft Wolfpack clustering is intended to support increased scalability through parallel processing.
SPI	■ The Microsoft service provider interface (SPI) abstracts away the details of a particular service implementation.
Telephony	■ The Telephony API (TAPI) provides a common API for integrating telephony functions, including modems, telephones, PBXs, and fax devices, with your application.
Threads	■ The Threads facility allows individual elements of an application to be decoupled from one another and executed independently, typically resulting in reduced blocking (waiting) and more overall parallelism. Beware, however, thread thrashing, which can occur when you spur too many threads and overwhelm the computer's processing capacity.
TP	■ The four essential ingredients of transaction processing are ACID: Atomicity, Consistency, Isolation, and Durability. ■ COM combined with MTS, Cedar, and Wolfpack offers a powerful transaction-processing system. ■ The Microsoft Cedar project provides a bridge between the desktop, NT server-based applications, and the world of IBM CICS and IMS transaction-based mainframe systems. Cedar leverages LU6.2 to connect with the mainframe. ■ The Resource Manager (RM) manages storage resources, and the Transaction Manager (TM) manages the sequence of events associated with the transaction. ■ MTS acts as a container for server-side COM objects and as a transaction coordinator for transactions involving them. MTS supports object pooling and resource sharing. MTS provides a platform upon which COM objects work together to meet the ACID properties of a transaction. ■ MTS objects are stateless and reusable. ■ MTS extends the NT 4 user/group security mechanisms into the transactional environment. Objects that are part of a transaction are combined into packages. Roles can be assigned to packages. Users and groups can be assigned roles. MTS also supports client impersonation. Client impersonation, if not managed properly, can degrade performance.
UDA	■ The Universal Data Architecture (UDA), of which ADO is a part, provides generalized data access and sharing between disparate applications. ADO and a lower-level object-oriented data access called *OLE-DB* are important parts of UDA.

Table 12.4 (continued)

Topic	Observation
Unicode	■ Windows NT 3.51, 4, and 5 support Unicode for internationalization. The initial release of Windows 95 requires the use of various workarounds in order to leverage Unicode.
Win32	■ The service provider interface (SPI) abstracts away the details of a particular implementation of a function, producing a common API to different implementations. For example, there are SPIs to support multiple network protocols, such as TCP/IP and NetWare IPX. There is then a set of common networking APIs that leverage these networks protocols through a common underlying SPI. ■ The Intel MP specification, supported by the Pentium Pro and II microprocessors, allows threads to run more efficiently when multiple processors are installed on a single computer motherboard. The Intel MP enables multiple processors to maintain their own caches instead of sharing a single one, as in the original Pentium architecture.
WOSA	■ The Windows Open Systems Architecture (WOSA) is often used to refer to the collection of APIs and standards that comprise the Microsoft network application framework.

Table 12.5 Novell

Topic	Observation
Bindery	■ The bindery is a database maintained by every server concerned with service availability and user/resource management. ■ The bindery can be thought of as the predecessor to NDS.
EIGRP	■ EIGRP supports NetWare.
IntraNetWare	■ IntraNetWare is NetWare 4.x bundled with Web and other value-added software.
IPX	■ IPX is a connectionless protocol. ■ An IPX network address is not numerically related to the host address (not, for example, through a subnet mask as in TCP/IP). Network addresses are selected by the administrator. They must be unique.

Table 12.5 (continued)

Topic	Observation
IPX (cont'd)	■ NetWare/IP in IPX emulation mode encapsulates IPX into IP packets. This means 20 bytes for IP, 8 bytes for UDP, and 30 bytes for IPX, bringing the total to 58 bytes per packet. NetWare/IP requires DSS servers, representing an additional administrative burden. ■ The IPX header is 30 bytes in length. NCP add another 10 bytes, bringing the total to 40 bytes.
LIPX	■ Large IPX (LIPX) allows for larger IPX packet sizes, potentially improving performance for applications involving large data transfers.
NCP	■ NetWare Core Protocol (NCP) provides an RPC-like mechanism for requesting NetWare services. ■ NCP provides NetWare services to applications through an API and application-layer protocol. ■ NCP employs a flow control mechanism that can significantly affect end-to-end performance of the application through the network. NCP burst mode can provide a significant performance improvement by making this flow control mechanism more efficient.
NDS	■ NDS uses a proprietary authentication and authorization scheme that leverages passwords and public key cryptography. ■ NWDS APIs are patterned after X.500 XDS APIs. ■ The NDS and X.500 DN address formats are essentially the same. ■ NDS is a development platform. ■ NDS for NT allows NT 4 directory services to be integrated with NDS. Username/passwords must be synchronized across the two directory services. ■ Through its rich APIs and integration, NDS is evolving into its own development platform. ■ NDS supports bindery emulation. ■ The NetWare Directory Service (NDS) was introduced as part of NetWare 4.x. ■ NDS provides single-user logon within the NetWare environment. ■ NDS supports LDAPv3. NDS objects for which access control is enabled require that the LDAP client be authenticated. This authentication mechanism must be reconciled between LDAP and NDS in some way.

Table 12.5 (continued)

Topic	Observation
NDS (cont'd)	■ NDS supports inheritance. An Inherited Rights Filter (IRF) can be used to control this inheritance. ■ NDS supports partitioning and replication. NDS supports peer-to-peer synchronization. Synchronization network traffic must be planned for. Partitioning can be used to isolate directory database changes and updates to specific areas of the network.
NDS/SAP	■ NDS reduces the need for SAP as the primary service availability communication mechanism in pure 4.x networks. In a pure NDS 4.x environment, SAP is used mainly for time synchronization and advertising the availability of NDS servers themselves. ■ There are network design and performance implications of mixed NDS and SAP broadcast networks.
NetWare 5	■ NetWare 5 offers the promise of many improvements, including native TCP/IP and broad support for Java, Java APIs, and CORBA.
NLM	■ NLMs are the historical way to extend NetWare services. ■ Java and CORBA may displace NLM over time through the use of IntraNetWare and NetWare 5.x. ■ NetWare loadable modules (NLMs) are installed on NetWare servers.
NLSP	■ NLSP is similar to OSPF. NLSP is a link-state protocol supporting IPX and SAP.
RIP	■ NetWare RIP rebroadcasts its table every 60 seconds, whereas IP RIP does it every 30 seconds. ■ NetWare RIP and TCP/IP RIP are nearly identical.
SAP	■ The default SAP broadcast interval is 60 seconds. Methods to control SAP broadcasts include filters, changing the rate of broadcasts either on the LAN or just between routers, and state-based update mechanisms between routers using NLSP or EIGRP.
SPX	■ SPX builds on IPX by providing a connection-oriented retransmission scheme. ■ Important NetWare utilities use SPX. SPX can time out in slow or congested networks. SPX maximum retransmission time-out values may need to be adjusted. ■ The SPX header adds an additional 12 bytes of overhead on top of IPX.
WinSock	■ WinSock version 2 supports NetWare.

Table 12.6 NT 4 Directory Services

Topic	Observation
DS	■ NT 4 directory services are proprietary, not based on an open standard such as X.500. ■ NT 4 APIs are provided allowing for username/password integration with an external directory service. Netscape uses this facility to integrate NT username/password with HTTP (Web) basic authorization and LDAP. ■ The enterprise is viewed in terms of users, groups of users, and resources. Users, groups, and resources are organized into domains. Domains are logical, not physical. Domains can ease management and enhance performance and reliability. ■ Domain controllers (DCs) manage user and group information. There are two types of DCs: primary DC (PDC) and backup DC (BDC). BDCs contain read-only versions of the SAM. Administration cannot be performed at a BDC. ■ There are three domain types: account, resource, and mixed. ■ Domains can require the maintenance of one-way and two-way directional nontransitive trust relationships, which can become overwhelming in large networks. Domain topologies include single domain, single master domain, multiple master domain, and complete trust. ■ A domain is configured with one PDC and one or more BDCs. ■ NT 4 directory services and Microsoft Exchange directory services are not fully integrated.

Table 12.7 NT 5 Directory Services

Topic	Observation
DS	■ Naming support is provided for the X.500 standard as well as a DNS style of naming ■ NT 5 extends the NT 4 concept of domains, provides transitive trust and inheritance among domains, and provides mechanisms to coexist with NT 4 directory services. ■ A domain is an administrative entity, equivalent to a Kerberos realm, consisting of users, groups, and resources. ■ Domains can be organized into a hierarchy, and transitive trust relationships can be configured among them. This hierarchy is called a *domain tree*.

Table 12.7 (continued)

Topic	Observation
DS (cont'd)	■ Support is provided for the LDAP protocol, the LDAP API, DNS, and the Active Directory Service Interface (ADSI), a proprietary directory service extensibility API. ■ Support is provided for directory partitioning and replication. A peer-to-peer replication model is supported. ■ A domain tree contains a global catalogue (GC). The GC provides a mechanism for the client (user or application) to quickly search for directory information within the domain tree based on attributes contained within the DN. ■ Domain controllers (DCs) hold directory information for the domain. Unlike NT 4, all DCs for a given domain hold a writable copy of the directory—there is no concept of primary or backup.

Table 12.8 OSF DCE

Topic	Observation
DS	■ Directory service is based on X.500 standard. ■ Both X.500 and DNS style of names are supported. ■ Users and resources are organized into DCE cells. ■ A cell must contain a CDS, security server, and distributed time servers. ■ DCE version 1.1 allows cells to be arranged hierarchically. ■ The X/Open Directory Service (XDS) API is supported.
File	■ DCE File Service (DFS) is a powerful distributed file service.
Objects	■ DCE and CORBA compete with and complement each other.
Security	■ The PAC is used for authorization. ■ Security is based on Kerberos version 5. ■ The IETF standard GSS-API security API is supported. ■ DCE supports authenticated RPC with Kerberos. ■ The security database should be heavily secured and highly available.
Time	■ DCE Time Service (DTS) is a time-synchronization protocol.

Table 12.9 TCP/IP

Topic	Observation
Addressing	■ IP addresses need to be assigned by an address authority. They are in scarce supply. Subnet masks are used to subdivide address space for your organization. VSLM is a method to further optimize address space usage.
Fragmentation	■ IP fragmentation can negatively impact the performance, efficiency, and stability of your network and applications. Techniques such as MTU discovery and maintaining knowledge of configured maximum IP datagram sizes within your network and applications can be used to avoid fragmentation.
Header overhead	■ With no options set, there are 20 bytes for IP and 20 bytes for TCP. That is 40 bytes minimum per TCP-based datagram. UDP adds 8 bytes. That is 28 bytes per UDP-based datagram.
IP	■ TCP rides on top of IP. UDP also rides on top of IP.
IPv6	■ IPv4 is in wide deployment today. IPv6 is the next generation of IP protocol having any likelihood of widespread adoption. Its main benefit is support for increased address space.
Max packet size	■ Maximum IP, TCP, and UDP packet sizes configured within your IP endpoint devices and your routers can greatly influence the overall performance of the network and user-perceived performance.
Ping	■ Ping can be used to measure performance within your network on a regular basis. Your SNMP management station may support a ping MIB, allowing pings to be issued and results recorded and analyzed against network objectives.
Retransmission	■ For error recovery and retransmission, the window may shrink if the network is congested or offers a high-bit error rate.
Security	■ TCP/IP loose and strict source routing can be used by hackers trying to override good (trusted) routes with their own.
TCP versus UDP	■ TCP offers a retransmission mechanism, but UDP does not.
TELNET	■ TELNET is a remote character echo application. Many terminal-based legacy applications, when ported to a LAN environment, leverage TELNET. In such a configuration, every character typed gets wrapped in a 40-bytes TCP header, sent across the network, then echoed back to the terminal. It is hard to imagine something less efficient across your network.

Index

N

Organizational units (OUs), 268–269, 270, 293
Origin field, 163
OS/2, 213
OSF (Open Software Foundation), 188–189, 355
OSF1, 189
OSI (Open Systems Interconnection), 59, 214
OSPF (Open Shortest Path First) protocol, 117, 153, 333
  basic description of, 122, 139–151, 168
  BGP and, 164–167
  case study, 149–151
  RIP and, 136
OUs (organizational units), 268–269, 270, 293

P

Packet(s)
  format, 96–100
  size, 22–23, 283
  SRB explorer, 327
  type, 282–283
Packet Type field, 282–283
PACs (privilege attribute certificates), 190–192
Parallel processing, 314–315
Partitions, 12, 298–301
Passive nodes, 154
Password in the Clear option, 79
Passwords, 72, 79, 302. *See also* Security
  cracking, 55
  NT directory services and, 248, 271
Path
  control layer, 320
  selection, 126, 142–143
  -vector protocols, 156, 168
Payload Length field, 175, 177
PBX systems, 207, 222
PCT standard, 44

PDCs (primary domain controllers), 251–252, 257–259, 274, 302, 354
Peer-to-peer model, 12, 272, 291, 313, 323
Pentium II processor, 209
Pentium Pro processor, 209
Performance, designing for, 298–301
Perl, 307
Permissions, 9. *See also* Security
PGP (Pretty Good Privacy), 33
Physical control layer, 320
Physical units (PUs), 317–319, 323, 324–325
Ping, 128, 129–130
PIP (Policy Information Base), 162, 163
Pipes, 210, 211–212
Platform-independent APIs, 5, 197–199
Plug-and-play, 109
Poison reverse technique, 136, 137
Policy
  -based routing, 139
  decisions, 156
Polling, 113–114, 325, 328–329
Polymorphism, 8
Port numbers, 96–98
POSIX, 191, 194, 197, 198
POTS (Plain Old Telephone Service), 222
Powersoft, 233
Prefix field, 180–181
Presentation services, 321–322
Principal Authenticator object, 72
Printer sharing, 1, 24
Print services, 9
Priority field, 174
Privacy, 30, 31, 33, 72. *See also* Security
Privilege service, 190–192
Process management, 207
Processors, 6–7, 103
  efficiency and, 114
  header compression and, 113
  IBM, 314–315

Q

R